Ulrike Meinhof and the
Red Army Faction

Ulrike Meinhof and the Red Army Faction

Performing Terrorism

Leith Passmore

First published in 2011 by PALGRAVE MACMILLAN® in the United States—a division of St. Martin's Press LLC, 175 Fifth Avenue, New York, NY 10010.

Where this book is distributed in the UK, Europe, and the rest of the world, this is by Palgrave Macmillan, a division of Macmillan Publishers Limited, registered in England, company number 785998, of Houndmills, Basingstoke, Hampshire RG21 6XS.

Palgrave Macmillan is the global academic imprint of the above companies and has companies and representatives throughout the world.

Palgrave® and Macmillan® are registered trademarks in the United States, the United Kingdom, Europe and other countries.

ISBN: 978-0-230-33747-3

Library of Congress Cataloging-in-Publication Data

Passmore, Leith, 1981–
    Ulrike Meinhof and the Red Army Faction : performing terrorism / Leith Passmore.
        p. cm.
    Includes bibliographical references and index.
    ISBN 978-0-230-33747-3 (hardback)
    1. Meinhof, Ulrike Marie. 2. Women terrorists—Germany (West)—Biography. 3. Women journalists—Germany (West)—Biography. 4. Terrorism—Germany (West)—History. 5. Rote Armee Fraktion—History. I. Title.

HV6433.G3P37 2011
363.325092—dc22   2011016072

A catalogue record of the book is available from the British Library.

Design by Scribe Inc.

First edition: November 2011

10 9 8 7 6 5 4 3 2 1

Printed and bound in Great Britain by
CPI Antony Rowe, Chippenham and Eastbourne

Contents

Acknowledgments

This book is based largely on a rich archival source base. The complete *konkret* catalog, Red Army Faction (RAF) texts, protest leaflets, amateur publications, posters, texts confiscated from defense lawyers and their offices, as well as material willingly donated by defense lawyers, writings found in RAF members' cells, police reports, and trial transcripts were viewed over many winter's days at the Hamburg Institute for Social Research (*Hamburger Institut für Sozialforschung*) and the Federal Archive (*Bundesarchiv*) in Koblenz. I owe the staff at both institutions a debt of gratitude for their interest in the project and, above all, for their tips. Without their help I would not have been able to navigate the reams of paper they brought me.

The process of producing a book from this material was a long one. The fact that it was also fruitful and—for my part at least—enjoyable is due in no small part to Alexandra Ludewig and Mark Edele. Their critiques and their advice made my long journey also a steep learning curve. I am proud to count them as colleagues, and very pleased to call them friends. There were also many scholars along the way who tolerated and responded to conference presentations, seminar papers, and ramblings over beer as this project took shape. Such feedback was invaluable. For their generosity, too, I am grateful to the anonymous reviewers of the book manuscript and to Sarah Colvin for her comments on a late draft.

Throughout the research and writing of this book I enjoyed the support of friends and family. My parents, Graeme and Denyse, were, in this endeavor, as with all others, incredibly supportive. For their wonderful friendship and their role in what could be considered the very beginning of this project, I thank the Weisser family and the broader communities of Neuenburg am Rhein and Müllheim. I am indebted to Clara Bowman for everything else. Everything else includes her company, her encouragement, her love, and her deep appreciation of where commas belong in a sentence.

Preface

Born into Hitler's "thousand-year Reich," Ulrike Meinhof made a name for herself as a journalist and spokesperson for a restless protest scene in a Germany split by the frontline of the Cold War. After her involvement in the 1970 liberation of Andreas Baader from prison, her face disappeared from the pages of the left-wing press and from West German television screens and appeared instead on wanted posters. The Baader-Meinhof Gang, as they were dubbed in the popular press, later took the name Red Army Faction (RAF) and launched a campaign of violence that would dominate the coming years. Meinhof's fall from journalistic prominence and disappearance into the terrorist underground is inextricably entwined with the story of the young Federal Republic of Germany. It is at once a tragic footnote to the waning student movement of the late 1960s and a preamble to the bloodiest period in Germany's postwar history.

Meinhof began her journalistic career while still a university student in the late 1950s. In 1959 she caught the eye of Klaus Rainer Röhl, cofounder and chief editor of the leftist magazine *konkret*, and soon gave up her studies to write for the magazine. Her recruitment coincided with a courtship, and she and Röhl married in 1961, shortly after she assumed the responsibility of chief editor. The following year Meinhof gave birth to twin girls, Bettina and Regine, before quickly returning to journalism. Her reputation grew alongside the *konkret* readership as she proved capable of capturing, and in many ways creating, the mood of a growing student movement. This "student movement" was a broad-based groundswell of protest representing interests from the liberal to the radical. A strong sense of solidarity emerged among the different elements largely in response to local political developments.

In 1966 the two major West German political parties, the left-of-center Social Democratic Party (*Sozialdemokratische Partei Deutschlands*, or SPD) and the conservative Christian Democratic Union (*Christlich Demokratische Union*, or CDU), formed a ruling "grand coalition" (*große Koalition*). Many on the left felt betrayed by the SPD and politically disenfranchised by the new partnership, and calls mounted for the student movement to become an extraparliamentary opposition (*außerparlamentarische Opposition*, APO). Led by figures such as

Meinhof and front man for the Socialist German Student Union (*Sozialistischer Deutscher Studentenbund*, or SDS), Rudi Dutschke, the APO mobilized against the grand coalition, against draft emergency laws, against the war in Vietnam, and for university reform. Debate within the movement about how best to confront authority and the legitimacy of violence heightened after a number of high-profile incidents.

On June 2, 1967, a crowd gathered outside the Deutsche Oper in Berlin to protest the state visit of the Shah of Iran to West Germany. The visit was seen by those who lobbed tomatoes and flour bombs at the official motorcade as tacit support for a regime guilty of human rights abuses against its own citizens. Meinhof had written an open letter to Farah Diba, the Shah's wife, taking issue with comments she made to the German press that ignored the poverty and exploitation of her people. The biting rebuke was printed in *konkret* and was also circulated in leaflet form as the Shah and his wife enjoyed a performance of Mozart's *The Magic Flute*.[1] The demonstration outside the opera escalated into violent clashes between police, Iranian loyalists who had come to cheer the Shah, and protesters. Amid the chaos, plainclothes police officer Karl-Heinz Kurras shot student Benno Ohnesorg. Ohnesorg's death was a watershed moment for the APO. After years of speaking about latent fascism in the Federal Republic, here was an example, embodied in a policeman, of an openly violent state.[2]

The following year, on April 2, 1968, a group that included Baader and his girlfriend Gudrun Ensslin placed a time-delay incendiary device in a Frankfurt department store. Ensslin was a university student who had left her fiancé and their young son for Baader, a petty criminal who had missed the events of June 2 after his arrest in Bavaria for traffic offenses. The fire caused minimal damage and injured no one. Such "violence against property" (*Gewalt gegen Sachen*) was intended as an attack against what they perceived as rampant capitalism, and during the October trial Ensslin stated the fire was also intended as a "protest against the indifference with which the people [were] watching the genocide in Vietnam."[3] Meinhof visited the accused arsonists in prison before writing an article that condemned arson, but celebrated the illegality of the protest as progressive.[4] Baader and Ensslin, as well as Thorwald Proll and Horst Söhnlein, were later convicted of arson and sentenced to three years in prison, in what many saw as an overreaction.

A little more than a week after the arson attack, on April 11, Dutschke was approached in the street by Josef Bachmann. The SDS figure enjoyed a high profile after years of speaking at rallies, leading demonstrations, and appearing on television. Pictures of him also appeared in a ring-wing newspaper article under the headline "Stop Dutschke now!" (*Stoppt Dutschke jetzt!*), which was in Bachmann's pocket when he drew a pistol and shot Dutschke in the head from point-blank range. The attack, which Dutschke survived, resulted in a violent protest at the Springer publishing house. Despite the fact that the article found on Bachmann was not published by media magnate Axel Springer, demonstrators saw the assassination attempt as a symptom of a wider media campaign led by Springer publications, most notably the *Bild* newspaper. They blockaded the publishing house and set fire to vehicles in an attempt to disrupt circulation of the *Bild*. Meinhof was at the demonstration, and in the wake of the Dutschke shooting she famously championed the blockade as crossing the line from verbal protest to physical resistance.[5]

The shooting of Ohnesorg, the attempt on the life of Dutschke, and the controversial sentence handed down to the Frankfurt arsonists were milestones in the evolution of what was, by 1969, an increasingly fractured and frayed student movement. Fundamental disagreements emerged over the legitimacy of violence, and the political conditions that had served to bind the disparate elements had shifted. Emergency laws were passed in 1968 after almost a decade of debate, and in 1969 the grand coalition came to an end when the SPD formed a government with Willy Brandt as chancellor. Brandt entered into a new dialogue with East Germany as part of his *Ostpolitik*, which won him the 1971 Nobel Peace Prize. In December 1970 he produced one of the iconic images of postwar German history when he knelt before a monument to the Warsaw Ghetto uprising as a symbol of conciliation. Many students returned to their studies to embark on Dutschke's "long march through the institutions," but some, mainly peripheral, elements became more radical.

By 1969 Meinhof's professional and personal relationship with Röhl had broken down, and she left *konkret*. She was now a well-known commentator as well as a television and radio personality and filmmaker, who focused increasingly on the issues faced by young people on the edges of society. Baader and Ensslin, too, began working with youth groups in Frankfurt upon their early release in June 1969, after serving only 14 months of their sentences. The three formed a friendship largely based on this mutual interest before Baader and Ensslin fled to Paris. Meinhof also housed the pair during their subsequent return to Germany before Baader's rearrest for violation of his parole conditions. With Baader again in prison, Meinhof agreed to be part of a plan to get him out. She used her profile to organize a meeting at a less secure research institute, and this was to be the extent of her role in the unarmed operation. However, the liberation did not proceed as anticipated. Amid the chaos of unexpected resistance put up by security guards and gunshots fired by a liberator roped in at the last minute, Meinhof fled with Baader through an open window. Posters with her picture appeared overnight advertising that she was wanted for attempted murder and that there was a reward of DM 10,000 on her head. This jump out of the window is widely considered to be both Meinhof's leap into the underground and the birth of the RAF.

Over the next two years the group underwent arms training in Jordan, put out political statements from the underground, held up numerous banks, and planted a series of bombs. The attacks and skirmishes claimed numerous lives—RAF members, police, civilians, and U.S. soldiers—before the core of the first generation of the group was arrested in 1972. Meinhof spent more time in prison than she spent on the run, and the texts she produced as an inmate would become at least as important as anything she produced while at large. This period climaxed with the most expensive trial in West German history in a purpose-built courthouse next to the Stammheim Prison, where the RAF leaders were held. In April 1977 Baader, Ensslin, and Jan-Carl Raspe were sentenced to life in prison, but Meinhof did not see the end of the trial, as she was found hanged in her prison cell in May 1976. Baader, Ensslin, and Raspe were all found dead, or close to it, in their cells on the morning of October 18, 1977, after the last of several bloody extortion attempts by second-generation RAF members to secure the inmates' freedom ended without success.

Violence in the name of the RAF did not end with the convictions of the founding members or with their deaths. Despite reaching its high point with the "German Autumn" (*Deutscher Herbst*) of 1977, acts of terrorism continued into the 1980s and 1990s. The RAF officially disbanded in 1998 after failing to recontextualize its struggle after the end of the Cold War and the fall of the Berlin Wall. The scarring is still evident, and unified Germany remains on many levels preoccupied with the RAF. This ongoing relevance is rooted in the fact that the group was central to a period that helped shape contemporary German society. Meinhof's story is key, as it weaves its way through decades of Germany's tumultuous postwar history: from the student protest scene of the 1950s and her fame of the 1960s, to her infamy in the 1970s, and her still-lingering twin statuses as master criminal or saintly martyr. She remains a highly polarizing figure capable of inspiring both fierce debate as well as more visceral reactions from the gut of the German public.

INTRODUCTION

Performing Terrorism

> At six in the morning the servant comes in with a light. He finds his master on the floor, the pistol, the blood . . . From the blood on the arm of the chair one could infer that he had done the deed as he sat before his desk, then slumped down in his chair thrashing about convulsively. He lay on his back near the window, exhausted, fully dressed, wearing his boots, his blue coat, and yellow vest . . .
> He had drunk only one glass of the wine. Emilia Galotti lay open on his desk.[1]
>
> —Johann Wolfgang von Goethe, *The Sufferings of Young Werther*

"*Matter of a corpse, Urgent!*" In the early morning of May 9, 1976, prison guards found Ulrike Meinhof dead and hanging from her cell window. The police report notes the position of the body and the untidy desk on which "no clues, leads, or notes relevant to the case" could be found, before remarking that "the sole thing on the desk to stand out was that, amongst other things, the book by Ludwig Wittgenstein with the title 'Philosophical Grammar' lay there. The book lay open at the pages 84/85."[2] It seems a curious detail to highlight, but just as Lessing's bourgeois tragedy open on Werther's desk was a clue to his frustrations, perhaps Wittgenstein is representative of Meinhof's sufferings: were the limits of her language indeed the limits of her world?[3] Questions may always remain about the circumstances of Meinhof's death, but what is clear is that she struggled with what she saw as the boundaries of communication as a writer, a fugitive, and a prisoner. This book examines her journalism and her terrorism in light of this struggle. It applies to her twin careers a communicative methodology that understands terrorism as a discursive construction: at once the result of, and itself a series of, performative acts of text, imagery, and physical violence.

Communicative approaches to terrorism rest on the assumption that terrorist violence is not meaningless. Dismissing acts of terrorism as senseless, and quarantining them as irrational, closes them off from analysis. They must instead be understood as having meaning and making a type of sense; as being rational attempts at communication, where the rationality of the act is separate from the rationality of the actor.[4] The rationality assumption represents an important shift in the writing on terrorism, as it enabled an examination of how acts of terrorism function.[5] Approaches that examine the communicative components of terror have since spanned disciplines, but they tend to share common starting points: sociologist Brian Jenkins's 1975 assertion that "terrorism is theatre," and linguist J. L. Austin's 1955 notion of the "performative."

The idea that terrorism is theater occupies an important place in the writing on terrorism. It also enjoyed a revival in the context of the spectacle of the attacks on New York in 2001, and comments such as those made by German composer Karlheinz Stockhausen one week after the event: "What has happened is—and you must now all reset your brains—the greatest work of art there has ever been."[6] Terrorism is not art, however, and the comparison to theater can be a groping attempt to handle the overwhelming and dramatic violence of terrorist acts.[7] In its original context, however, Jenkins's analogy was a simple but insightful observation: "Terrorism is aimed at the people watching, not the actual victim. Terrorism is theatre."[8] It is this acknowledgement of a third party that shifted thinking on terrorism.

Jenkins's recognition of the "people watching" broadened the traditional focus of terrorism research to include not only the terrorist and the state but also the victim and an intended audience. Terror was framed as communicative by scholars such as Walter Laqueur, and Alex P. Schmid and Janny de Graaf, before Peter Waldmann developed the idea into a sociological model for understanding terrorist violence as primarily symbolic, and terrorism as, above all, a communication strategy.[9] Whether by ensuring the attention of an audience for a message, the emotional terrorizing of the enemy, the mobilizing of sympathizers among the public, or the provocation of the state, terrorists use violence against an immediate victim or victims to communicate with and influence the behavior of a third party.[10] In Mark Juergensmeyer's study of religious extremism, this third party, the audience, is not simply present in the model, it is involved in the making of meaning. Juergensmeyer borrows the idea of terrorism as theater to write of acts of violence as having symbolic value and "performing" meaning, but that meaning is contingent on the context of the acts and audience perception. To make his point, he draws on Austin's notion of the "performative."[11]

Not long after her arrest, Gudrun Ensslin wrote in prison that "words, ideas are actions, actions are ideas."[12] Her prison note came almost twenty years after Austin outlined his, as he wrote, simple idea that "saying something" could be "doing something."[13] Depending on circumstance and context, he wrote, performative utterances—such as promising someone something, or pronouncing a couple married—do not simply report or describe something, they actually do something. They perform an effect by virtue of being uttered. In her work on gender, Judith Butler begins with Austin's work as a point of departure to develop performativity as a "reiterative and citational practice by which discourse produces the effects that it names."[14] That is to say, performative language "does" something, or performs an effect by drawing on recognizable linguistic conventions.[15] It was largely via Butler and Austin that the "linguistic turn," and a recognition of the power of discourse to constitute what it names, has been translated to the study of terrorism and counterterrorism.[16]

The discursive construction of the phenomenon of terrorism also makes room for the subjective element that sets terrorist violence apart from other forms of violence. The maxim that "one man's terrorist is another man's freedom fighter" is often cited to emphasize the subjectivity implicit in the terminology, and scholars have long struggled to find practical definitions of "who terrorists are" and "what terrorism is."[17] Definitions often remain clumsy and detached from the analysis, or so specific to a narrow case study that they are not broadly applicable. Understanding terrorism as a performative enactment, however, circumvents the definitional problems that have dogged research. Definitions are not crafted and then applied during the investigation; the definitional process, the process of naming, is instead part of the phenomenon itself, with the subjectivity of the language incorporated into the analysis.

In the context of West Germany, Andreas Musolff and Sarah Colvin have examined how Red Army Faction (RAF) terrorism and terrorist identity were linguistically constituted. Musolff identifies the rhetoric of war that framed the violence of the 1970s, and he sees the language used by left-wing terrorist groups as reactivations of terminology from historical contexts such as the French Revolution or World War II. The acceptance of this declaration of war in turn fuelled the conflict. By engaging in such militaristic rhetoric, the state and mass media enabled West Germany's own war on terror to become somewhat of a self-fulfilling prophecy.[18] In her work on Meinhof's writing, Sarah Colvin analyzes the use of language throughout Meinhof's careers as a journalist and a terrorist. Her close reading of Meinhof's texts identifies how, as a journalist and later a RAF member, she constituted postwar West Germany as a continuation of the Third Reich. Given the fascist threat and what she perceived as the ineffectiveness of talking, Meinhof was then able to craft a justification of violence. The brand of antifascism and the defense of the use of violence brought into being in Meinhof's texts were central to the RAF identity as soldiers of both the worldwide revolution and the belated resistance to German fascism. Over time, the stark line between black and white, good and evil, that enabled violence grew starker, and Meinhof's language eliminated any empathy for anyone outside the small and shrinking inner circle of the RAF. Succumbing to what Colvin calls the "language trap," Meinhof and the RAF isolated themselves. Any potential third party fell away, and the group identity became self-contained, its justifications circular.[19] The discursive creation of terrorist conflicts and identities, however, is not simply the work of words. This work is also "done" by images.

An interest in the imagery of West German terrorism was ignited with the dissolution of the RAF in 1998. Almost immediately, the group's iconography was absorbed into pop culture. The five-pointed star, the acronym "RAF," and likenesses of Andreas Baader and Meinhof soon appeared on T-shirts, underwear, and even condoms.[20] Reenactments of well-known photographs were even used in advertizing campaigns, including one of Baader lying in a pool of blood used to sell slippers, and one that used fashion models to re-create the discovery of the body of RAF victim Hanns-Martin Schleyer in the boot of a car.[21] The appropriation of terrorist imagery by the worlds of fashion and marketing—dubbed "Prada Meinhof"—sparked debate about the representation of RAF terrorism. The altogether more flippant use of the RAF logo as a pop-cultural reference fell out of fashion around the time of the 2001 attacks in New York, but an interest in the representation of West German terrorism remained.[22]

A 2005 art exhibition in Berlin, "Imagining Terror" (*Zur Vorstellung des Terrors*), sparked heated debate. Some found the artworks as well as the original working title for the exhibition, "The RAF Myth" (*Mythos RAF*) to be a glorification of RAF terrorists.[23] The controversy was the latest example of how the memory of the RAF is bound to visual culture: whether the Gerhard Richter's 1988 cycle of paintings *18 October 1977*, former RAF member Astrid Proll's 2004 attempt to reclaim images from the monopoly of the media industry with a book of photographs, or Uli Edel's 2008 desire to take back the realm of imagery for RAF victims with his film version of Stefan Aust's the *Baader Meinhof Complex*, the contested memory of West German terrorism and the RAF has often amounted to a contest over the interpretative control of its visual remains, what Susan Sontag called the basic units of memory.[24] Sontag argued that the visual record defines what and how societies remember, with photographic images serving as common triggers and signposts for a given narrative.[25] In terms of the RAF, these signposts are not in question; the contest has instead been over which narrative they trigger. Images are not only important, however, to the memory of RAF terrorism, they also were fundamental in creating it.

Sontag also outlined—in the same year as the German Autumn—how people in modern societies have a relationship to reality mediated predominantly by photographic images. This mediation is made possible by that unique quality of the photograph that sees it not relegated to mere representation, but instead allows it to overlap with the real. Collective experience of an event in industrialized societies can be understood to be a function of the relevant photographic record of that event.[26] In literature on terrorism, the power of the image is often couched in the context of an uncomfortable interdependence between terrorists and the mass media. The rise of modern terrorism can, in this respect, be linked to the development of the mass media since the 1960s, with the relationship between terrorists and the media framed as a convenient symbiosis: terrorists provide the mass media with the spectacular images and stories it needs, and in return the media supplies terrorist organizations with the coverage they crave.[27] Decades before the filmic language of the 9/11 attacks, the media-savvy RAF relied on the power of the image.[28]

Despite protests from former RAF member Astrid Proll that the group's "communication with the Left was still via words," and that they "never really tried to use the power of pictures," imagery was central to creating RAF terrorism.[29] Petra Terhoeven brought the "pictorial turn" to the study of the RAF in her acknowledgment that images are not passive reflections of events, instead they actively "make" them.[30] Pictures can be actions, too. For the RAF, images of dead member Holger Meins, for example, performed ideas of martyrdom and sainthood.[31] Pictures also were critical to the violence of the German Autumn, with images of Hanns-Martin Schleyer eliciting a sympathy from the public that his kidnappers had not expected. Intended to be the face of the system, the photos were, for many, evidence of individual humanity, and they dealt the RAF a heavy "communicative defeat" (*kommunikative Niederlage*).[32] Not long after, photos of the dead Stammheim prisoners were released as part of the official version of what happened on that night in October 1977. For many sympathetic to the group, however, the images triggered a narrative of state murder. The performative power of images to create and carry discourse is central to understanding RAF terrorism as also "a battles of images."[33]

The battles on the streets of West Germany were, of course, violent ones, and physical violence, too, can have a performative effect. This performativity lies beyond the symbolism of violent acts and the ability to refer to an existing, usually textual, narrative. It can instead be found in the messages inherent in the act itself, and the ability to augment the discursive construction of the terrorist conflict. In his work on the murder of Hanns-Martin Schleyer, Bernd Weisbrod understands terrorist violence as, in part, expressions of self-empowerment that are a means unto themselves. Beyond any intertextual or referential political statements, terrorist acts project claims of self-dedication, self-victimization, and self-transformation.[34] As opposed to the symbolism of the choice of target, the performative claim in the murder of the former SS (*Schutzstaffel*) man, Weisbrod argues, was the self-contained declaration of agency from the underground.[35]

Violence can also shift the discursive construction of a terrorist conflict, much like words and images. In his work on hunger strikes in Northern Ireland prisons, Allen Feldman treats violence as part of a suite of performed practices that allowed strikers to signify historical identities and narratives, and that have the power to transform these identities and narratives.[36] For Juergensmeyer, the element of transformation or creation is the difference between symbolic violence—violence that gives expression to symbolism—and a performative violence—violence that changes things.[37] An interest in the performativity of violent acts does not underplay the brutality of those acts or seek to obfuscate the fact that terrorist violence injures and kills people. Instead, it broadens the understanding of how terrorist acts function, and it helps create a fuller, more complete understanding of the roles that violence plays in those acts. It also better accommodates less obvious forms of terrorist violence, such as self-harm, self-starvation, and suicide, that are not as easily dealt with within models of attention-seeking or symbolic violence.

The sum of these developments is a conception of terrorism as a discursively constituted phenomenon that is created, and continually re-created, by performative acts of violence, acts of imagery, and acts of text. While presented separately here, these elements cannot be treated in complete isolation. There is significant overlap between the textual, the visual, and the physically violent: an analysis must also consider violence mediated by words or by pictures, violence in support of performative text or imagery, the reinforcement of images with words and vice versa, and so on. All three elements and the interplay between them are integral to understanding Meinhof's struggle to communicate. As the RAF scribe, understanding her struggle is pivotal to understanding how RAF terrorism was performed and reperformed. This approach runs counter, however, to much of what dominates the Meinhof story, as attention tends to have shrunk away from what she wrote and did in public to focus instead on a series of details from her private life.

At the time the RAF was planting bombs and on the run from police, understanding terrorism centered largely on finding psychological defects and a terrorist personality. The seeming paradox of the middle-class terrorist and the confronting nature of terrorist acts led researchers to assume that terrorists must insane.[38] The search for an underlying pathology went deeper in Meinhof's case than others. Shortly after the birth of her daughters in 1962, Meinhof underwent brain surgery. Doctors suspected a tumor, but surgeons instead found a widened blood vessel, around which they placed a silver clasp. As early as 1970, Meinhof's then estranged husband Klaus Rainer Röhl publicly linked the operation with her slide into terrorism when he cited a severe change in personality—a sudden callousness and sexual distance—resulting from the surgery, and potentially causing Meinhof to enter the underground.[39] Shortly after she entered prison, judge Georg Knoblich ordered an examination of her brain based on the possibility that her illness in 1962 was a contributing factor to her behavior of the early 1970s. Debate reignited in 2002 when, decades after it had been removed from Meinhof's body and disappeared, her brain was rediscovered and examined for a second time. Both the 1997 and the 2002 examinations were undertaken to find a cause for Meinhof's terrorism in a brain defect.[40]

Meinhof's early life also offered psychological profilers and demographers a range of factors that appeared to contribute to a terrorist personality: she lived through World War II, she belonged to the 5 percent of leftist terrorists who were orphaned by the age of 14, and she was one of the overwhelming majority of left-wing terrorists in the Federal Republic who grew up either Protestant or without denomination.[41] The statistics were cited in studies commissioned by the West German government in the early 1980s that formed part of a trend in terrorism research that attempted to psychosociologically profile terrorists by focusing on familial relationships and socioeconomic background. The usefulness of profiling is questionable, however, as the vague psychological picture painted of the typical terrorist could just as easily apply to the nonterrorist.[42] Moreover, no conclusive evidence was found that the West German terrorists or terror suspects were psychologically abnormal. In his examinations of RAF members, including Meinhof, Baader, Ensslin, and Jan-Carl Raspe, Wilfried Rasch found nothing that "could justify their classification as psychotics, neurotics, fanatics or psychopaths."[43] In a shift mirroring the abandonment of the assumption that terrorist acts were irrational acts of violence, research moved away from the idea that terrorists were psychologically abnormal.[44] Nonetheless, the curious demographics of West German terrorism and the focus on developmental years resonate still in the story of Meinhof.

Meinhof's Protestant upbringing has been noted as contributing to an intransigent terrorist morality. While studies in the 1980s stopped short of arguing for a direct causal link to terrorism, more recently, Meinhof's—and Ensslin's—Protestantism has been presented as at least a causal cofactor in their respective radicalizations.[45] In contrast, biographical accounts by Mario Krebs, Stefan Aust, and Alois Prinz have used Meinhof's faith and childhood as part of the basis for narratives of virtue and saintliness.[46] The Lutheran Meinhof—and readers are constantly assured that she was Lutheran (*evangelisch*)—is painted as "something of an angel," an angelic schoolgirl who becomes a virtuous, earnest young woman.[47] Her sense of Christian responsibility is later painted as a motivation for her early activism. Sarah Colvin argues that, on the one hand, this sanctification serves to create a neat dramatic arc for the story by setting up the impending fall,[48] and on the other hand, it underpins a narrative of purity that survives that fall. Meinhof is likened to the heroine Joan of Arc, and a correlation to a German heroine is frequently extrapolated from the "Sophie Scholl hairstyle" (*Sophie-Scholl-Frisur*) Meinhof sported as a student protestor.[49]

The comparison with Sophie Scholl, whose stand against Nazism in the final years of World War II cost her and fellow members of the White Rose (*Weiße Rose*) their lives, fits within a vague spirit of resistance. Meinhof has been placed within a dynasty of resistance fighters by foregrounding her maternal grandfather's membership in the Social Democratic Party (*Sozialdemokratische Partei Deutschlands*), and the fact he was consequently stood down from his job by the Nazis. Meinhof's father, in turn, hesitated to take up a position that would have meant joining the Nazi Party, and both her parents had connections to the Confessing Church (*Bekennende Kirche*). After her father died, her mother and Renate Riemeck—who would later become Meinhof's foster mother—continued to subvert the Nazi regime by helping escapees from Buchenwald or covertly listening to BBC radio. A young Ulrike upheld the tradition in her steadfast and virtuous confrontations with authoritative teachers.[50] More recent biographies by Bettina Röhl, Kristin Wesemann, and Jutta Ditfurth, however, have begun to move away from the sort of narratives that shaped previous accounts.[51] Röhl, in particular, sets out to undermine what she calls the "Meinhof myth," and dismantles Meinhof's lineage of resistance. She points out that Meinhof's father joined the Nazi Party in May 1933, long before any overt compulsion, and the upbringing described by Krebs and Prinz is a more accurate representation of Werner's childhood, not Ulrike's.[52]

The most telling of the statistical categories that defines Meinhof's story, however, is her gender. As a middle-class female terrorist, Meinhof represented a paradox compounded by a paradox. Faced with a high participation rate of women, West German terrorism was considered a particularly female problem. Attempts to reconcile the "unnatural" coupling of femininity and violence in 1970s West Germany drew on late nineteenth-century criminology. Colvin describes how a tradition of biological determinism runs through attempts to understand female terrorists in the Federal Republic.[53] Recycled ideas that link female crime with any number of aberrations from the gendered ideal can be found in the media portrayals of female RAF members, scientific reports on the group, and comments such as Günter Nollau's assertion that female terrorism was due to excess emancipation.[54] Violent women necessarily were damaged women, flawed women, manly—even "manlier" (*männlicher*) than men—women.[55] Statisticians recorded the percentage of lesbian and bisexual women among terror suspects, and government reports recounted tales of Ensslin's prudishness and Meinhof's promiscuity.[56] In the print media, however, Ensslin tended to be portrayed as the RAF's femme fatale and Meinhof its bad mother.[57]

Against the background of the construction of motherhood as natural and good, Meinhof's abandonment of her daughters has been made to fit within the explanatory framework of a broken, flawed woman. Meinhof left her children to enter the underground, and later arranged for them to be moved to a

Palestinian camp for orphans located in Jordan. En route, however, the two girls were intercepted in Sicily and brought back to Germany. All the children in the camp they were bound for were killed in an Israeli attack shortly after the twins were due to arrive. This incident especially is behind a broad condemnation of Meinhof, but there are also those who would ignore it, as well as those who offer instead an image of Meinhof as a good mother.[58] The trope of motherhood has not only damned her; it has also been used to rehabilitate her. Meinhof's former husband, in particular, used the fact that Meinhof was a mother of two to protest her innocence in his magazine.[59]

Whether in the condemnation underpinned by biological determinism, or in the redemptive zeal on the part of biographers, Meinhof's early years have been plundered in order to squeeze her story into an easily digestible, often gendered, narrative. The understanding of Meinhof, therefore, has typically pivoted around one of a series of decisive moments prior to her terrorist years, with the focus ratcheted back to her marriage breakdown, her brain surgery, the loss of her parents, and so on. Meinhof may have been, at various points, a pugnacious schoolgirl, an orphaned teen, a long-suffering wife, and single mother, but she was, above all, a communicator: a composer of words and an author of bombs. The chapters in this book focus on Meinhof's words and her deeds.

Chapter 1 traces Meinhof's underlying struggle for, and with, communication through her journalism, her time in the terrorist underground, and her years in prison. Meinhof began her journalistic career with a palpable desire to affect the world around her, however, this desire stood in constant tension with a perceived ineffectiveness that she would come to express in terms of structural violence. This tension spans any distinction between journalism and terrorism, and it was heightened over time and across three broadly chronological contexts: the anti-Springer campaign of the mid 1960s, her break from *konkret* in 1969, and her isolation in prison. In the end, the same limitations that Meinhof recognized in the West German media landscape, journalism, and eventually the process of writing, also crippled her relationship with words themselves.

Meinhof's ultimately unsuccessful attempts to tame language are true to a trajectory that runs counter to the conventional understanding of her entrance into the underground as an abandonment of language for deeds. Her move into the underground was messy, and her final decision to abandon her career in journalism came only after Baader's clumsy liberation and the realization there was now a substantial price on her head. Despite a creeping justification of violence that grew out of a frustration with language, Meinhof's shift toward actions did not mean she had given up on words. If anything, the circumstances in the underground and in prison influenced her battle to communicate more than that battle prompted her decision to follow Baader out a window in

1970. This arc of private doubt and frustration parallels Meinhof's public, and sometimes violent, communication.

Following Chapter 1 is a series of chapters that analyze the performative aspects and repercussions of Meinhof's words and actions during distinct periods in her life. Chapter 2 examines the time she spent in the underground, from the liberation of Baader in May 1970 until her arrest in June 1972. These years spent evading police are intuitively a self-contained period, but they can also be bracketed out as a distinct object of analysis in terms of the unique relationship with the media while on the run. The texts produced during this period are categorized as statements, declarations, and treatises on the basis of mode of distribution, format, intended audience, and intended function. In each case, production of the texts and their distribution are outlined before the performative function is analyzed. Within this framework, the statements reveal the development of the RAF's brand and audience recognition in the aftermath of the liberation of Baader. The evolution of this semiotic matrix of visual cues and cultural references became, over time, important to the standard format of the subsequent declarations and treatises.

The declarations are part of the most intensely violent period of the first generation's underground experience: the bombing spree of May 1972. Analysis of these texts together with the bombings clarifies Meinhof's specific role in the spree and addresses the centrality of the relationship between words and violence, not only in the literature on terrorism, but also in the RAF's own works. The group's conception of this relationship was not stable, but did at points align with established ideas of violence as attention seeking, expressive, and performative. The performative violence of the bomb was particularly important, as it worked together with images of the bombings and the text of the declarations to shift the public discourse on terrorism. This shift, in turn, had significant implications for counterterrorism efforts.

The analysis of the three RAF treatises, or major pieces of written work, focuses on the construction of ideology in these texts. It reveals the use of ideology in the treatises to be "picturesque," or isolated from its original context, and performing a function approaching that of the RAF logo. This instrumentalization of ideological text as a visual feature had significant implications, particularly for the relatively apolitical second generation. It saw the group's relationship to theory and leftist icons forming part of a terrorist "cool," an indicator of group identity and affiliation. Specifically, the "picturesque" ideology in the RAF treatises was able to sustain an aversion to theory and an insistence on "praxis" as well as perform discourses of violence, bravery and sacrifice, and betrayal and loyalty.

Chapter 3 isolates the prison hunger strikes as a way of understanding Meinhof's prison years from 1972 to 1976. It first outlines how first-generation prisoners overcame isolation to communicate between cells, between prisons, and with the outside world. Networks of smuggled texts enabled coordination and publication of the strikes, as well as aggressive constructions of self-starvation. Within the prison system, ideas of "holy" hunger maintained a collective identity and supported the internal discipline of the group. Externally, however, self-starvation was used to counter what the RAF saw as a mainstream medicalization of terror. Meinhof led the repackaging of the RAF struggle and its rhetoric of antifascism and anti-imperialism in terms of science, medicine, and the prisoner body for an external audience. Examining how she managed this process assigns Meinhof a central role in this period of RAF history, something established debates on the prison years have frequently denied her.

Having created a public relations machine from their cells, the media-savvy prisoners were offered more direct access to the West German public with the Stammheim trial. Chapter 4 examines the trial in the "multipurpose building" (*Mehrzweckhalle*) next to the Stammheim prison that dominated the final years of the incarceration of the first generation from 1975 to 1977. Both the state and the RAF prisoners understood the trial as an opportunity to reach their respective audiences, and both prepared for the long-anticipated proceedings: the government rushed through a number of focused legislative amendments, and the prisoners developed a series of tactics to stall or disrupt the judicial process. Such preparations set the scene for a battle over the staging of the trial and its reception beyond the courtroom. It was in this context that Meinhof led a remodeling of the RAF message for this new forum. The two central strategies of the group's defense were more spectacular than legal, and they were built around RAF constructions of the "political prisoner" and the "prisoner of war." Arguing for political prisoner status was designed to counter the idea of Stammheim being a "normal trial," while "project prisoner of war status" sought to hijack developments in international law. These twin tactics were only two aspects of a long and complex trial, but they are important to an understanding of a period in which legal procedure took a back seat to a much broader communicative process. They also reclaim a key position for Meinhof in the story of the trial, which is otherwise reserved for legal wrangling and Baader's and Ensslin's histrionics.

The conclusion of the trial was overshadowed by the events of the German Autumn, which ended with the controversial deaths of the prisoners. The "Stammheim deaths" and the debate surrounding them arguably lie at the heart of the group's continued relevance. Meinhof was found hanged on May 9, 1976, setting into motion a process of signification that gave rise to numerous interpretations. A similar process then emerged when Baader and Ensslin were found dead, and Raspe nearly dead, in their prison cells on the morning of October 18, 1977. Over the years, the main threads of interpretation to arise from these dual processes merged into the "Stammheim myth." This mix of seemingly incompatible explanations has survived on explosive accusations of state murder and a discourse equating suicide with murder.

Chapter 5 reveals how Meinhof was involved in cultivating a discourse of suicide that prepared the ground for the Stammheim myth. As a result, it establishes a place for Meinhof in the history of her own martyrdom. This final chapter also provides some symmetry to the book. On the one hand, it completes the chronological progression that begins with Meinhof's journalism and concludes with her suicide and the ever-present controversy that surrounds it. On the other hand, tracing back through prison communications, underground texts to her journalism, mirrors the analysis in Chapter 1: whereas Chapter 5 works backward to uncover a discourse of suicide that helped shape the potential responses to her own death, Chapter 1 tracks her struggle to communicate forward from her journalism until her death.

Meinhof's 1976 death did not, however, mean the end of her performative influence. What she set in place not only saved the group and enabled its violence during her lifetime; it also endured long after she was found dead. Much of what she created survived the German Autumn the following year to shape the RAF identity and violence into the 1980s. Parts, too, outlived the group itself, and linger still in the cultural memory of West German terrorism of the twenty-first century. The conclusion to the book gathers these echoing effects of Meinhof's struggle to communicate.

CHAPTER 1

Where Words Fail

man—it was grim—i COULD not write—EVERYTHING was just rubbish, mincemeat, not in my head but on paper.[1]

—From a letter by Meinhof to a fellow prisoner, 1973

It was in prison that words ultimately failed Ulrike Meinhof. Her writing toward the end of her life reveals a deep suspicion of language and its ability to convey the meaning she intended.[2] These prison texts were the final throes of her attempt to reconcile the tension between her criticism and skepticism of available means of communication and her employment of them. Far from being resolved in May 1970, this tension was a constant in Meinhof's work, and tracking her attempts to overcome this tension reveals not a self-assured abandonment of words in favor of deeds coinciding more or less with her entrance into the underground, but a trajectory of frustration and doubt independent of her status as a journalist or terrorist. With increasing desperation, her focus shrinks over time from sweeping analyses of the capitalist media, to a loss of faith in the genre of journalistic writing, to a paralyzing distrust of words themselves. The linguistic hopelessness so evident in her prison cell had its beginnings in her journalism and her work for *konkret*.

In the early months of 1958, Meinhof joined the Socialist German Student Union (*Sozialistischer Deutscher Studentenbund*, SDS) at the University of Münster and founded an antinuclear weapons committee (*Anti-Atomwaffen-Ausschuss*). The issue of nuclear armament had pushed to the fore since Chancellor Konrad Adenauer and Defense Minister Franz Josef Strauss had begun making a case for it in 1957. A group of 18 nuclear scientists put their names to the *Göttingen Declaration* (*Göttinger Erklärung*), denouncing the plans, and the debate soon came to dominate the political scene of the late 1950s. Elsewhere at this time, Klaus Rainer Röhl was also seeking contact with the antinuclear movement. The East German regime had subsidized Röhl's magazine *konkret* from as early as 1955, and with the antinuclear protests gathering steam in early 1958, it was decided that *konkret* should maneuver its way to the front of the growing movement. The 1959 *Atomkongress* was the vehicle to do this, and it was during the preparations for it that Röhl attempted to recruit Meinhof.[3]

While she would eventually overcome her oft-alluded to initial aversion to Röhl, it was not Röhl's efforts, but contact with the Socialist Unity Party (*Sozialistische Einheitspartei Deutschlands*, SED) and the Communist Party of Germany (*Kommunistische Partei Deutschlands*, KPD) that won Meinhof over. Röhl later described the steering of the *Atomkongress* as the first and last great success the KPD enjoyed in postwar West Germany, and while Meinhof was integral to that effort, her writing for the magazine would ultimately become far more important.[4] Her enthusiasm for the KPD and the East German regime spilled over into her written work for *konkret*. Her first article in October 1959— "Peace makes History" (*Der Friede macht Geschichte*)—celebrated both the launch of the Russian *Sputnik* satellite, as confirmation of Soviet technical prowess, and Khrushchev's recent visit to the United States, as an indicator of a thawing in the Cold War, a victory for the doctrine of coexistence. It was by no means a stretch for Meinhof, who had written articles previously for the student newspaper *das argument*, including a 1958 attack on the Adenauer government in which she, in the style and tone of the best pro-Soviet propaganda, completely inhabited Khrushchev's worldview.[5]

This first article was meant to be the extent of Meinhof's contribution to *konkret* as she left the editorial "boys' club" for Jena and research for her dissertation. It was only at the behest of the KPD, which paid for her move to Hamburg, that she returned to *konkret* and took up a permanent position with the magazine in early 1960.[6] In her second article— "Shadow of the Summit Westward" (*Gipfelschatten westwärts*)—she addressed a theme that would remain dominant in her writing: communism as the solution to a lingering national socialism in West Germany. She soon found a useful focus for this argument in the drafting of West German emergency laws (*Notstandsgesetze*).

The proposed laws took over from the nuclear armament debate of the late 1950s to become the dominant political issue of the early 1960s. The legislation under consideration would allow for the suspension of a number of basic rights (*Grundrechte*) in the case of an emergency, and Meinhof noted, as did many others, that "article 48 of the Weimar Constitution also abolished basic rights."[7] She opened her 1960 article "Emergency? Emergency!" (*Notstand? Notstand!*) with the observation: "Germany in 1960—every third person compares it with the Germany of 1933."[8] The column was also accompanied by a loose supplement that placed the Weimar Republic article alongside the 1960 draft emergency law legislation to allow for direct comparison. Meinhof followed the debate closely over the next eight years, until a somewhat watered-down version of the legislation was passed in 1968.

It was most notably via personal attacks, however, that she compared the Federal Republic directly with Hitler's Germany. Meinhof concluded her 1961 column "Hitler in You" (*Hitler in Euch*) with the line: "Just as we ask our parents about Hitler, one day we will be asked by our children about [Minister of Defense] Mr. [Franz Josef] Strauß."[9] This moved beyond comparing the Federal Republic with the Weimar Republic, the precursor to National Socialism, and instead equated West Germany with the Third Reich itself. Despite appearing at the end of a short text that accompanied a more comprehensive lead article by Jörg Haas, it was Meinhof's bold assertion that led to a defamation charge, protracted legal proceedings, and instant fame. The Strauss controversy was explicitly couched in the context of the Adolf Eichmann trial, and not long after, Meinhof found herself in Munich to cover the trial of Karl Wolff. Wolff was a high-ranking member of the Waffen-SS who after the war claimed to have only learned of the extermination of Jews in 1945. In 1964 he received a 15-year prison sentence for aiding and abetting the murder of three hundred thousand Jews. Meinhof's coverage of the trial resulted in a lengthy text that was shortened for *konkret* and served as the basis for her first radio feature, which aired in October 1964.[10]

Meinhof's Wolff portrait appeared in the second independent issue, after East German funding for the magazine had dried up. Despite the breakdown of their financial association, Meinhof maintained a working relationship with East Germany, which was important for the *konkret* investigation of West German President Heinrich Lübke's alleged Nazi past. She was involved in the research for articles written for *konkret* by Robert Neumann, alleging that Lübke had been responsible for building concentration camps.[11] In her efforts to gather information on his past she regularly met with Albert Norden, member of the politburo, and East German lawyer Friedrich Karl Kaul. Norden's recently published *Brown Book* (*Braunbuch*) listed close to two thousand West German politicians and other prominent figures, including Lübke, who were claimed to have held senior positions in the National Socialist regime. Kaul, who had continued to act as the lawyer for *konkret*, then passed on forged documents linking Lübke to designs for concentration camps.[12] The withdrawal of funding did not therefore mean a withdrawal of practical support. Nor did it mean a significant shift from party lines by Meinhof. It did, however, allow her wider scope in terms of subject matter.

Meinhof no longer focused solely on domestic political affairs. Instead, she continued her attack on the Federal Republic via radio and television with themes such as state-run homes for delinquent girls, workers, foreign workers, women, women workers, and the poor.[13] Her work on the outsiders of

West German society was incisive, if at times dogmatic, and addressed very real problems. The underlying thrust of these articles and radio features was the assumption of complete societal responsibility, that social forces alone were at work when laws were broken or crimes committed. While neither her sincerity nor the depths of the problems should be underestimated, Meinhof did use these domestic issues in a targeted attempt to reveal problems inherent in West German society. At this time, too, she increasingly turned to international issues to continue her attack on the state. In 1963 she wrote that "only if an issue becomes a scandal beyond the borders, if the standing of the Federal Republic amongst its friends abroad is at stake, do the victims and opponents of fascism gain political ground."[14] The idea that the international stage was the best place to make her case against the state came to dominate her journalism a few years later, with domestic debates replaced by international issues or German affairs in an international context: the Vietnam War, university reform, third-world countries, feminism, antiauthoritarianism, anti-Zionism, and antifascism.

The broad strokes of her journalistic career presented here have common elements: a commitment to communism and a firm belief that structural violence pervades West German capitalist society. She argued through this prism in all areas and topics she addressed in her journalism, and she applied the same logic of structural violence to processes of communication: to the mass media, to journalism, and to language.

Meinhof and the Opinion Industry

In a 1960 letter to her foster mother Renate Riemeck, Meinhof enthusiastically recommends Günter Grass's *The Tin Drum*. She gives a four-sentence synopsis of the colossal work before offering the (secondhand) interpretation that "the stunted figure of Oskar is a symbol for the situation facing the avant-garde writer in capitalist society—this seems to mean: cramped from all sides, unable to grow, condemned to the realm of scurrility and perversion."[15] While this is a contested reading of Grass's novel, it is representative of Meinhof's views on communication. The structural violence she saw as inherent in the capitalist Federal Republic also pervades the realm of expression and text production. Throughout her career she was torn between what she saw as the media's inherent restrictions and propensity to manipulate on the one hand, and her undoubted desire to communicate and "have an effect" on the other.[16] Tracing her attempts to resolve this tension reveals how the struggle that ended in a war with words began with her analysis of the West German mass media.

Meinhof was an astute observer of the media. From late 1959 she was responsible for reviewing a range of publications for *konkret*, and from this time there also appeared a regular feature, "What wasn't printed in *Die Welt*"

(*Es stand nicht in der Welt*). This section was a wrap-up of predominantly the international press: for example, *Neue Zürcher Zeitung*, *The New Statesman*, *The Guardian*, *The Observer*, *The Times*, and *Le Monde*. She would later monitor the press from the underground and continue in this role in prison. The internal prison discussions from June 1973 reveal how important and detailed the review of the press was to the prison communication system:

> what the thing must bring in:
> 1. Information on base organizations and particularly all that publish: newspapers, theoretical organs, discussion of the program, leaflets . . .
> 2. Press analysis (central in this office and via *one* clippings office) the keywords like RAF, Police, FBG [Federal Border Guard], organization, anti-terror, secret services, guerilla—more to come—Groenewold will finance it, and the useable stuff will be collected and copied . . . in his office and from there sent to the lawyers' offices and the prisoners.[17]

Also in 1973, a list of categories for the press archive devised by Meinhof was found in her cell. She organized the archive around themes and geographical areas. Not only is the collection and processing of media material understood as central to the Red Army Faction (RAF) practice of prison schooling, but the media itself is also one of the 39 categories.[18]

Beyond monitoring the media landscape, Meinhof provided a constant critique, focusing on the dangers of a monopoly and the potential for the manipulation of public opinion. Her critique centered on Axel Springer and his large market share as the embodiment of a manipulative media industry. In 1967 she famously called for Springer to be expropriated and his dominance of the market dismantled, as it prevented certain topics from reaching a wide audience:

> Political impulses like those that emanated from students in the example of the Shah visit, in the example of the Berlin counter-university, the Vietnam demonstrations, the protests against the police and the mayor of Berlin, Albertz, and like those that emanated from the *Emergency of Democracy* convention and from the emergency resolutions by the Confederation of German Trade Unions, today only reach a small sector of the public, a section of the population, and these impulses have only a small chance to even be noticed, to be part of the discussion.[19]

While this article was critical of the majority of the sector, its focus was Springer, and it argued his power was the direct result—though not a cause—of media concentration. Therefore, she wrote, any attempt to "re-democratize" the media failed in the face of Springer's market share, and she suggested limiting the circulation of newspapers from any one company to five hundred thousand copies. The demand to expropriate Springer, she wrote, "aims for a notion of democracy that Augstein [chief editor of the *Spiegel*] doesn't have in mind and Springer doesn't have in the BILD: instead of the manipulation of public opinion, it aims to use freedom of opinion and freedom of the press to abolish manipulation; instead of steering and blocking information, disseminating information; instead of hammering home political opinion, cultivating a critical consciousness; instead of putting the people to sleep, waking it up; instead of dumbing it down and letting it 'lounge about,' emancipating it."[20] This article came at the height of a much broader anti-Springer campaign that emerged within the student movement in the mid-1960s. This campaign decried his market share in the print news media, accusing him of abusing it to discriminate against minorities, launch campaigns against interest groups, and deliberately manipulate the consciousness of his readers. The notion of manipulation that underpinned the campaign drew heavily and explicitly on Theodor Adorno and Max Horkheimer's notion of the "culture industry," as well as Hans Magnus Enzensberger's "consciousness industry."[21]

Adorno and Horkheimer argued that the legacy of the Enlightenment of standardized forms of production had led to concentrated industries built around the mass production of culture. The interdependence of these industries tends toward sameness and a standardization of needs and desires that result in manipulation of the masses. The "culture industry" is characterized, therefore, by its ability to absorb "spontaneity" and "individuality" and maintain a "relentless unity." This "cycle of manipulation and retroactive need" allows for the standardization of improvisation, originality, and the accidental so that they are recognizable as such.[22] As a result, no room remains outside the culture industry for improvisation, originality, the accidental, or, by extrapolation, protest or dissent. Similarly, Enzensberger, who wrote a decade and a half after Adorno and Horkheimer, argued for the completeness of what he terms the "consciousness industry." Prerequisites for the industry are economic surplus (but importantly, not necessarily capitalism) and the new technical instruments of production such as radio, film, television, and public relations. The products delivered to the people are "opinions, judgments and prejudices, consciousness matter of all sorts." Important for Enzensberger was also the industrial-scale impossibility of alternatives via censorship, self-control and economic pressures, and monopoly in the means of production.[23]

For many in the Extraparliamentary Opposition (*Außerparlamentarische Opposition*, APO), Springer embodied this idea of a standardized culture or consciousness that was based on technological advancement and concentration of the means of production and was able to absorb difference. In her 1965 article "Springer Television" (*Springer-Fernsehen*), Meinhof commented on the removal of *Panorama* moderator, Gert von Paczensky, from the controversial political series due to political pressure from the Christian Democratic Union (*Christlich Demokratische Union Deutschlands*, CDU) in the wake of numerous reports critical of the government. She bemoaned the narrow range of interests enshrined in the "fascist" structure of the public television provider Second German Television (*Zweites Deutsches Fernsehen*, ZDF). Only a small range of interest groups was represented, she argued, on the ZDF's board, which itself was undemocratic. This point was emphasized by making a comparison between the appointment of Hitler as chancellor and the maintenance of an unelected Springer representative on the council responsible for all political reporting.[24]

The APO campaign against Springer continued to gather steam, and in February 1968, several months after Meinhof's *konkret* article calling for Springer to be expropriated, some 1,500 students gathered at the Technical University in Berlin to prepare for the "Springer hearings." Toward the end of the evening the audience watched a film by a young film student and later RAF member, Holger Meins, called *Instructions on how to Prepare a Molotov Cocktail* (*Anleitung zur Erstellung eines Molotowcocktails*, 1968). The four-minute silent film ended with a still of Springer headquarters in West Berlin. The night following the film's screening, and despite pleas that it would only hurt the campaign, windows of Springer branches were smashed with stones, some wrapped in pamphlets reading "Expropriate Springer!" (*Enteignet Springer!*)[25]

The hearings, which were originally planned for three days, lasted only one evening and were attended by roughly 1,800 students. The tone was clear, given contributions addressing, for example, the "manipulation mechanism of the Springer press" (*Manipulationsmechanismus der Springer-Presse*) and the "manipulation of public opinion in Berlin" (*Manipulation der öffentlichen Meinung in Berlin*).[26] The anti-Springer campaign reached its high point for most in the days following the shooting of Rudi Dutschke, when more than fifty thousand people took to the streets crying "Bild shot as well!" (*Bild schoss mit!*) and trying to stop the circulation of Springer publications by blockading printing houses in Essen, Esslingen, Frankfurt, Hamburg, and West Berlin. The high point of Meinhof's own campaign came in the underground.

After her RAF text *Serve the People* (*Dem Volk dienen*) had rehashed the SDS position on Springer from 1967, incorporating criticisms of the *Bild* and Heinrich Böll's media critique from 1972, Meinhof's personal attack climaxed with the bombing of the Springer offices in Hamburg. This bombing was her idea, and the only attack during the bombing spree of May 1972 she was personally involved in, beyond writing the declaration of responsibility.[27] In the Hamburg declaration she demanded, in the name of the RAF, that "[Springer's] newspapers cease the anti-communist campaign against the New Left, against acts of solidarity of the working class such as strikes, against the Communist parties here and in other countries; that the Springer Group cease the campaign against the liberation movements in the Third World, in particular against the Arab peoples fighting for the liberation of Palestine; that it cease the propaganda and material support for Zionism—the imperialist politics of Israel's ruling class; that the Springer press stops spreading racist lies about foreign workers."[28] The underlying logic of this aggressive defense of the operation was the same analysis of media concentration and manipulation.

Meinhof's interpretation of the capitalist media remained consistent throughout her incarceration, as is evident in her chosen reading material. RAF lawyers were allowed to order books via the prison administration on behalf of prisoners, and Meinhof read widely, including qualitative and quantitative studies of the media and public opinion. In February 1974, Klaus Croissant placed an order,[29] and among the works eventually received in December were Helmuth Diederichs, *Konzentration in den Massenmedien*,[30] and H. D. Müller, Der *Springer-Konzern: eine kritische Studie*.[31] In a separate 1974 order she requested[32] Horst Holzer, *Kommunikationssoziologie*,[33] Wolf D. Hundt, *Kommunikationstopologie*,[34] and Regina Schmidt and Egon Becker, *Reaktionen auf politische Vorgänge. Drei Meinungsstudien aus der Bundesrepublik*,[35] and in November 1974 she ordered[36] Hans Jürgen Koschwitz, *Publizistik und politisches System*, and Klaus Berpohl [sic], *Die Massenmedien*. These scientific studies of the media in industrialized, capitalist West Germany rely, more often than not, explicitly on Enzensberger as well as Adorno and Horkheimer's notion of the "culture industry." While Meinhof expressed doubts in prison that Adorno could be useful to the RAF because of his lack of a "class perspective" (*klassenstandpunkt*), this was in the context of the RAF's uncompromising denouncement of leftist intellectuals, and it must be noted that in the same breath she remained expressly aligned to his analysis of society's "broken communication" (*kaputte kommunikation*).[37]

The quantitative works also reinforce her long-standing interest in research into public opinion. Having first addressed opinion polling publicly in her 1963 article on Konrad Adenauer and public opinion, Meinhof monitored surveys from the underground.[38] She mentions in a 1971 letter to the North Korean Workers' Party, for example, that despite a concerted media campaign against the group, 10 percent of the population of the north German coastal states declared that they would harbor members of the RAF.[39] Later in the context of the trial, an unsigned prison text also mentioned surveys from 1972, 1973, and 1974 that show up to 20 percent of the adult population sympathized with the RAF.[40]

Meinhof's own campaign against Springer and the capitalist media in West Germany, and her interest in public opinion, shared their theoretical underpinning with a broader movement. Her fears of manipulation, press concentration, and the silencing of opposition via integration rested on ideas of a standardized, industrialized mass media, and these fears remained constant throughout her life. Amid mounting frustration, her unease manifested not only in more vocal and provocative attacks against the mainstream media but in a reflection on journalism itself. In what would be the final years of her journalistic career,

Meinhof increasingly brought the logic of her critique of capitalist society to bear on her own journalistic practice.

Meinhof and "Authoritarian" Journalism

Meinhof was not only an astute observer of the media; she was also a gifted exponent of its conventions. Her ability to inhabit vocabularies and styles was evident in her model examples of Soviet propaganda for *das argument*, in essays written under the name and in the style of Renate Riemeck, and the flawless assumption of party lines with *konkret*.[41] Her abilities as a journalist, however, stood in constant tension with her own analyses of the reporting of debates in the mainstream media. An inability to reconcile the two gradually gave way to frustration, scrutiny of her own practice, doubt in the genre of journalism, and ultimately attempts to create a new kind of writing.

Some of the work Meinhof did for *konkret* reveals in a playful way both her recognition of the stylistic and discursive strategies of other publications and her skill as a writer. The first episode in what became a series called "political fiction" appeared in 1964. Jürgen Holtkamp and Meinhof composed a number of fake articles in the style of various newspapers in response to an invented German Press Agency (*Deutsche Presse-Agentur*, dpa) release announcing that Walter Ulbricht had dissolved East Germany. They satirized publications such as *Die Welt* and *Die Zeitung* (a short-lived publication designed to compete with the *Der Spiegel*) with Holtkamp also penning the *Bild*'s response and Meinhof parodying Marion Gräfin von Dönhoff and *Stern* columnist Sibylle.[42] Ironically, elements of the parody were incorporated into the appearance of Meinhof's own columns: "We borrowed the concept," Klaus Rainer Röhl has subsequently admitted, "of how Ulrike was to appear as a columnist in the future, that is with a solid border and a photo, from the *Stern*, in which a certain Mrs. Sibylle regularly published."[43]

This first installment of political fiction appeared in the context of a new editorial freedom, given the breakdown of the working relationship with East Berlin. Other parodies followed. In 1966 "political fiction" reappeared when fake newspaper articles were written in response to a dpa release that Hitler had returned from exile in Paraguay.[44] Meinhof's contribution was articles written in the name of Heinz van Nouhuys, the editor of the magazine *Quick*, Jürgen Tern, the editor of the *Frankfurter Allgemeine*, and William S. Schlamm, columnist for Springer's *Die Welt*. A year later, media figures were not only the object of satire, but the industry also provided the scenario. The hypothetical situation saw *Der Spiegel* sold to Springer with Meinhof writing an editorial as editor of *Der Spiegel*, Rudolf Augstein, as well as a discussion between Augstein and Springer moderated by one of the political editors at *Die Zeit*, Hans Gresmann.

The authors prefaced this 1967 satire by conceding they "originally wanted to publish it on June 1, 1968, but the political development that the Spiegel has undergone in recent weeks and months forced us to bring it forward to July 1, 1967, as otherwise we ran the risk that this vision of the future would be overtaken by reality."[45] The tone was more earnest than the more fanciful ideas of East Berlin tearing down the Berlin Wall or Hitler returning from Latin America, and it was indicative of a shift in Meinhof's approach to her commentary of journalistic practice.

Throughout the mid to late 1960s the satire and polemics gave way to articles that amounted to discourse analyses of mainstream reporting. Once her plaything, journalism and journalistic methods themselves became the implicit, and increasingly the explicit, object of her critiques. In a 1966 article, for example, Meinhof used the debate surrounding a government proposal to extend the working week as an opportunity to address mainstream reporting. She identified in public debate the discursive linking of reduced hours with the threat of more foreign workers: "But even [the union] *Gesamtmetall* must have noticed that the extra hour of work in the Federal Republic is discussed in relation to foreign workers, that the preparedness to work an extra hour can be put down to not so much German work ethic as an antipathy towards foreigners."[46] More than a commentary of the issue at hand, this was a commentary on the reporting of the debate and what she saw as the instrumentalization of xenophobia to manufacture support for a longer working week.

In 1968 she tackled the reporting surrounding the case of convicted murderer Jürgen Bartsch. Bartsch murdered four young boys, and while condemning the killings, Meinhof took issue with the media's and the court's treatment of the case. She would have liked to have seen it used to provoke a discussion of the societal causes of criminality, "but the court did everything humanly possible to prevent the circumstances that inspired Jürgen Bartsch's development becoming the subject of the trial."[47] Meinhof used the case to contrast her view of the primacy of societal pressures and institutional violence with the construction of Bartsch as an exception and his criminality as abnormal. She wrote of a construction resting on the judge's own "Nazi biological determinism" (*NS-Biologismus*) used to spare the adoptive mother any blame, before she listed the societal failings that plagued Bartsch's life: bad parents, a bungled adoption, his treatment in a home, his treatment at the hands of adoptive parents, society's views of his homosexuality that denigrated love to an obscenity, and abuse at the hands of his adoptive father. By presenting Bartsch as an inexplicable aberration, she argued, the court and the press were able to confirm the given values and systems of the Federal Republic and silence any questions of causality.

Also in 1968, Meinhof addressed what she saw as the "paradigms of veiling" (*Verschleierungsmodelle*) in the reporting of the student movement. She attacked what she identified as the four dominant discourses in mainstream reporting in the wake of the shooting of Benno Ohnesorg as actively and deliberately hiding the underlying problem: the notion of "middle-class prosperity as a value unto itself," the assumed "innocence of the system" that frames the shooting as an inexplicable aberration, the argument that "the order is in order, it's the others who are confused," and the call for "action, but not like this," for constructive suggestions made appropriately.[48] What Meinhof consistently described was the performative power of mainstream discourse to "make" foreign workers a threat, victims of societal dysfunction complicit in their own fate, student protesters hooligans, and, she would argue, the system irreproachable. She did not express this recognition in terms of performativity, but in terms of violence.

In the same 1968 issue, Meinhof also wrote an open letter to Rudolf Augstein in which she attacked a *Der Spiegel* commentary of Bahman Nirumand's book on Iran, *Persia: Model of a Developing Nation or the Dictatorship of the Free World* (*Persien. Modell eines Entwicklungslandes oder Die Diktatur der freien Welt*). Nirumand's 1967 book criticizing the ruling regime in his homeland became an important work for the student movement, as the APO shifted its focus beyond Germany's borders. In her open letter, Meinhof went into great detail to counter claims made by the magazine and accuse it of using its "weapon of a massive circulation" to save Iran's face: "in this way the Spiegel represents the interests of the rich here like the Shah of Iran represents them in his country, the Spiegel—'consciously or otherwise'—with the means of misrepresentation, suppression, obfuscation (one can of course think of other words for it), the Shah with the means of a police state."[49] By comparing what she saw as the dishonest journalistic practices of *Der Spiegel* with the brutal oppression of the citizens of the police state of Iran, Meinhof made the analogous connection between highly visible and direct mechanisms of state control and the writing of West German journalists.[50]

While Meinhof was attacking mainstream journalism she was growing increasingly frustrated with her own work. In the face of a stark contrast between her desire to have an effect and her perceived ineffectiveness, she reportedly conceded to Joachim Fest in the mid-1960s that "the inappropriateness of my means is nearly killing me."[51] Her 1968 article "Counter Violence" (*Gegen-Gewalt*), for example, was an exasperated diagnosis of what she saw as the stymieing and simplification of debate. She writes of the protest movement being falsely and cynically reduced to a generational conflict and then presented as "mystically biological" (*mystisch-biologisch*), which allowed for "red" to be equated with "brown" and "oppression with the protest against oppression."[52] Later in the same column she declared that "they [students] have understood that ceremonial forms and the respectable system do not, without pain or being broken, allow any room for any critical content and democratic discussion."[53] Such frustration led not only to an intensified verbal provocation but, more importantly, to a period of self-reflection and attempts to find "room" for critical content and "democratic discussion." This search for alternatives, together with disagreements with Röhl over the magazine, prompted Meinhof to leave *konkret* toward the end of the 1960s.

Röhl employed two main strategies to fill the financial gap left for *konkret* after the subsidies from East Berlin dried up in 1964. He appealed directly to subscription holders for assistance, asking them to pay their subscriptions early, and he increasingly combined the magazine's promotion of a political revolution with an interpretation of the sexual revolution. Sex was not only entwined in the political analysis of the magazine, but the suggestive shots of young women that appeared on the covers in 1964 eventually became nude shots in 1969. Meinhof did not approve of the direction the magazine was taking. It was in this context of an intensifying frustration at her platform being dismantled and her disintegrating marriage that Meinhof, perhaps inevitably, turned her attention to her own journalistic practice.

In her 1969 article "Columnism" (*Kolumnismus*) Meinhof offered a self-reflective critique of her role as a journalist. She articulated her view that the unifying structural violence of capitalism has rendered the expression of an alternative worldview via the generic form of the column impossible. She now leveled at her own work the same criticism she had long since leveled at the media industry, as she accused columnists of submitting to the forces of capitalism: "We do not want saints, we only demand that resistance is offered and submission to the laws of the market is not sold as free journalism, and that the art of making deadlines is not confused with the art of communicating the truth to the people, and that editorial democracy is not a spanner in the works and the freedom of a columnist is recognized for what it is: a prestige and profit factor, deception of the reader, deception of oneself, cult of personality."[54] Journalists in her position were unable, she argued, to give expression to subversive messages in what she described as an "authoritarian" (*autoritär*) genre that inherently excluded room for subversion. Capitalism, she continued, has an ability to integrate and therefore nullify its enemies and "columnists," she wrote, "are the negroes in the State Department, the women in the Federal Government, a fig leaf, an alibi, an excuse."[55] In the wake of "Columnism," Meinhof declared in the pages of *Red Press Correspondence* (*Rote Presse Korrespondenz*)—an APO publication founded after the SDS dissolved—that *konkret* should not become a "consumer good" (*Ware*), but a forum, and she took concrete steps to try to rediscover journalism as a platform.[56]

In September 1968, and only months before "Columnism" appeared, Meinhof was part of "*konkret* Berlin." Röhl decided to allow this collective of authors, which included well-known writers such as Dutschke, Enzensberger, and Nirumand, to publish anonymously in *konkret*. A contract for 19 pages was drawn up, but the relationship fell apart after Röhl failed to publish some articles and made changes to others. This attempt at a "redemocratization" (*Redemokratisie-rung*) of her writing via collective authorship was something Meinhof revisited after the publication of "Columnism." Her final article written for *konkret*—"On the Situation in the Universities" (*Zur Situation an den Hochschulen*)—was rejected for publication by Röhl and did not appear in the magazine. It was produced collaboratively with the SDS in West Berlin, and was a conscious response to the personalization she had raged against in "Columnism." She later wrote that the "product of collective writing" is "in terms of content and formulation more exact and binding" than anything she could compose on her own.[57] It was after Röhl's rejection of the text that Meinhof publicly split from the magazine via a statement published in the *Frankfurter Rundschau* on April 26, 1969, that described *konkret* as being on the brink of becoming an "instrument of the counterrevolution" (*Instrument der Konterrevolution*).[58]

While committing herself to a new kind of text production, Meinhof had at the same time been establishing an alternative and clandestine editorial department for *konkret*. From West Berlin she won staff for her counterhierarchy and began interfering with the magazine by deleting planned articles or inserting new ones without Röhl's knowledge. In the early months of 1969 she was often in Hamburg to lead this alternative editorial department. The struggle for the magazine intensified and, despite her public statement in April that she was giving up the fight, culminated in plans to occupy the *konkret* offices. On May 7, 1969, a group of about thirty people drove to Hamburg to take over the offices and prevent circulation of the next issue. Röhl was warned of the plan, however, and the offices were emptied. The group left a leaflet at the scene accusing the magazine of being as "authoritarian" as Röhl's managerial style, before a number of them made their way to his house and trashed it. Meinhof had in the meantime flown to Hamburg, and arrived at what had once been her home shortly after the police, photographers, and journalists who had come to report the attack.

After the spectacular finale to her relationship with *konkret*, Meinhof continued her search for a medium capable of carrying her message. She had worked in radio since 1964 producing lengthy features, but she also reflected on the role of radio in mass communication. According to a police report, she was part of the New Left Radio Committee that formed in the aftermath of the demonstrations over the 1968 Easter weekend in response to the shooting of Rudi Dutschke and sought to negotiate an hour of airtime per day with West German public radio.[59] Toward the end of 1969 she was invited by Harry Pross, of the Institute for Journalism and Communication Studies (*Institut für Publizistik- und Kommunikationswissenschaft*) of the Free University in Berlin, to teach a seminar on radio.

Pross wanted to teach communication studies with a more practical component, but within the framework of his theoretical understanding of a journalist as someone who leads the reader through the "world of signs and symbols."[60] The majority of students, however, saw journalism as something to be bent to a political end, and this was reflected in Meinhof's series of lectures during the 1969–70 winter semester called "Radio Laboratory. Possibilities for Agitation and Enlightenment in the Radio Feature" (*Funklabor. Möglichkeiten von Agitation und Aufklärung im Hörfunk-Feature*). In one of the seminars Meinhof told her audience, "We don't want to produce radio features suitable for state-owned stations, rather features designed for the agitation work in the basis groups of leftist organizations."[61] This point was reinforced when she framed the seminar as a recruitment drive for specific groups by telling students that "the seminar does not serve to train journalists who work politically against the Left; the results of this seminar are to serve the work of agitation; the participants of the seminar are to make contact with the Red Guard and the Red Spartacist League."[62] The Red Guard and the Spartacist League had strong organizational links to the West German Communist Party and the East German Socialist Unity Party. The choice of these groups reflects Meinhof's continuing loyalty to communism and the East German model as the future for Germany.

Meinhof's nascent attempts at journalistic reform and activism were many and varied, but none were terribly successful. Journalistic practice, which had previously been her playground, proved a source of increasing frustration, self-reflection, and doubt. She extended the accusation that the capitalist media monopoly integrated and extinguished alternative views to journalistic writing, which she charged with adhering to market forces, of becoming a consumer good, and rendering subversion impossible. Her attempts to "redemocratize" and "emancipate" journalism ranged from sweeping attempts at collective authorship to her focused struggle for control of *konkret*, from her idea of radio as the agitator for a broad-based leftist movement to the short-lived International News and Research Institute (*Internationales Nachrichten- und Forschungsinstitut*) of the SDS.[63] In the end, however, there is little evidence of a solution to the underlying tension that continued to simmer, even after Meinhof entered the underground in May 1970.

Meinhof, the Media, Writing, and Language

Meinhof's entrance into the underground is often understood to be preceded by a neat evolution in her relationship to physical violence that sees her leave language for action. Such a development must be seen within the context of the discussions in the protest movement at the time that revolved around questions of whether verbal protest was sufficient, whether or not acts of physical violence were justified, and whether such acts could legitimately target people or just things. A number of moments in her writing can be cited as points along the path of this radicalization. These moments reveal a shifting attitude to the legitimacy of violence. The inevitability of the evolution is undermined, however, by the clumsiness of Meinhof's entrance into the underground, and in the fact that in the end she did not give up on words.

Meinhof wrote an article in 1967 for issue 5 of *konkret* entitled "Napalm and Custard" (*Napalm und Pudding*) on the failed attack on U.S. vice president Hubert Humphrey by the *Kommune I* (KI). The commune had planned to rain Humphrey with balloons filled with custard, but the plan was betrayed to police and the "attack" never happened. Nonetheless, the *Bild* newspaper led with a headline implying an assassination plot, and *Die Zeit* likened the plotters to the man accused of the 1963 Kennedy assassination.[64] Meinhof celebrated the planned stunt as a "brilliant means" (*brillantes Mittel*) for provoking the police, the press, and politicians, but condemned the group for not steering the attention they received toward the war in Vietnam:[65] while Meinhof was lamenting that "the napalming of women, children, and the elderly is not criminal, but protesting against it is," prominent KI member Dieter Kunzelmann was asking "what do I care about Vietnam . . . I have orgasm problems."[66]

In the aftermath of the shooting of Rudi Dutschke and the resulting blockade of Springer branches, Meinhof defended the at times violent actions as "resistance" (*Widerstand*). She opens her column "From Protest to Resistance" (*Vom Protest zum Widerstand*) by paraphrasing a slogan from the Black Power movement in the United States: "Protest is when I say I don't like this and that. Resistance is when I make sure that which I don't like no longer occurs. Protest is when I say I refuse to participate. Resistance is when I make sure that no one else participates."[67] A year after her recognition of the potential of the spectacle of the KI's planned stunt, Meinhof slipped into a justification of violence against automobiles, buildings, and windows. Not long after this justification of violence against things, she would go on to defend an act of violence against consumer goods, but this time in terms of breaking the law.

"Setting fire to Department Stores" (*Warenhausbrandstiftung*) was written after a group including Baader and Ensslin set a fire in a department store. According to Meinhof's interpretation, "the progressive moment of a department store arson attack does not lie in the destruction of consumer goods, it lies in the criminality of the deed, the breaking of the law."[68] Meinhof wrote that the burned goods would simply be replaced by insurance and their destruction was "system confirming" (*systemerhaltend*) and "counterrevolutionary" (*konterrevolutionär*), but breaking of laws that protect things more than people was progressive. She opens the article by stating, "In general, the fact that people could be put in danger who should not be put in danger, speaks against arson."[69] While this is cited as proof of her maintaining an opposition toward violence against people, there is, even here, some ambiguity, in that the statement implies the existence of people who should be put in danger.[70] Not long after, however, any ambiguity was put to rest.

In issue 25 of *Der Spiegel* in 1970, Meinhof again launched a defense of a violent action, only this time she was intimately involved and the defense had to be smuggled out of the underground. In "Of course, we can Shoot" (*Natürlich kann geschossen werden*), Meinhof, for the first time, explicitly justified violence against people. According to the logic within the group, which at this time was the precursor to the RAF, the people named as legitimate targets had been thoroughly dehumanized: Meinhof began using the Black Panther Party (a U.S. group founded in 1966 as part of the Black Power movement) term for the police—"pigs"—and deemed police, both men and women, to be functionaries of the system, nonhumans that "of course, could be shot."[71]

Connecting the dots reveals an evolution in Meinhof's relationship to physical violence. The neatness of the evolution is complicated, however, by the messiness of the final step—her panicked jump out of a window with Baader in 1970—and the sudden need for a retrospective justification. Meinhof's frustration with writing was surely behind her creeping justification of violent acts.[72] It undoubtedly also contributed—along with factors such as her affinity with Baader and Ensslin, the unfounded accusations of attempted murder immediately leveled at her, and the precedent of perceived judicial overreaction in the department store arson case—to the inertia that kept her in the underground once there. This frustration did not, however, see her abandon written language in favor of physical violence. Despite the dichotomous thinking in the protest scene at the time, and often in Meinhof's own analysis, that pitted actions against words in the endgame of the student movement, Meinhof's relationship to physical violence developed not at the expense of, but rather alongside her conception of the role of writing and language.

Far from choosing between words and deeds, Meinhof's underground activities reveal an understanding that actions can say something and that writing can do something. The third RAF treatise, written by Meinhof shortly after her arrest, offered a critique of the events in Munich in September 1972 and framed the murders of Israeli athletes during the Olympic Games as having "documented a courage and a power."[73] The analogous linking of action with language was reiterated on the second day of the Stammheim trial when Baader asserted that "the language of the guerilla is action, you shall listen to it,"[74] and a 1975 declaration denying the group's involvement in the bombing of the central station in Hamburg announced, "we can confirm, with regard to the attempt of state propaganda to blame the attack on the hamburg central station on the raf: the language of this explosion is the language of r e a c t i o n ."[75] The idea that actions could be expressive was also clearly accompanied by the notion that writing had its own agency. Meinhof's primary role in the RAF bombing spree of May 1972 was as the author of the declarations claiming responsibility. Released after the fact, the declarations sought to clarify the expression of the attacks by influencing their reception. The goal was a focused and usable publicity, in contrast, for example, to the opportunity she thought the KI wasted after the planned custard stunt. For the RAF, and in particular for Meinhof, language and writing were integral parts of violent actions in the underground. In prison, her focus on writing intensified.

The attention Meinhof paid to the written word in prison cannot be separated from the physical dimensions of her cell. While the trajectory of frustration and skepticism during her incarceration was true to a preexisting trend evident in her journalism and underground work, the confines of prison undoubtedly forced a more intense focus on language.[76] She was convinced of the potential of the written word to carry the RAF's campaign from prison. She wrote of providing "offensive information" (*offensive informationen*) when discussing the press conferences of the group's lawyers, and championed using "counterinformation as a weapon" (*gegeninformationen als waffe*).[77] Meinhof also afforded language a performativity of its own by dismantling the distinction between RAF theory and praxis as a false one: "revolutionary theory is critical theory. where we formulated it in order to publish it, it was intended as a *weapon* and always applied to clearly defined problems of the praxis of the struggle from illegality . . . the theoretical writings of the raf were . . . intended as weapons, because a weapon is something that helps the struggle from a position of illegality."[78] Writing was part of the revolutionary struggle and quickly became the overriding path to that revolution in the isolation of the penal system. At the same time, however, there emerged a deep and increasing suspicion of the ability of words to be mastered. Language became, then, not only her greatest hope but also her deepest despair.

At the beginning of her journalistic career, Meinhof bent language to her end with great skill, even relish. At a Hamburg party in the mid-1960s, she fended off accusations from Joachim Fest that she used "set phrases" (*besetzte Formeln*) and "hand-me-down clichés" (*lange abgelegte Klischees*) as the means to an end. In the early years of her incarceration, however, she leveled similar accusations at Horst Mahler. In May 1973, and amid mounting desperation since that party in Hamburg, Meinhof charged Mahler with using terms like "possessions" (*besitz*), like "titles of ownership" (*eigentumstitel*): "your central phrase is: 'every struggle must unequivocally be a struggle for the interests and needs of the masses'—there is no more meaningless, more inflated word than 'unequivocally'—but: if you don't see the comrades for sheer mass fetishism or as far as i'm concerned: kitsch, then enjoy being a cadre, but you're not one."[79] Mahler's arrest and imprisonment in late 1970 meant he was isolated from the leadership group during its time in the underground. The alliance never overcame this isolation, and he was excommunicated from the RAF in June 1973. A year later, in July 1974, Meinhof critiqued his 1971 text *On the Armed Struggle in Western Europe* (*Über den bewaffneten Kampf in Westeuropa*), arguing that what the RAF did not need was "yet another theory: incantations, reeled off mao quotations."[80] She went on to accuse Mahler's text of conforming to "market forces" (*gesetze des marktes*), arguing that it is fundamentally wrong to "go into the content of opportunistic shit, because its roots don't lie in fine-sounding verbiage, but in the internalized, internally accepted self alienation, he who, regardless of what he babbles, as the voice of the system and his complicity, rationalizes via a conscious or unconscious identification with the enemy (however it's communicated)."[81] The idea that this use of language was an inherent confirmation of the system, that Mahler's written words were themselves an internalization of the capitalist status quo, is reminiscent of the argument presented in "Columnism." Meinhof began her stinging attacks against Mahler's work demanding he carry out self-criticism, a confession-like practice of the RAF that became routine throughout the prison years. Given this context of self-criticism and Meinhof's continued isolation, it is unsurprising that she shifted focus to her own use of language.

At this stage she had come to see the structural violence she identified elsewhere in society permeate language itself, and she became increasingly skeptical of the possibility of words being able to express her thoughts, or any subversive thought. In a 1973 letter, Meinhof wrote of the disjuncture between her thoughts and her writing: "man—it was grim—i COULD not write—EVERYTHING was just rubbish, mincemeat, not in my head but on paper."[82] This admission in a letter to a fellow prisoner is representative of her doubt that words could correspond to truth or intent. In March 1976 she wrote, "maybe you have to understand—i don't know—that one can only achieve something with words if they communicate the concept of the actual situation, the situation in which everyone in imperialism finds himself; that it is senseless to want to agitate with words, as *only* enlightenment agitates, truth."[83] She was increasingly convinced that words do not by their very nature transport truth.[84] Without a way to usurp the "authoritarian" form of language and its power to integrate alternatives, words were reduced to platitudes: "put it this way: the proletariat becomes a class in that it acts as one—which is a process with the formula: through revolutionary initiative of the guerilla the proletariat becomes a class—expressed in such a simplified way, that it comes across as a cliché. that's how i see it anyway. simply too reduced, set phrases . . . damn it—there are things that only become true when one does them, not when one says them."[85] The playfulness with which Meinhof had once bent and employed terms to her own end gave way to desperation as she lost faith in her ability to steer the reception of her words and that words could even convey an intended meaning at all.

Toward the end of her life, the struggle with the means of communication played out for Meinhof at the level of words. In the *info* in October 1975 she wrote of "hunting" down terms and described the struggle to express oneself through language: "one means what he says. if he means something different, he should say it, he should fight to be a b l e to say it, *find*, that is *seek out* the words, sentences, facts, terms."[86] She wrote in March 1976 in the *info* of understanding the world in solitary confinement through the "strain" of "putting reality into words."[87] However, despite an obvious pessimism, Meinhof had not given up trying to find a way around this inability to express an alternative. Whether it was the verbal provocation and taboo-breaking of her journalism or the rejection of standardized orthography by the exclusive use of lowercase letters in prison, Meinhof had long since extended the idea of rule breaking to language, but these did not offer the alternative she sought.[88] She wrote in September 1974 in the *info* that "it is somehow clear that the old writing no longer works at all and the new writing hasn't yet arrived."[89] She went on to describe a broad notion of a "new writing" and her conviction that

> with this type of writing it's not about presenting the reader all these details, individual thoughts. it's about giving expression to identity.
>
> facts are also tricky. in an instant and on the quiet they become consumer goods—that is, proof, evidence, examples, shit . . .
>
> now—vertical class analysis. it was incredibly important to the learning process, at least for me it was, but tell me—what for? why class analysis? again it can only become a consumer good.[90]

This entry is particularly revealing as it juxtaposes her increasingly desperate pessimism toward an "authoritarian" language with an unwavering belief in linguistic redemption. On the one hand, the logic of the argument that saw Meinhof condemn the genre of the column and later Mahler's use of words as confirmations of the status quo is brought to bear on the "consumer good" of facts, analysis, and language. On the other hand, she takes tentative steps toward a new conception of writing and a redefinition of the rules.[91]

There is little evidence to suggest that Meinhof revolutionized the rules of communication, or even that she found a resolution that satisfied her.[92] Language remained, until her death, the frontline for the same tensions and the battlefront against the same structural violence that had defined her journalistic career. In the face of mounting frustration and deepening doubt, the horizon of Meinhof's critique shrank from the capitalist media industry to the genre of journalism, to language and words. This private, and often lonely, struggle with communication parallels her public, and often violent, struggle to communicate from the terrorist underground.

CHAPTER 2

Writing Underground

Publish this![1]

—Note accompanying RAF texts sent to major media outlets

The day before Meinhof was arrested in Hamburg in June 1972, a package was sent to the offices of the *Frankfurter Rundschau* newspaper. It contained pages four and five of the first Red Army Faction (RAF) treatise, *The Urban Guerilla Concept* (*Das Konzept Stadtguerilla*), from April 1971, three RAF declarations regarding bomb attacks in Frankfurt, Karlsruhe, and Hamburg in May 1972, and a simple typewritten demand on a loose piece of paper: "Publish this!" This package is representative of the relationship between the RAF and the media during the first generation's two years in the underground. Meinhof composed most of the texts that were produced in the name of the group and disseminated via existing communication networks. Texts were sent to mainstream media outlets, alternative publishers, as well as private mailing lists, and in each case the message was tailored to the particular forum and audience. In this context, Meinhof's words were integral to the underground interplay between language, image, and physical violence: they established what would become the RAF brand and its sharp sense of audience recognition, they played a central role in the bombings of May 1972 and the mainstream appropriation of the radical rhetoric of war, and they used ideology to perform distinctly nonideological discourses. All this was set against the background of life on the run, armed robbery, and skirmishes with police on the streets of West Germany in the years after Meinhof's entrance into the underground.

On the morning of May 14, 1970, Meinhof arrived at the German Central Institute for Social Issues in Berlin to work on a book project. Andreas Baader, who had been brought across from the Tegel Prison, was shown to the same room shortly after. The two of them smoked heavily while appearing to settle down to work, before an officer eventually opened a window to let in some fresh air. A little while later, a shot was fired outside the door of the room before Ingrid Schubert and Irene Goergens burst in firing tear gas pistols. An armed Gudrun Ensslin and a man, who had just shot and wounded a guard, followed them in. In the ensuing scuffle, shots were fired by both sides into the walls; in the panic Baader, Meinhof, and the four others jumped out of the open window. The group fled the scene to the apartment of a friend of Meinhof's, which had been chosen as the place to hide out should anything go wrong. And things had gone wrong. The "live" firearms and the fourth member of the liberating group, who shot the guard, were not part of the original plan. Nevertheless, the overarching goal had been achieved: Baader was free.

The group met later in another apartment, but without Meinhof, who was lying low. She was found by members of the group two days later in an apartment with newspapers spread across the kitchen table sporting headlines about the liberation and the "Baader-Meinhof Group." She undoubtedly knew that she was now wanted for attempted murder and had a DM 10,000 reward on her head. Meinhof was picked up that evening, and it was only then, days after the liberation, that individuals who had come together to realize a specific and short-term goal, and were quickly dubbed the "Baader-Meinhof Group," seemed to adopt a group identity. Shortly after, they flew out of East Germany under false names headed for a training camp of the Popular Front for the Liberation of Palestine (PFLP), outside of Amman. The Germans spent two months receiving rudimentary arms training before returning to the West German underground.

Back in the Federal Republic, and on the run from the police, RAF members were constantly on the move. Meinhof relocated every few days between safe houses or between cities.[2] On September 29, 1970, she was in Berlin taking part in the armed robbery of a bank as part of a heist that saw the RAF hit three banks simultaneously, netting more than DM 200,000. Three more bank robberies were planned for December but did not happen because of the arrest of several group members.[3] Two banks were held up in January 1971, another in December 1971, and a final one in February 1972. The raids on West German banks preceded the RAF bombing campaign of 1972, when, in two weeks in May, the group carried out six bomb attacks in six different West German cities, killing four people and injuring many others. The search for the RAF intensified after the attacks, and the leaders, including Meinhof, Baader, Ensslin, and Jan-Carl Raspe, were arrested in quick succession in June 1972.[4]

The police files on Meinhof's activities while on the run reveal an efficient and assured criminal. Meinhof—also known as "Anna," "Marion," and "Lilli"—was responsible for fitting out RAF members with forged identification papers after stealing the necessary documents, stamps, and official seals during break-ins at the town halls in Neustadt am Rübenberge and Lang-Göns in late 1970. She also forged automobile and truck documents to "makeover" (*umfrisieren*) those she allegedly stole. She procured weapons for the group, and at one point in December 1970 bought about thirty firearms in a Frankfurt pub before distributing them among the RAF members. She organized safe houses, either staying with sympathizers or renting hideouts under false names—"Sabine Marckwort" in Polle/Hameln in November 1970, and "Sigrid Motz" in Heppenheim a month later, for example—and she was involved in the planning and carrying out of brazen armed attacks on military targets and armed raids on banks.[5]

This image of the master criminal is at odds with various recollections of Meinhof. Dr. Johanna Meyer, Meinhof's physician, who last saw her in the beginning of 1970, described a woman who after her operation was in constant fear for her head. This was why, Dr. Meyer supposed, she remained in the background of protests, preferring to observe or pass stones, not throw them.[6] The calculating and brazen terrorist and the passive, harried woman who was eventually arrested with vast quantities of sleeping tablets are not easily reconciled, but they are indicative of the RAF's contradictory brand of terrorism. A glance through the list of objects collected by the group paints a picture of the group's underground experience as an oddly homogeneous mix of its limited paramilitary training and a desperate absorption of knowledge from textbooks and popular culture. The group was well armed, and Meinhof—described in police files as "Luckow"—was in possession of numerous weapons, substantial ammunition, and two hand grenades when arrested.[7] But Astrid Proll has claimed the fourth, armed member of the group that liberated Baader was brought in because the others were not confident with firearms.[8] As late as the 1969 storming of the *konkret* head offices, for example, the group led by Meinhof was still arming itself with water pistols filled with butyric acid, a fairly harmless liquid that a police forensic report concluded may have been used to make people "smell bad" (*stinken*).[9]

The hardware was accompanied by books on Marxism, Leninism, and Maoism, as well as Carlos Marighella's *Mini-Manual of the Urban Guerilla*. In addition to these, a number of practical supplements to the RAF's brief weapons training were found in 1970 in the safe house rented by Meinhof calling herself "Renate Hübner," including *The Science of Weapons and Ballistics for Hunters*, a weapons magazine with various offers of automatic weapons and handguns marked with a ballpoint pen, and a textbook on organic chemistry.[10] Further to the practicalities of learning about weapons, techniques of secrecy and espionage were investigated. Empty bottles of "ash blond no. 105" and "light blond no. 100" hair dye and used tubes of "hair color cream" littered the "Hübner" safe house.[11] Police also found in the house a magazine article, underlined, about the company Micro-Electronic and a brochure for its listening devices branded "mini-spies" (*minispione*). Among the hair dye, the ads for listening devices, and the ingredients for a bomb was a copy of the book *Spies, Agents, Soldiers* (*Spione, Agenten, Soldaten*).[12] Published in 1969, Janusz Piekalkiewicz's work presented a war at times as fantastic as a James Bond case with exciting case studies of espionage, bluffing, and beguilement by secret commandos during World War II.

Meinhof's underground experience was indeed the stuff of spy fantasies. While Baader has since been presented as the gunslinging antihero of Western films behind the wheel of fast and expensive cars, Meinhof's illegal activities, both in and prior to entering the underground, are better suited to a Cold War spy novel. She was involved in clandestine border crossings and the outlawed Communist Party of Germany (*Kommunistische Partei Deutschlands*, KPD) as a journalist with *konkret*, and found obvious enjoyment in the secret activities.[13] Once the group was on the run, Heinrich Hannover, a lawyer and later counsel for Meinhof, met with Horst Mahler in Berlin, who was as "pleased as Punch" that his disguise fooled, initially at least, his colleague.[14] It is perhaps unsurprising then that Mahler chose for himself the nickname "James" as in Bond, James Bond.[15] A subsequent meeting between Hannover and Meinhof saw them rendezvous in Bremen opposite the police station before strolling around the block with Thomas Weisbecker hanging thirty meters back, a submachine gun under his jacket. Hannover arrived at yet another meeting in a Bremen park to see Meinhof and Klaus Jünschke sitting on a park bench with what he recalled as a sinister look in their eyes: "Both had—so very inconspicuous—strange, oblong suitcases on their laps, the contents of which was to be used to hold the 'pigs' at bay if necessary. As on other occasions, I could not take the outward appearance of our meeting completely seriously."[16] Such filmic elements of West German terrorism also resonated with the public, with Meinhof later receiving fan mail in prison addressed to "Bonnie and Clyde."[17] It was in this context that the RAF produced and disseminated texts that are categorized here as statements, declarations, and treatises according to their intended function, intended audience, and distribution.[18]

"Statements" were short texts in direct response to a specific event or situation beyond the group's control or that it considered to be not of its own making. These texts usually performed a retrospective explanatory role and were generally printed in some form in the mainstream media. "Declarations" were also short, but they were written consciously as part of acts of violence staged by the RAF, and they were directed toward the mainstream media. Finally, the three completed "treatises" were more major pieces of written work, stand-alone theoretical texts up to sixty pages long. They were distributed primarily by hand and via the alternative media, and were aimed less at the wider public and more at sympathizers and potential members. Working with this categorization, underground texts were produced or appeared as follows:

Printed June 5, 1970	Statement: "Build up the Red Army" (*Die Rote Armee aufbauen*)
Printed June 15, 1970	Statement: "Of Course we can Shoot" (*Natürlich kann geschossen werden*)
Appeared April 1971	Treatise: *The Urban Guerilla Concept*
Printed February 1972	Statement: "The Struggle has only just Begun" (*Der Kampf hat erst begonnen*)
Appeared April 1972	Treatise: *Serve the People. Urban Guerilla and Class Struggle* (*Dem Volk dienen. Stadtguerilla und Klassenkampf*)
Dated May 14, 1972	Frankfurt Declaration
Dated May 16, 1972	Munich Declaration
Dated May 20, 1972	Karlsruhe Declaration
Dated May 20, 1972	Hamburg Declaration
Dated May 25, 1972	Heidelberg Declaration
Dated May 28, 1972	Statement: "To the news editors of the West German press" (*An die Nachrichtenredakteure der westdeutschen Presse*)
Dated May 29, 1972	Statement: "The two bomb threats composed of letters cut out of magazines" (*Die beiden aus Buchstaben zusammengestückelten Bombendrohungen*)
Printed May 31, 1972	Statement: Teach-in recording and text
Appeared November 1972	Treatise: *The Black September Action in Munich* (*Die Aktion des Schwarzen September in München*)
Never completed	Treatise: referred to in prison communication as "bassa."

This list includes the third RAF treatise *The Black September Action*, which was written by Meinhof in the early months of her incarceration, because it was distributed much the same way as previous underground texts. It also shares both its intended audience and its function with the two previous treatises. The list does not include, however, *On the Armed Struggle in Western Europe* (*Über den bewaffneten Kampf in Westeuropa*) by Mahler. This text was written in prison in 1971 after a significant physical and ideological isolation from the remainder of the group. The RAF leadership distanced itself from Mahler's effort when it appeared under the codename *The New Traffic Regulations* (*Die neue Straßenverkehrsordnung*), and the text even prompted the composition of a response in the form of the first RAF treatise *The Urban Guerilla Concept*.[19]

The texts were composed predominantly by Meinhof, although this can be established only to varying degrees for respective texts. They were produced and copied primarily on a number of typewriters that the group had access to in the underground. The RAF text denouncing a fake declaration published in the *Frankfurter Rundschau* mentions six typewriters that the "pigs" (*bullen*) knew about, and the police files list seven (five matched to texts and two found in the possession of the RAF) as well as a further two suspicious machines.[20] The dissemination of texts was also a haphazard affair. They were distributed via the group's personal contacts and sent via the postal system to individuals or groups, as well as to mainstream and alternative media outlets. They were also dropped around university campuses and handed out at demonstrations. Beyond what can be reconstructed in terms of direct distribution of the original texts and reprints in the mainstream and alternative media, West German authorities conceded that reproductions were also in circulation.[21] The police noted at the time that it was impossible to know the number of copies in circulation, and that a policy of confiscation would not have been able to recover them all.[22]

Although the exact extent of the reproduction of statements, declarations, and treatises cannot be known, there are a number of examples of significant reproduction. In June 1972, the Frankfurt, Munich, Karlsruhe, and Hamburg Declarations, as well as *Serve the People*, were reprinted by the Fackel publishing house in an anthology titled *Treatise on Method* (*Traktat über Methode*), which was available in leftist bookshops.[23] The publisher Red Sun also produced an anthology, complete with the RAF logo, called *Armed Struggle: Texts of the RAF: Discussion and Critique* (*Bewaffneter Kampf. Texte der RAF: Auseinandersetzung und Kritik*). This anthology included the three RAF treatises, as well as the declarations (which it lists as leaflets and press releases, suggesting the declarations also circulated as amateur leaflets), the teach-in text, as well as critiques from outside the group. Given the content, this was probably produced around 1974.[24] The specific details of the production and dissemination of Meinhof's underground texts and the details of their performative effects can be further differentiated within the categories of statement, declaration, and treatise.

Opening Statements: Formation and Branding

The initial public statements by the RAF were short pieces produced in response to the liberation of Baader. These opening two statements were produced around the same time with a slight lag, which saw them emerge from the underground within ten days of each other. They were not conceived of as part of the action; instead, they provide defensive, retrospective justifications. They also include the early development of elements of RAF practice, such as the recognition of and discrimination between audiences and a recognizable brand. These aspects are crucial to the understanding of the RAF declarations and treatises.

"Build up the Red Army" appeared on June 5, 1970, some three weeks after the liberation of Baader, in the leftist magazine *agit 883*, after the publishers were sent the text. At this early stage the RAF brand was only beginning to evolve, and this first statement was not signed by the "RAF." The name "Red Army Faction" did not appear until the first treatise in April 1971, however, the term "Red Army" did feature prominently in the hand-drawn title of this first statement. A firearm also took pride of place in the center of the layout, in a clear space among the paragraphs, although it is also possible that the editors of *agit 883* included the machine gun image in the final layout. The words and the firearm were two foundational elements of the subsequent RAF logo (the third being the five-pointed star), and their presence in this statement give an indication of the group's later self-promotion.[25]

In handwritten notes passed to French journalist Michèle Ray on June 5, the day the *agit 883* article appeared, Meinhof addressed the issue of the group's name: "Name: 'Build up the Red Army'—not a name but a sentence: it includes what we are doing. At the same time, it implies what now needs to be done."[26] The name also plays on a number of cultural references. The "Red Army" refers to the Soviet Red Army, while the acronym RAF is also that of the British "Royal Air Force." To the RAF, both references alluded to the liberators of Germany from fascism: the Russians from the east and the British from the air. They are also, however, linked to the "terror" of the rape of Berlin and the bombing of Dresden in the final months of World War II. The simple name "RAF" therefore constitutes a complex semiotic field that represents both the promise of liberation as well as a terrifying threat. This name and logo would later evolve into a visual staple in the RAF treatises and was even refined in consultation with a graphic designer.[27] At this early stage, however, the mix of visual and textual elements evident in "Build up the Red Army" were printed alongside, and superimposed onto, an already developed and recognizable logo: that of the Black Panther Party (BPP).

The BPP was a militant, African American organization founded in 1966, and its activities attracted a lot of West German attention. Protests against the Vietnam War in November 1969 in West Berlin and Frankfurt were simultaneously demonstrations of solidarity with the BPP. As a result, *agit 883* dedicated increasing amounts of page space to the American group. So when the soon-to-be RAF sent its text to the magazine, the BPP's famous black cat had long since prowled the pages of *agit 883*.[28] Meinhof was well aware of the BPP and the civil rights movement in America. She opened one of her more famous *konkret* articles—"From Protest to Resistance" (*Vom Protest zum Widerstand*) (1968)—by paraphrasing a slogan from the civil rights movement. Ironically this paraphrasing became one of the most famous quotations attributed to her. Meinhof also cited the BPP as an ideological role model for the group in correspondence with Ray.[29] Despite such links, the presence of the BPP logo in "Build up the Red Army" is likely the result of the magazine editors tailoring the RAF text to the popular (both within the magazine and within the protest scene more generally) BPP brand by adorning "Red Army" words with a black cat.[30]

"Build up the Red Army" was a bitter defense of the liberation of Baader. With this statement and its publication in the alternative *agit 883*, the group clearly identified its audience as it turned away from the "intellectual windbags, the cowards, the know-it-alls" to the "potential revolutionary sections of the people."³¹ The liberation operation was, the text continued, just the beginning, not an isolated incident. The group framed their actions as part of an existing worldwide movement against imperial exploitation that had already begun in Vietnam, Palestine, Guatemala, Cuba, and China. Breaking Baader out of prison was therefore not a novelty, it was simply the first deed of its kind in Germany. The authorship of the text must fall to the group. While it bears many of the hallmarks of a Meinhof text, Ali Jansen, for example, recalled his own role in cowriting the text that later appeared in *agit 883* while speaking at a rally in 1996.³² The production of the second opening statement is a little better understood, if not just as complex.

On June 4, the day prior to the appearance of the first statement in *agit 883*, the group met with Ray. Meinhof had first encountered Ray when working with *konkret*, and the group now summoned her to West Berlin by promising involvement in "something important for the Left."³³ Ray was taken to see Baader, Ensslin, and Meinhof before being taken back to a safe house where she later received a cassette with a recorded text spoken by Meinhof. She passed the cassette on to *Der Spiegel*, which published excerpts from it on June 15, 1970, under the title "Of Course we can Shoot." This second statement is not only a defense of the Baader liberation but also a defense of the use of violence. In this context, Meinhof distanced the group from the "intellectual Left," a differentiation that in the treatises becomes increasingly bitter. Importantly, this text sees the complete reification of the police and, by implication, all other "functionaries" of "the system."

The two opening statements of the RAF are indicative of ad hoc formation of the "Baader-Meinhof Group" and, a little later, the RAF. They were released to the West German public when the group was yet to solidify its identity and public image, and just before the group left the country to undertake guerilla training in the deserts of the Middle East. Meinhof later distanced the RAF from these statements in the group's first treatise. She described "Build up the Red Army" as too general and her cassette recording as taken out of context in the *Der Spiegel* article.³⁴ Despite Meinhof's subsequent misgivings, the texts are representative of the nascent media practice of the RAF. It is one of the lingering ironies in Meinhof's story that after struggling for years to escape the commodity fetishism of culturally industrial West German journalism, she made vast concessions to the way the capitalist media operated as part of the RAF. From the beginning, the group distinguished between its mainstream and alternative audiences, and even borrowed techniques from advertising to begin developing a logo and a brand. One the one hand, such branding is indicative of how Meinhof and the RAF would work within the maxims of news media practices, and it was no doubt a pragmatic choice to plug into existing networks of distribution. On the other hand, it was nevertheless contrary to the desire Meinhof showed right up until the 1970 liberation to dispense with the rule-book and push through boundaries. Just how the RAF's audience awareness and visual branding evolved into a refined operation, and how the group was able perform its terrorism through them, is evident in its declarations and treatises.

Declarations: Words, Bombs, and the Visual War Narrative

The RAF declarations represent a short burst of public engagement as part of a series of violent and deadly attacks in the month before the arrest of the first generation. The relationship between the words and the bombs in this final underground flurry is complex. Understanding this relationship requires a clear chronology of both the bombings and publication of the associated declarations, and clarification of the authorship of both the texts and the bombs, before an examination of the role of terrorist texts and terrorist violence in the bombings. Models for conceiving of the relationship between language and violence are implied in RAF texts. These models draw to varying degrees on historical models and correspond with contemporary literature to frame the bombings as an attention-seeking medium for a written message, an expressive attack capable of giving symbolic voice to an existing conflict, and a performative moment, not merely representing, but creating and re-creating the conflict between the RAF and the state. It is this performativity that offers an insight into how the bombings helped create a mainstream framework for understanding RAF terrorism as acts of war, a framework that had significant ramifications for counterterrorism policy and RAF recruitment.

The RAF bombing spree began on May 11, 1972, when Ensslin came up with the idea of bombing the U.S. Army Corp headquarters in Frankfurt. She, along with Baader and Raspe, placed three bombs that caused severe damage to the building and claimed the life of an American soldier. Two subsequent bomb attacks took place the following day: the first when Angela Luther and Irmgard Möller bombed the police headquarters in Augsburg, injuring five policemen, and the second, two hours later, when a car laden with explosives and left by Baader, Holger Meins, and Ensslin exploded in the car park of the State Criminal Police Office in Munich, destroying sixty cars. On May 15, the "Commando Manfred Grashof"—Baader, Raspe, and Meins—planted a car bomb in Karlsruhe, targeting Judge Wolfgang Buddenberg.[35] On this particular morning, however, the judge's wife was worried about her husband and wanted to pick him up from work. The car exploded when she turned the key. She was able to crawl, severely injured, from the wreckage.

The "Commando 2nd of June"[36] bombed the Springer building in Hamburg on May 19. This attack was Meinhof's idea, but was given the go-ahead by Baader and Ensslin, who supplied the three bombs used in the attack.[37] The commando, which included Siegfried Hausner, Klaus Jünschke, and Ilse Stachowiak, called the switchboard of the building twice to warn of the bomb. Both operators that took the calls dismissed them as crazy and the building was not evacuated. Seventeen people were injured, two of them severely, in the subsequent blast. The next day the police were told via telephone of three more bombs in the Springer building. These devices were found and disarmed. Within the group and among its supporters, this attack was also the most disputed bombing. Sympathizers did not see the workers in the building as legitimate targets, and Baader and Ensslin tried to disown the attack during the trial, despite originally giving the operation their blessing.[38] The final bombing in the spree took place on the evening of May 24, 1972. The "Commando 15th of July"[39]—Baader, Meins, Möller, and Luther—planted two bombs in cars outside the U.S. Armed Forces European Headquarters in Heidelberg. The explosions claimed the lives of three American soldiers. While she played a direct role in all aspects of the Hamburg bombing, Meinhof was involved in all the bombings via her typewriter.

The declarations claiming responsibility for these attacks were each sent to mainstream media outlets throughout Germany in the days following each bombing. An original of the Frankfurt Declaration dated three days after the bombing was sent to the German Press Agency (*Deutsche Presse-Agentur*, dpa) in Munich on May 15, while an original of the Munich Declaration was sent to the dpa in Hamburg from Lörrach on May 17. An original of the Hamburg Declaration in an unstamped envelope and dated May 19, the day of the bombing, was hand delivered to broadcaster *Norddeutscher Rundfunk* in Hamburg that same day, and originals of the same Hamburg Declaration (but now dated May 20 and reporting the events as happening "yesterday" instead of "today") were sent to the dpa in Hamburg, United Press International, the *Bild* newspaper in Hamburg, and the *Süddeutsche Zeitung* in Munich on May 22. Originals of the Heidelberg Declaration were sent to the dpa in Munich and the *Westdeutscher Rundfunk* in Cologne, a carbon copy was sent to the *Frankfurter Rundschau* on May 26, and a subsequent original and carbon copy were sent to the dpa in Hamburg and *Der Spiegel* in Hamburg, respectively, on May 30.[40] A majority of the texts were sent again up to weeks after the bombings. For example, packages containing carbon copies of the Frankfurt, Karlsruhe, and Hamburg Declarations, as well as pages four and five of *The Urban Guerilla Concept*, were sent to the *Frankfurter Rundschau* and the *Westdeutsche Allgemeine Zeitung* on June 12.[41]

While media outlets differed in their handling of the texts they received, the group's writings were reported, contrary to RAF claims of a media blackout. Almost all newspapers and radio networks reported the declarations, often printing them verbatim, albeit mostly in the context of a negative article.[42] The Frankfurt Declaration, for example, was not only reprinted but reproduced in its original form in the *Frankfurter Rundschau* only four days after the text first entered the postal system. The declarations were reproduced in the alternative media as well. The Frankfurt, Munich, Karlsruhe, and Hamburg Declarations were printed in issue 9 of *Red Aid West Berlin*, and the Heidelberg Declaration was printed in *Red Aid Hamburg* (copies were also found in the offices of the magazine's publisher *Roter Stern*).[43] All the declarations were later reprinted in the anthology *Treatise on Method*, which could be found in leftist bookshops.[44] Despite these alternative modes of distribution, the undoubted primary focus was on mainstream newspapers and radio stations. It was via these mainstream outlets that the RAF sought contact not just with sympathizers and potential members but with the wider public.

The style of the declarations is reminiscent of Meinhof's writing, leading analysts at the time from the Federal Criminal Police Office (*Bundeskriminalamt*, BKA) to assume Meinhof played a significant role in the composition of the texts.[45] Gerhard Müller, a former RAF member who turned witness for the state, testified that "from conversations within the group, I know that Ulrike MEINHOF composed the declaration distributed after the Hamburg attack, as well as all other declarations released after explosions."[46] Cross-referencing the information on the typewriters, safe houses, and draft texts gathered by police does not allow for any more definitive statements on authorship. However, handwritten amendments were found on a copy of the Munich Declaration, which after comparison were found to be written by Meinhof.[47] This copy was also composed on a typewriter that produced all other copies of the Munich Declaration known to police and a majority of the remaining declarations. It thus seems reasonable to assume that Meinhof played a significant role in the composition of the declarations. This assumption is reinforced by the relative certainty that she wrote, or was the most significant contributor to, most of the statements and all the treatises. It would therefore represent a sharp and short-lived shift in established RAF practice, under conditions that were more or less constant, if she were not involved in writing, or at least cowriting, the words that were so integral to the physical violence of the RAF bombing spree. A number of conceptions of this relationship between revolutionary writing and revolutionary violence coexisted and overlapped in RAF thinking. Models of attention-seeking, expressive, and performative terrorist violence can be tracked from their appearance in RAF texts back through their contemporary and historical influences, and forward through scholarly literature on terrorism.

In May 1972, the *Frankfurter Rundschau* published a communiqué signed by the RAF and warning the citizens of Stuttgart to stay off the streets between 1 p.m. and 2 p.m. on the afternoon of June 2. By staying home, opening their windows, and retreating to their cellars, they would be able to avoid the carnage caused by three car bombs, each with the explosive power of thirty kilograms of TNT (trinitrotoluene). The RAF did not write the text.[48] The unique use of letters cut from magazines contrasts sharply with the easily recognizable and exclusively typewritten RAF format. The content, too, is in stark contrast to the RAF practice of releasing declarations in the days following a bombing. Only once, in Hamburg, was a warning issued, with a written declaration released after the fact. The fake threat came on the back of a false report in April of Meinhof's death and a report in the *Bild* newspaper in January that Baader wanted to give himself up, which drew a vehement denial famously signed with a thumbprint. In a statement written in direct response to the text in the *Frankfurter Rundschau*, the RAF challenged the mainstream press to publish genuine declarations, what it described as the "political content" (*politischer Inhalt*) of the bomb attacks.[49] This reveals one RAF conception of the relationship between the violence of its deadly campaign of bombings and its words: words as the "political content" carried by the "empty" medium of violence.

The idea of violence as a bare medium for a written message can be situated within a European tradition of revolutionary violence and, more specifically, the anarchist tradition of "propaganda by deed." This concept developed in the 1870s against the background of the invention of dynamite and the spread of the mass print media. In his 1880 text "Spirit of Revolt," Russian anarchist Petr Kropotkin wrote of the need to spread ideas "by actions which compel general attention." "One such act," he continued, "may, in a few days, make more propaganda than thousands of pamphlets."[50] It was in the context of comparable and rapid technological developments in the mass media of the postwar years—the dominance of the daily newspaper and the rise of (color) television—that the RAF revisited the historical, pan-European concept of "propaganda by deed." The group accessed the anarchist tradition, however, not via Kropotkin, but via Carlos Marighella's then contemporary makeover of the idea: "armed propaganda."

Marighella was a Brazilian revolutionary and self-proclaimed urban guerilla. His *Mini-Manual of the Urban Guerilla* (1969) was a mainstay of RAF literature, with copies accompanying the group in the underground. Baader also quoted him directly in his statement "The Struggle has only just Begun."[51] The manual outlined the strategy of the urban guerilla that the RAF later adopted as well as that of "armed propaganda." Marighella writes of the inevitability of robberies, ambushes, and bombings becoming stories within the mass communication system. This must, he continues, be combined with a clandestine press producing pamphlets, tape recordings, and letters "explaining the meaning of the urban guerilla's armed action."[52] Meinhof's prison notes on the "relationship [between] public work [and] urban guerilla" describe the coupling of

Marighella's "urban guerilla" with "propaganda through leaflets" as "very important, tremendously important."[53] The idea of "armed propaganda" developed by Marighella and expressed by Meinhof is not out of line with subsequent sociological notions of terrorist acts as being primarily attention seeking.

Waldmann's model of terrorist violence as a strategy used to communicate with and influence the behavior of a third party can be read parallel to the idea of "political content" in the form of a preconceived interpretation, or declaration, piggybacking the medium of an act of violence. This parasitic relationship between terrorist words and violence falls within a broader symbiotic relationship that sees terrorists provide the mass media with the spectacular images they need in return for the coverage terrorists' require. In this context, the 1972 bombings were indeed constructed to heighten the likelihood of being reported.[54] In terms of the declarations, the RAF did its best to maximize the chance of them being printed by writing texts that already conformed to the logic of the news media: the shorter, more clear-cut, and more recognizable a press release, the greater the probability of it being reported. The release of RAF declarations was also timed to ensure the story remained current. The initial bombs guaranteed a story several days of coverage, and when this story was reaching the end of its natural cycle, the declarations appeared. They revitalized the story, provided new details, as well as new questions, and ensured the images of destruction remained in the papers a while longer.[55] Hijacking the logic of the mass media in this manner was necessary for the RAF, which did not control any communication or media infrastructure beyond its access to the postal system and the handful of typewriters it had spread across the Federal Republic.

The reliance of the RAF on established and mainstream media to carry its message was pivotal to its strategy, and it is clear that the group used violence to engage the media. However, there is more to terrorist violence than the symbiotic relationship between terrorist and the media, and the associated parasitic relationship between terrorist words and terrorist violence. While the spectacle of a violent act can be harnessed to draw attention to a message, it can also be understood as an expression unto itself. This idea was implied in the formulation of "propaganda by deed," which dominated anarchist debate in the 1870s, and was thrashed out at a small annual meeting of the Jura Federation and later adopted by the International Anarchist Congress in London 1881. The congress's resolution included an explicitly expressive element arguing that deeds were intended to contain an inherent message, so those on the land and importantly those who could not read could be "spoken to."[56] The 1881 resolution hints, too, that violence draws much of its expressive power from the targets of attacks. Waldmann would later write of terrorists seeking out symbolic targets and of the symbolism of the targets, sites, and modes of attack as speaking their own language.[57] This is no different in the case of the RAF, with the main strands of RAF rhetoric symbolically represented in the choice of targets: the judiciary, the conservative media, and the U.S. Army.

The declaration released after the attacks on the Munich and Augsburg police buildings makes clear the bombs were planted to avenge the shooting death of Thomas Weisbecker, member of the Second of June Movement, at the hands of police. The targets were those Munich detectives and Augsburg police the RAF thought responsible for Weisbecker's death and the judiciary in general.[58] The attempted attack on Judge Buddenberg in Karlsruhe was likewise intended to avenge a RAF member. In her declaration, Meinhof accuses Buddenberg of hastily transferring Manfred Grashof from the hospital to prison and endangering his health: "He launched," she wrote, "a renewed attempt on the defenseless Grashof's life, after the pigs had failed in theirs."[59] The bombs laid in Hamburg were also directed against one of Meinhof's long-standing preoccupations, the Springer media group. The declaration demanded the publications owned by Springer cease what the RAF considered to be slander against the New Left, unions, Communist Parties in West Germany and abroad, foreign workers, and revolutionary movements in third-world countries.[60] The U.S. military bases in Frankfurt and Heidelberg were likewise chosen as targets for their symbolic value as proxies for the U.S. Army, and by extension the U.S. administration. Meinhof described the Frankfurt attack as a direct response to the U.S. offensive in Vietnam and stated that West Germany and West Berlin "shall no longer be a safe hinterland for the strategists of extermination."[61] Similarly the Heidelberg bomb was a reaction to a U.S. policy: "The attack was carried out," Meinhof wrote, "after General Daniel James . . . declared on Wednesday in Washington: 'In the future, no target north or south of the seventeenth parallel was off-limits for the US Air Force.'"[62] The RAF idea of expressive violence may echo in practice the anarchist idea of targeting "existing institutions," and the symbolism may appear straightforward, but the RAF bombs are not merely symbolic, they also have a performative element. This performativity became important with the "language of the explosion," which by 1975 had replaced the analogous firestorms of 1968 in RAF parlance, proving central to the creation of a mainstream narrative of war.[63]

A narrative of war was, from the outset, central to the protest movement of the late 1960s and the extraparliamentary opposition. The conception of the Federal Republic as a fascist state and the self-conception of the protestors as a belated resistance was also a prominent theme in Meinhof's articles. She consciously employed the term "resistance" (*Widerstand*) to draw on its powerful World War II connotations. This understanding was taken to the streets, in particular, in the skirmishes with police after the attempt on Dutschke's life, and became very much a central tenet of the student rebellion. But these connotations of a recent, German past were also blended with an exotic present to create a narrative of war that served as a model for many protesters' understanding of their experience in West Germany.[64]

The Vietnam War saw the capitalist West pitted against the communist East in an isolated, hot theater in an otherwise cold war. The broad ideological strokes were the same as those that split Germany down her middle, meaning the conflict found particular resonance in the West German protest scene. Those who took to the streets of West Berlin saw themselves as part of a worldwide struggle. Moreover, the protests against the U.S. invasion of Vietnam recalled the ill feeling in occupied West Germany toward the American presence. Slogans such as Dutschke's "Yankees out of Vietnam" (*Amis raus aus Vietnam*) therefore rode an international wave of protest but also echoed the well-known slogan "Yankee go home" (*Ami go home*) specific to West Germany in the immediate aftermath of World War II.[65] Meinhof, too, recognized the conflict in Vietnam as having spilled over national borders. In her 1967 article "Vietnam and the Germans" (*Vietnam und die Deutschen*), she wrote of the Vietnam War as not a locally or ideologically isolated conflict, but part of a new type of world war.

A mix of antifascist resistance and postcolonial liberation became a defining element of the RAF self-image, and it was integral to Meinhof's declarations. Having a different commando claim responsibility for the bombings, for example, was an attempt to give the impression that numerous guerilla cells in the Vietcong mold were in operation in West Germany. This narrative was also established visually in the alternative media, such as the Red Aid publication *Preparation for the RAF Trials via the Press, Police, and Judiciary* (*Vorbereitung der RAF-Prozesse durch Presse, Polizei und Justiz*). In this booklet and in the context of an article on the "Campaign against the lawyers CROISSANT & LANG" (*Kampagne gegen die Rechtsanwälte CROISSANT & LANG*) press photos of the arrests of Meinhof and Baader sat alongside, and without any commentary, an image of a captured Vietcong. The photograph from Vietnam visually informing the photographs of the RAF arrests is one example of RAF supporters visually producing and reproducing the war narrative by aligning the West German guerilla with the Vietcong.[66]

While the war narrative was embraced and actively promoted among protestors, RAF terrorists, and the alternative media, the mainstream media did not initially take it up.[67] It was actively resisted within the conservative media and conservative sections of the broader public. In February 1968, for example, tens of thousands gathered in John F. Kennedy Square with the slogan "Berlin must not become Saigon!" (*Berlin darf nicht Saigon werden!*).[68] Despite resistance, politicians and mainstream media outlets did eventually adopt the model for understanding terrorism, and importantly counterterrorism, as acts of war. This appropriation of the radical war narrative was important, as it provided a "script" for commentators to follow, but it only emerged in mid-1972.[69] The trigger for taking up this ready-made script was the performativity of the RAF bombing spree. The bombings were able to perform war by inserting the Federal Republic into that visual space in the West German consciousness occupied by the conflict in Vietnam. In this manner, RAF words and images worked together to align the mainstream discourse of terrorism with the alternative narrative of war.

In 1970 literary scholar Karl Heinz Bohrer described in artistic terms a surrealist scene. The image was not a painting, but a journalistic photograph of the conflict in Vietnam showing U.S. ambassador Elssworth Bunker inspecting the bodies of dead Vietcong on the embassy grounds. Surrealist images, he wrote, terrorize the imagination, and the reality of wartime photojournalism had caught up with and overtaken the imagination. Bohrer argued that whether "the incineration of three American Cosmonauts in their capsule, the self-immolation of a Saigon monk, Japanese suicide-happenings, Godard's Film 'Weekend,' a poem by Robert Sward—these are at once aesthetic and real events, which have become substantively interchangeable, such is the extent to which the once opposed spheres of art and reality have merged towards congruency: The perception of reality is increasingly stylized, art is almost exclusively only tolerable as a particle of reality."[70] In West Germany such imagery defined the experience of the Vietnam War. Contemporaneous developments in mass media and photographic technology combined with unprecedented journalistic practices to present the western world with a "live" war experience. This stylized reality was "uncensored" (a relative term), as journalists had direct access to the conflict and reporting on the ground was not run through the U.S. military. It also played out in "real time" (likewise a relative term, there was still a lag of some thirty hours) and in color. In West Germany, too, the conflict was televised and relayed in newspapers and photos. Wolfgang Kraushaar writes of the Vietcong seeming to be everywhere at the end of the 1960s, appearing every night on the evening news, but experienced exclusively virtually.[71]

The power of photography was significant in creating an emotional connection to this virtual war. The conflict was shaped in West Germany by iconic photos such as those of the young, naked girl running along a street after a Napalm attack, the man holding in his hands a baby only a few weeks old and with its skin hanging in tatters, and the Saigon chief of police shooting a defenseless Vietcong in the head from close range for television news cameras. Eddie Adams's photo of this execution along with the 1966 photo by a Japanese photographer of a dead Vietcong dragged through the jungle by a U.S. tank and the 1967 image of a small and delicate female militia leading away an enormous U.S. pilot also helped shape the phantom of the Vietcong as it evolved in the Federal Republic.[72] The importance of mass-mediated imagery to the production of a stylized reality cannot be overstated, and the performative capability of the RAF bombings can be found in interplay between this imagery and the well-established war rhetoric.

The *Frankfurter Rundschau* from May 13, 1972, ran images of the destruction caused by RAF bombs with the accompanying headline: "Such attacks only in Vietnam until now" (*Solche Anschläge bisher nur in Vietnam*). The language here undoubtedly influences the interpretation of the images, a process described by Roland Barthes as the "quickening" of image comprehension by text.[73] W. J. T. Mitchell describes this process as the "discursive or narrative suturing of the verbal and the visual." More importantly, however, Mitchell argues that the text necessarily encroaches on the pictorial, that even "pure" images are understood by recourse to verbal discourses or narratives.[74] Such interdependence is important for understanding the performativity of the images of bombings, which went beyond mere intertextuality. It did more than create referential bridges between two texts, it directly affected the medial experience of war in West Germany. Given such a visual mode of comprehension, the bombs created a seamless collage, cutting and pasting recognizable West German elements into a stylized experience of war. For example, the *Stern* magazine from May 11, 1972, ran a two-page spread showing destroyed VWs, BMWs, and Mercedes in a scene of warlike destruction with a member of the military police (MP) in the foreground.[75] Here, the Federal Republic was slipped into a scene reminiscent of the Vietnam War as experienced by the West German public. Just as the 9/11 attacks were carried out in a filmic language and had already been imagined over and over again in apocalyptic action movies, the RAF bombings were able to tap into a preimagined war narrative.

Such an alignment also manifested as entwined newspaper articles. Pieces on RAF bombings and Vietnam bombings appeared side by side: the *Süddeutsche Zeitung* from May 12 ran a story titled "USA bombs Hanoi and Haiphong" (*USA bombardieren Hanoi und Haiphong*). Appearing physically within the Vietnam article, and with a headline that seems at first a subheading of the article, was a piece on the Frankfurt bombing titled "One dead in the attack on the American officers' mess" (*Ein Toter bei Anschlag auf amerikanisches Offizierkasino*). The discursive entanglement was therefore also carried by reporting where no photographs were used.

Instead of bringing a "Vietnam feeling" to the Federal Republic as Baader and Ensslin attempted in their 1968 act of arson, May 1972 aligned the mainstream discourse of terrorism with the radical narrative of war by inserting the Federal Republic into the stylized reality of the Vietnam War. The RAF bombings of May 1972 were able to force their way into the existing medial experience of the Vietnam War, "quickening" the mainstream discourse of terror and effectively imposing on public debate the RAF's model of understanding. The now merged war/terrorism discourse held sway from the 1972 bombings, and it was only seriously questioned after the demise of the first generation of the RAF in 1977.[76] The ramifications during these years were significant.

As early as 1972, Heinrich Böll had argued against any acceptance of the RAF's declaration of war in his *Der Spiegel* article "Does Ulrike Meinhof want a Pardon or Safe Conduct?" (*Will Ulrike Meinhof Gnade oder freies Geleit?*).[77] He sarcastically described the situation as a war of 6 against 60 million, undermining the perceived danger that the group posed at that stage. Accepting a declaration of war and solidifying a stark frontline would, he warned, take the group more seriously than it deserved. More than this, accepting a terrorist declaration of war re-creates the strict dichotomy of good and evil, and the absolutist logic of terror. Agreeing to play the game by terrorists' own discursive rules risks establishing an endless loop of justification for violence and counterviolence. The idea of war rhetoric being counterproductive to counterterrorism policy has reemerged in the aftermath of the 9/11 attacks.[78] In the context of West Germany's own war on terror, Andreas Musolff argues that engaging in such discursive excess played a role in the violence in the mid to late 1970s by allowing RAF rhetoric to become somewhat of a self-fulfilling prophecy.[79] Specifically, the acceptance of the radical war narrative by politicians and the mainstream media provided external confirmation of the RAF's self-image as soldiers in an army. Not only was this now legitimized conception of themselves as combatants in a war a great source of internal solidarity, but it also had the ability to mobilize a new generation of members.[80] In this sense, the narrative of war that was so central to the protest scene's conception of the West German experience from the early 1960s, and that was made mainstream by the 1972 RAF bombings and declarations, was also able to spark a resurgence in support for the group after it had become increasingly isolated.[81] This unifying effect of the declarations and bombings was complemented by the "picturesque" ideology of Meinhof's treatises.

Treatises: Picturesque Ideology

In a note from July 7, 1973, and not long after her arrest, Gudrun Ensslin declared, "marcuse belongs to us . . . the joke that i for example see in that is that one deals with marcuse in a manner in which marcuse of course does not deal with himself."[82] This obscure prison note is indicative of the RAF engagement with ideology and intellectuals, many of whom—like German philosopher Herbert Marcuse—explicitly denounced the group's actions. The function of ideology is described here as "picturesque," as isolated, detached, and being as much a visual as a textual element of the treatises. This use of ideology meant that despite being ostensibly theoretical and purporting to outlay an ideological position that justified the group's actions, what the RAF treatises more effectively established was a moral program: a sustained meditation on the themes of sacrifice, loyalty, treachery, martyrdom, and glorious violence that became important for a group identity.

The first treatise, *The Urban Guerilla Concept*, appeared in the Federal Republic in April 1971, a year after the RAF went underground and some ten months after its last public statement. It was an attempt, in six sections, to justify RAF actions and ideologically rationalize its chosen course. Section one addressed the reporting of RAF operations in the press. Specifically, it denounced the editing of Meinhof's interview with Michèle Ray in *Der Spiegel* and defended the liberation of Baader. The second lamented the close ties between Bonn and Washington, as well as what the group saw as the ability of the Grand Coalition to absorb the discontent that had surfaced during the student movement. Section three claimed the history of the student movement as the prehistory of the RAF, and section four bemoaned the return of students to their desks. After outlining the case for the intervention of a revolutionary avant-garde, section five presented the chosen method for that intervention: the urban guerilla. The last section dealt with the anarchist slogan "destroy what destroys you" (*macht kaputt, was euch kaputt macht*). This 14-page text was written by Meinhof and sent by post to leftist groups and radical individuals throughout West Germany from a fake Bonn address.[83] It was distributed by hand in Republican Clubs (*Republikanische Clubs*) and other "socialist" centers as well as at demonstrations, such as those held on May 1 and 9, 1971, in West Berlin. It was also included as a supplement to issue 80 of *agit 883* from May 11 and sold in leftist bookstores for between fifty pfennigs and two marks.[84]

The second treatise, *Serve the People*, was distributed approximately a year after the first, in April 1972, and was largely a continuation of *The Urban Guerilla Concept*. Sections one and two dealt with Chancellor Brandt's visit to Tehran and the 1971 strike in the chemical industry, respectively. Section three was a response to criticism from the Left of the RAF's concept of the urban guerilla, and section four sought to provide answers to "current issues." Meinhof also wrote this second treatise. It is stylistically consistent with the first text, and a draft copy found by police in Switzerland showed amendments in Meinhof's handwriting.[85] The distribution of this sixty-page document was also similar to that of *The Urban Guerilla Concept*. It was sent via the post to mainstream media outlets from a Regensburg address, with *Der Spiegel* publishing excerpts in issue 18 in 1972.[86] Copies of pages four and five also arrived at the offices of the *Frankfurter Rundschau* and the *Westdeutsche Allgemeine Zeitung* on June 14, 1972, but were not printed.[87] Selected individuals also received the entire text directly by mail.[88] While it is impossible to know the size of the mailing, the 71 copies in 9 separate packages that were stranded as undeliverable mail at a single Regensburg branch of the Federal Mail give an indication of the numbers involved.[89] *Serve the People* was also dropped in large numbers across the campus of Göttingen University. In addition, copies were found in RAF safe houses and in the Information Centre Red People's University (*Informationszentrum Rote Volksuniversität*, IZRU) in Heidelberg.[90] There were even short-lived plans to reprint and distribute the text beyond the German borders with the sister organization Red Army Faction Zurich (RAFZ). In April 1972 Irmgard Möller, or "Gabi" as she was known, passed on a copy of the treatise to the RAFZ, but Swiss police swiftly foiled the planned expansion.[91]

Meinhof composed the third treatise, *The Black September Action*, in her Cologne prison cell.[92] The police assumed she wrote the text between September and October 1972, before a handwritten draft was either smuggled out of the prison by a defense lawyer or sent via uncensored mail. *The Black September Action* represents in many ways a bridging text between RAF communication in the underground and RAF communication in prison. In terms of content, there was a shift in argument once in prison, which was accompanied by a change in terminology and phrasing. Most notably, the long-coveted urban guerilla strategy fell out of favor and, in terms of operational strategy, the focus shifted from realizing the revolution to the liberation of Meinhof, Baader, Ensslin, and Raspe.[93] Despite being written in prison and the adjustment of focus, the distribution of this third text was very similar to that of the first two treatises.

Once it had cleared the first initial hurdle of escaping the prison system, it was typically hand delivered or sent by mail. An undeliverable package with a fictitious sender reveals that the text was posted directly to "interested parties." It was also made available in leftist bookshops. On November 23, 1973, copies of the text were found dropped across the campuses of educational institutions in three different West German cities. In what appears to be a coordinated drop, copies were found in a telephone booth on the grounds of Frankfurt University, in the main building of Cologne University, and in the Technical College in Berlin. The total number of copies is not known in any of these cases. Three copies were also found in the IZRU in Heidelberg.[94] The treatises can be grouped together not only because of the comparable modes of distribution but also because of other important similarities.

The intended audience for the texts was sympathizers, members, and potential members. In contrast to the declarations, which were primarily directed toward the general public, the group targeted the alternative media and direct distribution in sympathetic forums for the distribution of the treatises.[95] Like the declarations, however, the treatises did follow a strict, standard format, albeit tailored for a different audience. In their original format the treatises had a cover page featuring the RAF logo. The main body of the text was prefaced with quotations from either Mao or Marx and was significantly longer than either the statements or the declarations. Within the main body, each section was also prefaced with citations from various sources, but mainly Mao. Ideology, in the form of these quotations, thus played a very conspicuous role in the RAF texts.

The world of the 1970s was still sharply divided, with the Berlin Wall and the border between East and West Germany constituting the geographical and symbolic frontline. The RAF operated against the background of this clash of ideologies, conceiving of itself as part of a worldwide struggle and draping itself in political rhetoric. The group's own texts as well as the high-profile involvement—wanted or otherwise—of intellectuals such as Marcuse, Böll, and French philosopher Jean-Paul Sartre in the debates surrounding West German terrorism ensured the struggle was an ostensibly ideological one. The traditional assumption that terrorism is primarily ideologically motivated has, however, been called into question. Typically ideology is instead attributed a symbolic or communicative role rather than a causal one.[96]

In a critique of Mahler's work, Meinhof conceded that she, in contrast to Mahler, came to theory via praxis.[97] This path is representative of the route taken by many RAF members who only began to engage with theory once in prison and exposed to the group's schooling system. Ideology, it seemed, came second, and can be seen as neither decisive in, nor the foundation for, the formation or operation of the group.[98] The group's positions do not appear to be based on any deep understanding of political thought, and this, together with an insistence on the primacy of praxis, reveals an overall aversion to theory.[99] Critiques of Meinhof's stated position have focused largely on her understanding of socialist theory, particularly the works of Marx and Lenin. They confirm a fuzzy and superficial understanding of leftist political theory and the highly selective nature of Meinhof's relationship to theory. Government studies presented such cherry picking as in line with the practice of the RAF, which reduced ideological and theoretical debate to issues of morality in the face of criticism. They present Meinhof's "ideology" as a reductionist retreat from the economic, social, and political to the psychological, and the subsequent, stark division of these psychological elements into a rigid duality of good and evil.[100] Foreshadowing such work is a body of anecdotal evidence that Meinhof did not directly engage with political theory.[101]

It makes sense then to approach Meinhof's employment of ideology as not purely, or not even in the traditional sense, "ideological," but rather as consciously communicative. She used staccato quotations that become as much visual as textual features of the standard treatise format. More significantly, Marx, Mao, and Lenin are used almost exclusively to sustain thoroughly nonideological, nonpolitical theoretical discourses. At work is an "ideology" stripped bare of its context and resignified to perform discourses of antitheory and an insistence on "praxis," violence, bravery and sacrifice, and betrayal and loyalty. These rhetorical threads were important to the group dynamic of the RAF, and they rested largely on an engagement with "picturesque" ideology.

At the peak of her journalistic career, Meinhof acknowledged a certain brand awareness and the broad symbolic value of ideological mainstays such as Marx, Mao, and Marcuse during discussions with Joachim Fest. She defended her use of what he termed "long-since moth-balled, set phrases of Marxism," a curious mix of clichés from politics and religion, and a mixing of "brown" and "red" metaphors, by framing it as a "language of protest."[102] It aided, she insisted, the speedy uptake of ideas among comrades. They could not, after all, hold an explanatory lecture before every protest. Such ideological signposts were intended as symbols, which could tap into broad narratives among her audience. It was, as Rohrmoser and Fröhlich have described it, a mobilization of anarchistic energy behind the facade of borrowed vocabularies.[103]

This process of symbol making resembles the production of Theo Ligthart's 2000 work *avantgarde*. Ligthart places photographs of the Chrysler "Avant-garde" automobile and user manual alongside close-up, painted sections of RAF texts showing the word "Avantgarde." His intention here is to comment on the contemporary commodification of the political term and describe the shift from politics to style associated with the 1990s revival of RAF iconography.[104] His notion of picturesque (*pittoresk*) language as detached, isolated, and reappropriated recalls Dick Hebdige's idea of "style." Hebdige describes a "process by which things are made to mean and mean again."[105] He points to the radical aesthetic practices of Dada and surrealism as examples of appropriating objects and meaning only to redeploy them, and he also draws heavily on Barthes's notion of "myth." Barthes writes of "myth" as a "second-order semiological system" that "transforms history into nature" by stripping signs of their history and resignifying them.[106] He described a "speech *stolen and restored*. Only, speech which is restored is no longer quite that which was stolen: when it was brought back, it was not put exactly in its place. It is this brief act of larceny, this moment taken for a surreptitious faking, which gives mythical speech its benumbed look."[107] The picturesque resembles the processes of "style" and "myth" making but is additionally useful as it incorporates the element of the word as an image. These twin elements help in conceiving of Meinhof's ideology as a visual feature that helped bring into being a moral imperative and group identity.

The ideology in the treatises was picturesque in Ligthart's sense. It took a "close-up" view of schools of thought and removed them from their context and history in a manner not dissimilar to his painted and detached text. Icons of the left were never incorporated into the new context, appearing instead almost exclusively as isolated quotations. They are, then, twice removed: once from their original context and again from the body of the RAF texts as leading quotations prefacing the entire text or individual sections. In the original documents, such quotations appeared on the title pages and dominated lead-in pages, to the point that their role approached that of the RAF logo.

In this manner, theory and theorists became important signifiers for a group identity and indicators of affiliation. For the second generation of the RAF in particular, a picturesque ideology was just another element of a terrorist "cool." Volker Speitel, a former RAF member who described himself as being rather apolitical before being radicalized by the prison campaigns of the first generation, describes ideology as being on par with other visual, often pop-cultural symbols of belonging. "Affinities," he writes, "were established via a formal context, the same appearance, the same music, the same habits, the same catch phrases and slogans."[108] He continues: "The soundtrack to the guerilla differed from that of John Wayne films and Cowboys and Indians only in that with the RAF real blood flowed from torn bodies."[109] Ideology, then, had become an important element of a terrorist image. It was a shortcut to belonging that tapped less into a weighty ideological discussion than the cultural currency of socialist thinkers and vocabularies. It was a development that did not go completely unnoticed at the time.

Disgruntled members of the "Proletarian Front" (a publishing house in Hamburg that succeeded "Trikont" and existed between 1970 and 1972), who referred to the RAF members as comrades, addressed the picturesque quoting practice of the treatises in a 1973 article:

> The quotations from Mao, Lenin, Marx, Il Manifesto, from the Tupamaros or whomever else, which they cite as supporting evidence for the correctness of their course of action, serve in their first programmatic text on the "Urban Guerilla Concept" and in the "Treatise on Method" almost exclusively only as mottos for the individual sets of problems dealt with . . . Furthermore, one gets the impression that the cited, and very specific, experiences from Marx, Lenin, Madel, or for example even Mao are used more as general pearls of wisdom and as such are projected onto the fundamentally different, insufficiently understood and particular situation in the FRG; in other words, that the aforementioned guideline from Mao Tsetung was not observed or at least not always abided by. For this reason, quotations, even those used by the RAF comrades, approach the edge of dogmatism.[110]

What the authors refer to as dogmatism, Butz Peters describes as, at best, a negatively defined ideology.[111] A more accurate description would be a psychological onslaught in response to increasing criticism and isolation from the Left. This onslaught saw Meinhof make use of ideology as a mode of communication not to further theoretical debate or delineate a philosophical position, but to constitute distinctly nonideological discourses: (paradoxically) a discourse of antitheory and insistence on praxis, and discourses of violence, bravery, sacrifice, betrayal, and loyalty.[112]

Despite Meinhof laying claim to the student revolt of the late 1960s as the RAF's prehistory, and its legacy as the group's motivation, the RAF was subject to heavy criticism from the Left. In the face of this ideological critique, Meinhof's texts sought refuge initially in an aggressive antitheory stance. The turn away from the mainstream Left began with a refusal to enter into a dialogue, which was evident from the first line of published RAF text. In "Build up the Red Army" the group announced its arrival by saying "there is no point wanting to explain the right thing to the wrong people."[113] This sentiment was reinforced in the opening section of *The Urban Guerilla Concept*, borrowed from Mao: "I insist that anyone who has not engaged in enquiry, has no right to say anything."[114]

Meinhof continues in *The Urban Guerilla Concept* to attack leftist intellectuals. She denounces the "paper-production" (*Papierproduktion*) of leftist organizations as simply "the infighting of intellectuals, all competing for the best interpretation of Marx before an imaginary jury, which cannot be the working class because their [the intellectuals'] language precludes their [the working class's] access to the decision making process. When considering your praxis, it is more embarrassing for you to be caught out with an incorrect Marx quotation than with a lie. The page numbers that you include in your references almost always add up, the membership numbers that you give for your organizations almost never do."[115] This section is an insight into the relative lack of importance she placed on accurate citing of (in this case) Marx. Internal coherence was not the goal, rather it was the ability to pull in followers that mattered. Meinhof, whose "praxis" as a journalist had involved the instrumentalization of sentiment and symbolism to engage her readership, had a relatively late and secondhand introduction to leftist theory. Her texts also reveal a deep mistrust of Leftist intellectuals.

In her third treatise, Meinhof attacked Marx's disciples who unthinkingly arm themselves with nothing but quotations.[116] Similarly, then RAF member Horst Mahler also attacked the citation practices of the RAF's critics in *On the Armed Struggle in Western Europe* (1971), citing Lenin to do so: "Legions of 'Marxists' will come forward and will 'prove' with entire batteries of Marx quotations that the path described here is 'pure adventure,' 'Blanquism,' 'putschism,' 'anarchism.' Well and good. We'll gladly leave such exercises in isms to the scribes; if we only come a step closer to the revolution in Germany. 'Poor Marx and poor Engels, what abuses have been committed with quotations out of your works!' "[117] Meinhof's attack on Marxist disciples prefaced a personal attack on Leftist social theorist Oskar Negt, then professor of sociology at the Technical University in Hannover. In June 1972 he publicly denounced RAF violence as "apolitical" (*unpolitisch*).[118] Meinhof viewed Negt as representative of the academic left and dedicated an entire section in *The Black September Action* to him. Meinhof, perhaps ironically, also cited theorists to denounce theory and "mere quotations," as her texts shrank from a theoretical dialogue with increasing venom. In *Serve the People*, for example, she cites the Uruguayan urban guerilla group Tupamaros: "In the present stage of history, it can no longer be disputed that an armed group, as small as it may be, has a better chance of developing into a large people's army than a group that limits itself to annunciating revolutionary tenets."[119] Alongside this rejection of theory, a complementary and explicit insistence on "praxis" also emerged.

As part of her rationalization of the violence of the armed liberation of Baader in *The Urban Guerilla Concept*, Meinhof cites Mao as describing "armed struggle as 'the highest form of Marxism-Leninism.' "[120] She then concludes the justification with a Lenin citation: " 'If you would like to know what the Communists think, then look to their hands and not to their mouths.' "[121] Moreover, *The Urban Guerilla Concept* included a section dedicated to the "primacy of praxis." It was prefaced with Mao:

> He who wants to directly learn about a thing or complex of things, must personally participate in the practical struggle to change reality, to change the thing or complex of things, for this is the only way he can encounter the event of the thing at hand, and only through the personal participation in the struggle to change reality is he able to reveal the nature of that thing or complex of things and understand it.
>
> However, Marxism only attaches any significant importance to theory because it can be the instructions for action. If one has the right theory at one's disposal, but only treats it as something to chat about before putting away in a drawer, and as something that one never realizes as praxis, then this theory, as good as it may be, becomes meaningless.[122]

The self-marginalization is indicative of Meinhof's target audience being supporters and sympathizers, people already amenable to RAF arguments. Parallel to an aggressive rejection of theory, the insistence on the "primacy of practice" and a closed theoretical monologue were important refuges for the group. In the context of increasing theoretical and practical isolation, the group found further solace in the psychological. Meinhof, in particular, preferred to rebut theoretical criticism by insisting on the primacy of courage, strength of conviction, and a willingness to act.[123]

In *The Urban Guerilla Concept* Meinhof justified the RAF's role as the violent spearhead of the revolution. As part of the justification she attacked "proletariat organizations" (*proletarische Organisationen*) that remained within the given power structure and lacked the necessary conviction to be victorious. To clarify what she meant by victory she cited Debray: "To be victorious means to accept in principle, that life is not the most precious asset of a revolutionary."[124] She goes on to address the methods of the *Bild* newspaper and the Springer press. Given the power of the dominant media and its construction of the group, Meinhof counsels stoic fearlessness, using Mao to reinforce a sense of duty and strength of conviction. The urban guerilla, she wrote, could expect nothing but bitter hostility from the dominant media, but had "only to orientate itself around Marxist criticism and self-criticism. 'He who has no fear of being quartered, dares to tear the emperor from his horse,' Mao says."[125] Only a few lines later Meinhof reminds the urban guerilla of his or her duty, this time via Blanqui. One should take action, she wrote, "without leaving open a return to a middle-class life, without being able to leave the revolution on a hat-stand in a terrace house, and without wanting to, thus with the pathos expressed by Blanqui: 'the duty of a revolutionary is to fight always, to fight regardless, to fight to the death.' "[126] This emphasis on both courage in the face of death and the courage to seek out death continued in the second treatise.

Serve the People, the title of which is borrowed from Mao, opens by citing Mao in turn quoting Sima Qian: "In ancient times in China there was an author by the name of Sima Qian, who said: 'though death befalls all men alike, the death of the one may be weightier than Mount Tai and the death of the other lighter than swan down.' "[127] This celebration of courage and glorification of death prefaces a short discussion of the then recent deaths of RAF members Petra Schelm, Georg von Rauch, and Thomas Weisbecker.[128] Meinhof celebrated these shootings as examples of "weighty" deaths.[129] Later in the same treatise, when discussing the Springer-led "counterrevolution," she finishes her train of thought with Kim Il Sung: "the issue is . . . whether we can be successful in transforming the reactionary militarization into a revolutionary one, whether it is better, 'to simply lie down and die or stand up and offer resistance.' "[130] The rhetoric of courage built on a collage of channeled leftist thinkers only continued in the third treatise.

The Black September Action addressed the murder of Israeli athletes and coaches during the Munich Olympic Games. As part of her critique of the attack, Meinhof praised the killings as "anti-imperialist, anti-fascist, and internationalist," before rationalizing the murders and linking them to the RAF experience.[131] She concluded the text with the now standard stanza of capitalized exclamations and by again evoking Mao's quotation to declare "the deaths of the Arabian comrades to be weightier than the Mount Tai."[132] This same "Mount Tai" reference became a favorite and was used later in a prison tirade unleashed by a starving Holger Meins on Manfred Grashof.[133] Meins was furious at what he saw as Grashof's lack of conviction during a RAF hunger strike. The verbal attack exemplified the internal group dynamic at work both in the underground and in prison, a dynamic maintained largely via psychological domination and peer pressure.

Meinhof also nurtured in her treatises a stark distinction between friend and foe. Her construction of the "enemy" was similarly performed in the treatises by picturesque ideology. *The Urban Guerilla Concept* was prefaced by two Mao quotations reinforcing the strict separation of friend and foe: "Draw a clear line between us and the enemy!"[134] and "When the enemy battles against us, it is good; for it is proof that we have drawn a clear line between us and the enemy. When the enemy vigorously confronts us, paints us in the blackest of blacks and accepts nothing of ours, it is even better; for it attests to the fact that we have not only drawn a clear line between us and the enemy, but that our work has yielded great successes."[135] Meinhof later returns to this second citation when putting a positive light on the dark portrayal of RAF actions in the conservative media. The fact that the media had painted them in the blackest of black, she said, said something of the enemy.[136] In section five of *The Urban Guerilla Concept* Meinhof used Mao to further define the enemy as formidable, but ultimately vulnerable: "Therefore one must in his very being; with a long outlook, and in strategic terms, see imperialism and all reactionaries for what they really are: paper tigers. We must base our strategic thinking on this. On the other hand, they are in turn real, living tigers that are as hard as iron and eat people. We must base our tactical thinking on this."[137] This is indicative of a desire to galvanize hope among supporters, as well as the group's us-and-them mentality. However, as the support network of sympathizers began to diminish and the group's isolation began to bite, the focus shifted from defining "them" to defining "us."

From the second treatise, betrayal and solidarity became major issues. The final section of *Serve the People* began with a subsection on the trial of one-time RAF member Karl-Heinz Ruhland. Ruhland was arrested in 1970 before turning on the group and becoming a witness for the state. Meinhof dismisses him as unimportant and not close to the group.[138] In the very next subsection, "On Betrayal" (*Über Verrat*), she leaves no doubt that "traitors must be removed from the ranks of the revolution. Tolerance of treachery produces further treachery."[139] Solidarity, the other half of the binary opposition, completes the second treatise. "On Solidarity" (*Über Solidarität*) describes solidarity as a "weapon," a sentiment that would later become a catchphrase during the prison hunger strikes. Meinhof then concludes the section, and with it *Serve the People*, with a quotation: "We must, where possible, avoid unnecessary victims. Everyone in the ranks of the revolution must look after one another, must be caring towards one another, help one another."[140] Though strangely not attributed, this concluding citation nonetheless appears in quotation marks and comes from Mao's *Serve the People*.

Collectively the nonideological themes supported by Meinhof's picturesque ideology informed the RAF's intransigent moral program, and this terrorist morality in some ways outlived the treatises. The RAF's three major pieces of written work from the early 1970s remained intact for many years, with the political worldview articulated by Meinhof dominating the second generation. It endured the arrests of the group's leaders and was not significantly redressed until the third generation released its treatise *Guerilla, Resistance, and the Anti-Imperialist Front* (*Guerilla, Widerstand und antiimperialistische Front*), also known as the *May Paper* (*Mai-Papier*), in May 1982.[141] This paper confirmed the shift in strategy from the urban guerilla to the establishment of a "Western European Front" of allied terrorist groups, and the characteristically eclectic mix of ideological threads of the first three treatises fell away in favor of a strictly pragmatic view of the armed struggle.[142] A more important legacy, however, than the language used to articulate the RAF's worldview is the moral program and group dynamic that it performed. As psychological drivers of RAF identity, the themes of betrayal and solidarity, bravery and sacrifice, and loyalty and duty remained important regardless of fluctuations in personnel and strategy. They were particularly important when the parameters of the revolution collapsed from worldwide insurrection to the conditions within West German prisons.

CHAPTER 3

The Art of Hunger

The longest period of fasting was fixed by his impresario at forty days, beyond that term he was not allowed to go, not even in great cities, and there was good reason for it, too. Experience had proved that for about forty days the interest of the public could be stimulated by a steadily increasing pressure of advertisement, but after that the town began to lose interest, sympathetic support began notably to fall off.[1]

—Franz Kafka, *A Hunger Artist*

By the tenth and final collective hunger strike in 1989, the West German public had grown tired, and the Red Army Faction (RAF) prisoners, for their part, had grown both sick and tired.[2] The hunger strike declaration from February 1989 combined familiar demands with a new tone of desperation and a recognition of the physical toll the campaign of self-starvation had taken: "We have embarked on nine hunger strikes, two prisoners have died as a result, the health of many of us has suffered. Now this eighteen-year-long torture must end."[3] Exhaustion had dulled it, and historic circumstances had marched by the RAF strategy of political self-starvation, but for a decade and a half the collective hunger strike shaped West German terrorism and counterterrorism. The carefully choreographed spectacle of hunger dragged the organization up from its knees after the arrest of its leaders, it helped underpin a RAF prison identity, and it allowed the group to confront what it saw as a mainstream medicalization of terror. The performative strength of the hunger campaigns rested on Meinhof's ability to tailor the RAF struggle to the prison environment by encoding the starving prisoner with the group's established rhetoric and victimhood during the three major strikes of the first generation.[4]

The Strikes

Toward the end of 1972, Andreas Baader took the stand during the trial of Horst Mahler and was prompted by the defense to comment on the prison conditions: "from today, I won't eat any more until the prison conditions are changed."[5] Baader's words appeared the next day in newspapers, and a statement was distributed by RAF lawyers Eberhard Becker, Jörg Lang, Klaus Croissant, and Kurt Groenewold on January 17, 1973. This strike would end on February 16, 1973. Forty prisoners joined the strike and the RAF lawyers went on a much shorter, symbolic hunger strike in front of the Federal Court of Justice (*Bundesgerichtshof*) from February 9 through 12. The goal was the abolition of the oppressive prison conditions. Although a concession saw Meinhof transferred out of the "death wing" (*toter Trakt*) during the strikes, she was soon returned to her original cell once the prisoners were eating again.

Individual prisoners had used the tactic of the hunger strike previously, with Gudrun Ensslin, for example, embarking on a private hunger strike shortly after her arrest over access to her defense lawyer, Otto Schily.[6] The strike announced by Baader from the witness stand, however, was the first of the strikes that were conducted not in response to conditions and demands within the prison, but in accordance with the publicity they generated and a timeline of press releases. A note updating the situation reveals the pressures that governed the strikes:

> 7 still in Berlin. In addition, 4 are still starving in Cologne, 1 in Wittlich, 2 in Zweibrücken, 1 in Gotteszell! Except those in Berlin, everyone is more or less regularly artificially fed.
>
> Baader, Braun, Grundmann, Goergens, Mahler, Hoppe have interrupted the strike for health reasons—unbearable pain—colic etc.—with the will to start up again when better. I have no details on the others.
>
> Baader is for stopping
> 1. because nothing of any significance is afoot outside any more.[7]

Shortly thereafter, RAF lawyers wrote to the prisoners: "we, that is, the lawyers and the hunger strikers in Berlin, assume that the strike will end on Friday once press conference in Paris has taken place."[8] These comments were made in June 1973 and in the context of the second major strike that had begun weeks earlier on May 8.

Eighty prisoners—both RAF members and sympathizers—embarked on this second hunger strike.[9] Meinhof composed a declaration outlining the demands of the strikers that was circulated widely and printed in the alternative media. After 52 days, the strike ended on June 29, 1973, largely due to fading public and media interest.[10] It was during this second strike that force-feeding was used for the first time. The process was extremely painful and had remained largely unchanged since the beginning of the century. The prisoner was strapped, held down, or both, and a mouthpiece with a hole in it was placed in his or her mouth (making the practice of removing teeth redundant). A greased tube was then passed through the hole and down the throat into the stomach.[11] One advance was the use of a stethoscope to prevent the lungs being pumped full with food. A thick liquid was then forced down the tube. Vomiting afterwards was both a normal side effect and a frequently self-induced means of resistance. Consequently RAF members were often left strapped to the table for an hour after the procedure to allow for some digestion.[12]

Shortly after the second strike came to an end, and with it the force-feeding, a search of Meinhof's cell on July 16, 1973, turned up a manual for starvation.[13] The five-page document described the symptoms associated with self-starvation, provided the ideal daily weight loss, and even outlined the critical phases of the body's deterioration: pulse less than sixty or fifty, blood protein level of between 3 and 5 percent, a shift in the pH of the blood. The prisoners prepared themselves for the strikes, during which they suffered extreme weight loss and were at times very ill, but it was the third strike that would prove to be fatal.[14]

Meinhof launched the third and longest hunger strike on September 13, 1974, during the Berlin trial relating to the 1970 liberation of Baader. In internal discussion, this trial was chosen by Baader as a "tactically opportune moment," while in the courtroom a visibly ill Meinhof spoke softly for forty minutes before declaring the RAF was entering its third hunger strike.[15] Her written declaration, which was also circulated in the courtroom in print form, listed demands that centered on prison conditions but also included pensions and social security for all prisoners, prisoner access to doctors of choice, unobserved sexual contact, and the abolition of mail censorship.[16] Eighty prisoners joined this third strike, and it was always intended that some would not make it.[17] By the time the strike was called to a halt 145 days later on February 5, 1975, two prisoners were dead, including Holger Meins. A tall man, Meins died weighing only 39 kilograms.

Allegations of fraud, which recall those leveled at "miraculous maidens" and "hunger artists" of previous centuries, have subsequently been used to imply the strikes and the suffering of the prisoners were not "real." Such allegations are based on the fact that the prisoners hoarded food and secretly ate during the strikes.[18] While we cannot presume to know the reasons or motives for eating, there is medical evidence that suggests the feeling of hunger disappears (as is stated in the RAF starvation manual) after a few days. Eating was instead used during the third hunger strike to manage the rate of deterioration and ensure RAF prisoners starved in a predetermined order, allowing for a staggered yet constant stream of prisoner deaths. Dogmatic adherence to the argument of

torture and dismissive allegations of fraud may be understandable symptoms
of the historical immediacy of West German terrorism and a severely polarized
debate, but they both miss the point. The success of these hunger strikes lies not
in the flawless adherence to food abstinence, but in the discourses provoked.
The constructions of hunger and the starving body were very much real, and
they helped set the discursive parameters for West German terrorism for years
to come.

Strikes carried out after Meinhof's death adhered largely to the model established in the first three, however, they were ultimately less successful in garnering broad public sympathy. The brutal and roundly condemned violence of
the German Autumn robbed second-generation strikes of the possibility of any
broad-based support. The Stammheim deaths also stripped the protest of the
strength of the cult of personality that surrounded the first-generation leaders.
Moreover, these effects were compounded by the shifting official response to
the strikes, which reduced the uncertainty and scope for the type of emotional
extortion the strategy of political self-starvation relies on.

After heated debated in the years following Meins's death, legislation was
enacted in 1977 that clarified how prison authorities were to deal with prisoners refusing food: the new section 101 of the Prison Act (*Strafvollzugsgesetz*,
StVollzG) respected the autonomy of prisoners, but included an obligation to
force-feed if an "acute danger to the life" (*akute Lebensgefahr*) of the prisoner
could be established.[19] While this move provided legislation specific to the situation of a hunger strike for the first time, and with it greater clarity, it did not
provide absolute certainty. The new law was a compromise of two extreme positions, and the vagueness of the terms provided for neither an inviolable right
for prisoners to refuse food nor concrete obligations for prison doctors. The
state's position was refined in 1985 when the autonomy of the prisoner to refuse
food and treatment unless he or she was deemed incompetent was recognized.[20]
In practice, this new policy—labeled the "coma solution" (*Koma-Lösung*) by
prisoners and their supporters—meant waiting until the prisoner was unconscious before commencing artificial feeding. This staggered clarification of the
expected response effectively called the prisoners' long-standing bluff.[21] While
the ability of the strikes to mobilize widespread sympathy eroded, the second
and subsequently the third generation of the RAF continued to rely on constructions of self-starvation that were developed in prison and were transmitted
from prison via complex and effective communication networks.

Communicating the Strikes: The *Info* and the *Out-fo*

Among the East German military magazine *militärtechnik*, individual *Der Spiegel*
issues, and countless other publications prevented from entering the prison system

was issue 20 of *Wir wollen alles*. This particular magazine was stopped before it reached Meinhof, the intended recipient, because page 10 included a RAF hunger strike declaration.[22] Meinhof's declaration had circumvented the prison measures to prevent information from getting out, only to be halted on the way back in. The fate of issue 20 is representative of the frontline in the penal system: behind the debate that framed the harsh initial prison conditions in terms of either "security" or "torture" raged a battle for control over the flow of information.

The initial prison conditions experienced by the RAF leadership group were severe. After her arrest on June 15, 1972, Meinhof was placed in a cell in the otherwise empty psychiatric wing of Cologne-Ossendorf prison. Among the numerous "special instructions" (*besondere Anordnungen*), it was stipulated that the lights should burn day and night and neighboring cells should be left empty.[23] Isolation was standard for most RAF prisoners, and especially for the leaders, who were spread across penal institutions throughout West Germany: Baader was sent to Schwalmstadt, Jan-Carl Raspe to Cologne, Meins to Wittlich, and Ensslin to Essen.

Over the course of the five-year incarceration, prison conditions were highly fluid. There were differences between prisons, and prisoners were moved between facilities. Ensslin was transferred to Cologne-Ossendorf and a cell next to Meinhof in February 1974, before the two of them were moved to the seventh floor of the purpose-built Stammheim facility near Stuttgart in April. Along the way Meinhof spent time in the Moabit prison in Berlin to appear at trials regarding her involvement in the 1970 liberation of Baader and the trial of Horst Mahler. Baader and Raspe arrived at Stammheim in October 1974, but Meins's health had, as the result of a prolonged hunger strike, deteriorated so drastically that moving him from Wittlich was not an option. Conditions were also subject to change as a disciplinary measure or due to shifting "security needs."[24]

Against this background of general fluidity, there was a slow trend of relaxing conditions. Nevertheless, the commentary on the conditions often succumbed to the traditional rut of RAF historiography of defending one or the other political perspectives. Anecdotal evidence is also wide-ranging and at times highly contradictory without necessarily being untruthful.[25] On the one hand, for example, the RAF prisoners lived in larger than normal cells, which more closely resembled academic offices than prison cells, toward the end of their lives and were allowed to spend much of the day with each other. They had access to books, individual televisions, and privileges not enjoyed by other prisoners. On the other hand, they suffered terribly under earlier prison conditions. One of Cologne-Ossendorf prison's own medical experts, Dr. Bernd Goette, found in February 1973 that "in the case of Ms [Meinhof], whom I have twice examined, the limit of her resilience, in psychiatric terms, has *now* been reached."[26] His recommendation to ease conditions was not immediately, or even quickly, implemented by prison authorities because it was deemed to pose too great a risk to the control of the flow of information between RAF prisoners and their "helpers" (*Helfer*).[27] More important to understanding the discursive construction of hunger, however, is understanding the motives behind prison conditions rather than judging their merits.

The flow of information became an important battleground during incarceration of the first generation. The official legal reason given in 1972 for the heightened *Untersuchungshaft* was the danger of suppression of evidence (*Verdunkelungsgefahr*) and the need to prevent prisoners from communicating with the outside world and interfering with the criminal investigation.[28] Visitation as well as incoming and outgoing mail was restricted to lawyers and immediate relatives. Packages and letters within this scope were also subjected to differing levels of censorship. Prisoners could only receive newspapers and magazines requested through the prison administration, and those publications approved were then appraised on an issue-by-issue basis. Radios were also withheld from prisoners until—in Meinhof's case at least—late 1972, and the use of cassette recorders was likewise highly regulated.[29] The constant emphasis on control of the flow of information, which was behind many of the fluctuating prison conditions, saw the prisoners and lawyers attempt to circumvent the measures imposed.

Early efforts at circumvention were messages smuggled from prisoners to other individuals, presumably by individual lawyers. However, information also needed to flow the other way. In March 1973, Baader demanded the lawyers finally "build an info-system," which in May became highly organized.[30] A text found in Meinhof's cell summarized the internal prison discussion as it stood on May 25, 1973, and described how any texts a lawyer received were to be delivered to the Hamburg office of RAF lawyer Kurt Groenewold, the "central contact," before being collated, copied, and disseminated to the RAF prison population. This became known as "das info" (*info*), and it was received by a regular group of about thirty prisoners.[31]

The *info* was a flexible system that could easily deal with prisoner transfers and changes in prison conditions. It relied heavily on the relatively easy passage of material marked "defense mail" (*Verteidigerpost*) between the prisoners and lawyers. The rules governing defense mail were, however, detailed and subject to change, which meant packages were often subject to search and censorship. The system, then, was not perfect, but given the efforts to stop communication between prisoners, it was relatively reliable. The *info* was also hierarchical, and after initially being two-tiered, it soon had three levels. Prisoners who received the *info* at level I, also received levels II and III. Those who entered at level II, also received level III, but not level I. Level III was the lowest degree of access. Anyone could contribute to the *info*, but final decisions on the content and stratification were made by Baader and Ensslin. The *info* functioned well as a prison communication system, and it also helped maintain a sense of group identity, a strictly hierarchical structure, and a certain discipline. However, another network was required to communicate with the outside world.[32]

Meinhof saw the group's "central problem" as the "dissemination [and] publication of [its] ideas," and the system subsequently developed for communicating RAF ideas from prison to the wider world was built on the logistics of the *info*.[33] The immediate contacts remained chiefly RAF lawyers, but instead of turning the flow of information back in on itself, communiqués were passed on to a variety of organizations. This system, referred to here as the *out-fo*, became more than a line of communication between comrades, it evolved into a network of publication and event management. Some avenues of publication were extensions of those used in the underground, such as the relationship with Red Aid (*Rote Hilfe*).[34] The Red Aid organization was an arm of the Communist Party of Germany (Development Organization) (*Kommunistische Partei Deutschlands [Aufbauorganisation]*, KPD/AO) and published leaflets and a magazine. Hunger strike declarations written by Meinhof appeared unedited in the magazine. Red Aid also organized demonstrations and teach-ins. The cooperation stretched back to before the group's arrest, when Red Aid published RAF declarations and ran a teach-in in May 1972 in Frankfurt at which a cassette recording of Meinhof from the underground was played. Once in prison, Meinhof wrote of her hope that Red Aid would perhaps develop into an "organization of the political prisoners, of the prison politics of the guerilla."[35] The Information Centre Red People's University (*Informationszentrum Rote Volksuniversität*, IZRU) also printed RAF texts, RAF lawyer texts, and hunger strike declarations, both in its magazine *Red People's University* and in leaflet form, as did the Information Service for Suppressed News (*Informationsdienst für unterbliebene Nachrichten*, ID).

Perhaps the biggest single development in terms of the *out-fo*, however, was the founding of the "Committees against the torture of political prisoners in the FRG" (*Komitees gegen Folter an politischen Gefangenen in der BRD*). The appeal to the public to form committees was drafted by lawyers in consultation with RAF prisoners, and committees soon appeared in 23 West German cities.[36] The groups attracted about 450 people in their first year, however, the most active members remained RAF lawyers and relatives of prisoners. In July 1974 Wienke Zitlaff wrote of the committees' work as being done by a couple of people in Hamburg and Heidelberg. Many of the young committee members thought of themselves as the "legal arm of the RAF," the expressed purposes of which were to inform the public, mobilize liberals, and raise funds.[37] These very active groups published leaflets and booklets, led demonstrations, held press conferences, appeared on television, collected money, and organized teach-ins.

In total, they held no less than 75 information events in the year following their formation.[38]

The printing of unedited RAF texts as well as frequent cross-publication of texts and images produced a common vocabulary of phrases, slogans, photos, cartoons, and a surprisingly homogeneous message in these alternative publications. The prison texts that were published on the outside were composed by Meinhof in her cell with Ensslin and Baader exercising scant editorial veto via the *info*.[39] The strikes and, more importantly, the external protests and events coordinated via the *out-fo* were designed to capture the attention of the commercial media, which tended not to publish RAF texts or report the self-starvation of prisoners as an event unto itself.[40] Contrary to the widespread reporting of RAF texts from the underground, prison texts, which were often sent directly to media outlets, did not often appear in mainstream publications.

Mainstream reporting of the strikes tended instead to gather around three areas. First, a relative suppression compared to the alternative media: in a rare interview conducted via correspondence and published in *Der Spiegel*, the RAF leadership group denounced what it termed a "news boycott" (*Nachrichtenboykott*) and the role Meins's death played in breaking it.[41] Second, a number of longstanding themes, such as the fitness of the prisoners to stand trial, the role of the defense lawyers, and the extended debates over the ethics and medicine of force-feeding shaped coverage. These debates represented the in-house discussions of politicians and medical professionals, and they addressed the strikes to the extent that they encroached on their immediate professional responsibility. Prisoner texts appeared in articles, but these were almost exclusively originally intended as internal correspondence and were cited as part of the self-contained debates among lawyers, politicians, and doctors. The third node of reporting was the external events staged in support of the strikes, and it is here that the event management of the *out-fo* ensured a media presence for the RAF construction of hunger.

The most prominent of the events sanctioned and designed by prisoners to attract publicity was Jean-Paul Sartre's 1974 meeting with Baader in Stammheim. Meinhof wrote the invitation to Sartre, and drafts that circulated through the *info* reveal the clear intention behind the visit was to create media hype capable of "transporting political content."[42] The visit, or more accurately the subsequent press conference with the French philosopher and RAF lawyer Klaus Croissant, provided the RAF with the platform it sought, as it was reported widely by the domestic and international press. The West German newspapers presented the visit predominantly as foreign interference in the internal affairs of the Federal Republic but also gave column space to RAF accusations of "torture" and "fascism," with terminology such as incarceration of "isolation" (*Isolationshaft*) and "extermination" (*Vernichtungshaft*) finding its way into articles, for example, in the *Frankfurter Allgemeine Zeitung* (*FAZ*), *Süddeutsche Zeitung*, and *Der Spiegel*. Baader's own words from his conversation with Sartre were even reported in the *FAZ*, albeit via a prison interpreter, Sartre himself, and then a second interpreter at the press conference.[43]

Such an increased level of abstraction is representative of the route RAF slogans and phrases took to make it into the pages of mainstream publications. Protests in the aftermath of Meins's death, for example, saw RAF words reported verbatim: the *Süddeutsche Zeitung* reported the slogan "Holger Meins—murdered by bourgeois class justice," as it appeared on wreaths laid at his funeral, and "Fight the bourgeois class justice," "Fight Holger Meins' murderers," and "Freedom for all political prisoners" as was plastered across placards after the funeral.[44] A similar sentiment was relayed by pictures of, and articles on, graffiti that appeared on West German churches. The *Süddeutsche* ran a photo of a spray-painted "Holger Meins murdered in prison" and cited similar graffiti such as "Holger Meins starved to death—amen" in the caption.[45] Pictures of a protest by RAF lawyers outside the Federal Court of Justice (*Bundesgerichtshof*, BGH) showing, among others, posters painting the justice system as fascist—"BGH = Brauner Gangsterhaufen"—appeared in *Der Spiegel*.[46] While such Nazi analogies, accusations of murder, and the preferred terminology of the RAF were unlikely to make it directly from prison to the newspapers, they regularly did so via the subterfuge of the reporting of demonstrations either directed from prison via the *out-fo* or sprouting organically from the supporter milieu it maintained.

By circumventing the prison conditions imposed on them, RAF prisoners maintained contact with each other and allowed their words to filter out of the prison system and into the alternative and commercial media. In many ways, the prison communication networks were more effective for the group than anything in the underground, and the importance of the notion of hunger performed via these networks can scarcely be overstated. Externally hunger was central to a medical discourse capable of transmitting already established RAF themes by enabling prisoners to occupy the twin victim statuses of their rhetoric: the object of Nazi atrocities and the colonized third world. The resulting debate and public campaigns surrounding the hunger strikes and prison conditions, in turn, were the catalyst for radicalizing underground members of the Socialist Patients' Collective (*Sozialistisches Patientenkollektiv*, SPK) and many young committee members, giving rise to the second and eventually the third generation of the RAF.[47]

Having revived sympathy for the RAF in the mid-1970s, the prison campaigns maintained a base of sympathizers throughout the 1980s, and proved capable of mobilizing elements of the Left well into the 1990s. This legal base was in turn instrumental to RAF recruitment, as it served as a gateway to the levels of the group's hierarchy that existed and operated illegally.[48] Such potential to radicalize and prompt violence remained a concern up until the final 1989 strike. Authorities pushed for a solution to be found in response to this tenth strike, which was carried out in the context of a renewed rash of bomb attacks.[49] In a reference to the German Autumn, a member of the Federal Republic's domestic intelligence agency noted, "If the next 14 days do not see negotiations that are sensible and have a sense of proportion . . . we will have conditions like 1977."[50] The deadline underpinning this urgency was not the likely death of a prisoner, but prisoners' even more likely loss of consciousness: the trigger for the force-feeding of prisoners. The state feared that a reactivation of the debate on force-feeding alone would be enough to spark more bombs.[51] In this sense, it is very difficult to imagine RAF violence being sustained into the 1980s and 1990s without the starving prisoners of the 1970s. The lingering potency rested on constructions of hunger and the prison experience established during the first-generation strikes. Internally, hunger was part of the psychological discipline exercised by RAF leaders on the rest of the group. It maintained a group identity and helped foster the martyrdom necessary for people to put their lives on the line.

Self-Starvation as Holy Hunger

Contemporaneous examples of prison hunger strikes were at hand for the RAF. Most prominent among them was an Irish Republican Army (IRA) strike just prior to the first major RAF strike. In 1972 IRA prisoners launched a successful 37-day hunger strike to attain the status of "political prisoners," which also became an important campaign for the RAF. In 1974 the Price sisters went on strike demanding repatriation after being arrested in London for their part in a series of car bombings in March 1973. This strike lasted for more than two hundred days and was sustained by force-feeding. These contemporaneous examples echoed throughout the *info*, and the language of these Irish strikes, contributed a sacralization of self-starvation among RAF prisoners.

Unlike in West Germany, the hunger strike has a long history in Ireland. The IRA strikes can be placed in a tradition of self-starvation that can be traced back to pre-Christian oral legal codes allowing an aggrieved party to "fast against his debtor." The Irish hunger strike has also attained unique importance in Irish Christian traditions and has taken its place in a history of religiopolitical martyrdom.[52] Allen Feldman argues, however, that while the hunger strikes of the IRA have been interpreted as acts of "religious transcendence," this has more to do with their reception outside of prison. He writes—drawing on extensive interviews with former prisoners—that striking prisoners insisted theirs was a secular hunger strike with political goals, but they were well aware of the sacralization of the hunger beyond the prison walls.[53] Such "holy hunger" led to a rush of support and grief, which the strikers seized upon for their own political ends. Nevertheless, a clear line remained between the internal conception of hunger and the construction of it outside the prison. The distinction between internal and external exists, too, in the case of the RAF, but, in some senses, the group reversed the Irish logic.

The RAF prisoners were well aware of the IRA and its hunger strikes, with a history of the Irish group and its long history of the "torture and extermination camps in ireland" circulating in the *info* from 1973 to 1974.[54] In an *info* entry from November 1974, Baader refers to the hunger strike as " 'the holiest weapon' as the ira says."[55] The term was adopted days later by Ensslin in another *info* entry, in which she also kept the quotation marks.[56] In addition, an unsigned *info* (most likely written by Raspe) hails the Price sisters as living for "10 times 10 times 10-thousand years!"[57] The Price sisters were at this stage not dead; in fact, both survived the strike and were eventually released from prison.

The appropriation of Irish hunger with its connotations of virtue, sacrifice, and holiness were introduced into the *info* system in late 1974, in the early stages of the third RAF hunger strike, and only weeks after the death of Holger Meins. This third strike was intended to cost lives. As early as February, Baader wrote in the *info*: "I think, this time we won't stop the strike. That means people will break."[58] In March 1974 Meinhof wrote in the *info* of the hunger strike needing to be backed up with sick and even dead prisoners.[59] Ensslin also made specific suggestions as to the timing of prisoner deaths, arguing that deaths needed to be accepted and proposing a staggered program of self-starvation that would see one death every third week (or second or fourth; on this point she was flexible).[60] The prisoners were able to eat by storing food when not on strike and later resorting to these hidden hordes, meaning the policy of staggered deaths was manageable. Though they starved themselves, the RAF leaders were never part of the program of death by self-starvation.

The importance the leadership group placed on other prisoners putting their lives on the line was matched by the need for numbers of participants. An internal communiqué regarding the planning of the third strike clearly states that strikes should only take place if supported by a large number of prisoners: between fifty and one hundred.[61] Elevating self-starvation to a pseudoreligious practice also helped to maintain a group sense of purpose, particularly as the members were isolated from each other. The appropriation of a discourse of virtuous and holy hunger to foster a sense of duty and willingness to sacrifice complemented the already existing group structure and disciplinary system of the RAF.

Verbal abuse and peer pressure were integral to the group dynamic of the RAF from the moment it entered the underground and the public consciousness.

Baader was the leader and cultish figure around which the RAF gathered, and in the underground he wielded his power largely via verbal abuse, humiliation, and by cultivating a cumulative peer pressure. Baader's verbal abuse of those who stepped out of line continued in prison via the *info*. He threatened, for example, to excommunicate Astrid Proll from the *info* when she discontinued her hunger strike, and Meinhof followed up on the threat by warning that she could be thrown out of the RAF altogether.[62] The efficacy of such threats is supported by Gerhard Müller's testimony that while no concrete pressure was exerted via the lawyers to participate in the hunger strikes, the stakes were obvious: "For me it was nevertheless clear that not participating would automatically lead to expulsion from the RAF and with it expulsion from the info with the consequences that entails."[63] When Margrit Schiller was in fact banished from level I of the *info* during the third hunger strike, she responded with desperation: "send me 1 again immediately. I need it, to stick with the hs [hunger strike] and particularly the ts [thirst strike] until the end."[64] Meins also attacked Manfred Grashof after the latter broke off his strike: "you stupid idiot. / start again immediately and continue—if you haven't already done so. that and nothing else . . . the only thing that counts is the struggle."[65] During the third strike, lawyers reported the weights of striking prisoners to Baader, who would then admonish those he thought were not fasting quickly enough. In addition to the peer pressure and unquestioned common goal, the prisoners received regular collections of letters written by other prisoners under the heading "critique and self-critique" (*kritik und selbstkritik*) which served as a type of confession. Prisoners could confess to how they had failed to adhere to the particular brand of revolution the RAF had developed.

As a pseudoreligious tool, the "sacralization" of hunger was an integral part of the internal group dynamics of the RAF. The group cited an Irish history and discourse of hunger, reversing the logic of the IRA strikes: the external discourse of hunger in the Ireland case was used by the RAF to support an internal holiness and sense of martyrdom. It provided an important basis from which the number of strikers could be maintained and a willingness to sacrifice exalted, but it never left the internal *info* system. Beyond the prison walls, hunger was referred to as a weapon, but never a "holy weapon." If the internal dynamics of the RAF were the playground for the domineering Baader, the external discourses of hunger were the domain of Meinhof, the RAF scribe. Externally, hunger formed part of an intense effort to counter a discourse of terrorism that married contemporaneous scientific thinking on terrorism with the construction of terrorists in the commercial media. Not only was Meinhof's medical history central to the mainstream pathologizing of terror, but she also led the RAF effort to combat it by medicalizing the group's own struggle.

Self-Starvation as Countermedicalization

The scientific community and sectors of the commercial press actively sought to present Meinhof's 1962 brain surgery as a potential cause for her radicalization. The surgery was widely reported at the time, and her medical history was written up in 1968 in a medical journal.[66] Years later, issue 26 of the weekly magazine *Stern* from 1972 printed the article "The tumor in Meinhof's brain" (*Der Tumor im Gehirn der Meinhof*), complete with a Röhl family portrait and her 1962 brain X-ray. The conception of the damaged or crazy terrorist was only reinforced by the decision to keep her not in prison, but in a prison psychiatric wing. It was here that identifying Meinhof also became an issue for doctors. Her fingerprints did not exist on file and the prisoner refused to cooperate with police, or even acknowledge her name. So the decision was made to X-ray her head and compare the results with the now famous image. Even the search for the terrorist became a matter for medical experts charged with identifying the terrorist deep within the body of the accused.

In line with this wider trend of doctors being considered the appropriate experts to assess terrorists, psychiatrists were soon assigned the task of assessing the criminal responsibility of the prisoner. At the beginning of 1973, and in the context of the first hunger strike, the chief medical officer, Bernd Goette, used the 1962 surgery to justify his finding to Federal Prosecutor Peter Zeis that "according to the results of the inquiries conducted to date, an impaired criminal responsibility for the accused Ulrike Meinhof between June 1970 and her arrest cannot be easily ruled out."[67] The role of the psychiatrist would soon shift again to assessing the damage, if any, to the prisoners' mental health as the result of prison conditions. It was the common assessment of prison doctors that the physical and mental well-being of the prisoners was suffering and already damaged, but these concerns were deemed subordinate to security needs.[68] Even the deaths of the prisoners were viewed through the medical prism, as the debate surrounding the deaths in Stammheim, particularly Meinhof's, proceeded in terms of conflicting sets of medical evidence. The 1979 report by the International Investigation Commission (*Internationale Untersuchungskommission*, IUK) countered the official autopsy finding that the "results of investigations suggest, in fact, that Ulrike Meinhof was dead when she was hanged and that there is alarming evidence, which indicates the involvement of a third person in this death."[69] Identification of the terrorist, the cause of his or her actions, the conditions of his or her incarceration, and the nature of his or her death were all to be understood through the gaze of a doctor.

In response, the prisoners armed themselves for the prison experience with a manual for countering diagnosis and treatment. Removed from Meinhof's cell in 1973, this seven-page text lists the tools of diagnosis and treatment—from observing speech and interactions and performing X-rays to hypnosis and carotid angiographies—as well as methods for sabotaging such attempts, including remaining silent, thrashing around to guard against needles, or tensing and relaxing muscles and yawning through the nose to sabotage electroencephalograms.[70]

The body developed as the frontline not only inside but also outside the prison system, with the medical or scientific construction of the terrorist feeding off the science and continuing in its own right in the press. Meinhof's brain became a defining image of West German terrorism. In August 1973, shortly after the second hunger strike, *Der Spiegel* published the article "Clear-headed or sick?", which included the 1962 image of Meinhof's brain.[71] The *Frankfurter Rundschau* from August 16, 1973, ran a similar piece, with the article "Fight surrounding the head of Ulrike Meinhof," which also included the X-ray.[72] The medicalization, or, as the prisoners and sympathizers often wrote, the "psychiatrization" (*Psychiatrisierung*) of the prisoners, particularly Meinhof, in the media did not go unnoticed or unanalyzed. Red Aid published a 192-page book that included a review of the reporting on terrorism and cited examples from the time of the arrests, such as "Ulrike Meinhof, a 'severe psycho,' who has lost touch with reality (Welt, 19.6.72)" and "The fear of the nation—a case for psychiatrists? That's the way it is! (Bild, 5.6.72)."[73] The RAF and its sympathizers saw the reporting as a coherent and coordinated campaign across the entire spectrum of the mainstream media. In a letter from April 1974 to fellow RAF lawyer Heinrich Hannover, Jörg Lang writes of what he sees as a prolonged, almost two-year campaign to "make" Meinhof a mad person in the public consciousness.[74] It was the job of the defense, Lang wrote, not to let this happen.

Meinhof herself wrote of the "scientification" (*Verwissenschaftlichung*) of the public discourse on terrorism as a tool of domination being used to replace all political concepts with scientific terms.[75] She also led the way in showing how this was to be countered: by its appropriation and subversion. In a letter to her lawyers, Meinhof demands that they "finally bring the committee arguments up to the same scientific level, that the pigs have, and onto the political level of the RAF."[76] Meinhof's comments are indicative of the shift she ushered in to create the group's own scientific discourse of terrorism. She shared the view of the *Red People's University* that "science is political and politics is scientific."[77]

From prison, Meinhof regularly edited committee texts and gave directions on press conferences to be held by the committees or RAF lawyers. In this manner she was able to insert desired terms and phrases, such as "brainwashing," which she demanded be added to committee publications and included at lawyer press conferences.[78] A 1975 written interview with the leadership group printed in *Der Spiegel* is likewise laden with the term brainwashing, seemingly irrespective of the question posed.[79] Meinhof also suggested recruiting the expert opinion of Dr. Jacques Hassoun, and that Dr. Hassoun use the word "brain" instead of "personality."[80] The appropriation of the discourse of science proceeded, then, by lacing texts and speeches with medical and scientific language.

Perhaps the most famous linking of the RAF prison experience to the human body, and the basis for much of the prison campaigns, is a poem. It was written by Meinhof and reproduced completely or in part in almost all texts produced in the cloud of activity surrounding the RAF:[81]

> the feeling, your head is exploding (the feeling, your skullcap will actually rupture, chip away)—
>> the feeling, your spinal cord is being pressed into your brain—
>> the feeling, your brain is gradually shriveling up, like dried fruit, for example—
>> the feeling, you're always and imperceptibly live with electricity, that you're remote-controlled.[82]

The poem was presented as a personal account of Meinhof's time in the Cologne-Ossendorf prison under the heading "letter from a prisoner in the death wing" (*brief von einem gefangenen aus dem toten trakt)*, and draws much of its impact from its intimacy. However, the *info* of 1974 includes a discussion between Meinhof and RAF lawyers in which it was decided to use the poem externally: "I'll write a few things down and you should tell me, whether it can be of any use in the fight against the obscene mess."[83] "These things" included the entire 1973 poem. Having given the "wing stuff" (*traktkram*) more thought, Meinhof had reservations that the release could backfire and provide propaganda for the fascists "precisely because i did not write it down for publication, but rather to provide material that could poss. help bring the counterinformation up to the same scientific level as the obscene mess."[84] If the poem had already been used publically, however, she was "ok" with it. It was used, and Groenewold reported back to Meinhof on a speech he gave on January 30, 1974, in Stuttgart to about nine hundred people and the success of the poem in relaying the reality of prison torture.[85]

Just as experts served to bolster the official scientific discourse of terrorism, the support of doctors was also integral to legitimizing the RAF's medicalized politics. Physicians mobilized against the treatment of prisoners by publishing declarations and open letters, as well as by supporting events. One leaflet produced by a group of eight practitioners with no obvious links to the group took the form of a RAF or committee text, typewritten with an underlined heading and concluding slogans written in capital letters with exclamation marks.[86] Doctors also put their names directly to committee publications, such as the 35 medical professionals who signed and delivered an open letter to the Federal Court dated August 1973, which was printed by the Committee Against

Isolation Torture.[87] Sympathetic doctors also lent their support to events such as the committee teach-in about the hunger strike on November 26, 1974, where Dr. Ekkehard Seckendorff appeared alongside sociologist Professor Christian Sigrist and RAF lawyers Groenewold and Schily.[88]

Meinhof also actively solicited medical support. She was aware of the importance of medical opinions and suggested to lawyers in April 1974 doctors she thought would be useful for their purposes.[89] An *info* from that time describes one of the main tasks of the committees as mobilizing doctors and recording their support "in *one* broad statement that in the best case is issued and signed by *multiple* 'experts' (theuns!)."[90] Such support was fundamental to the forming and success of the committees, particularly the support of psychiatrist Sjef Teuns, who famously wrote of isolation and sensory deprivation as torture in an article in *Kursbuch 32*. Ensslin wrote of the hunger strikes bringing the committees to life, that this was the measure of the success of the self-starvation, and that this process was enabled by the public support of medical professionals.[91] In her 1974 letter suggesting suitable experts, Meinhof also wrote of medical expertise as an organizational tool for developing what she thought Teuns had in mind: a countermedicine.[92]

The RAF had always expressed their struggle in political terms. Now in prison, a model for the expression of the political in terms of the medical was close at hand. The Socialist Patients' Collective (*Sozialistisches Patientenkollektiv*, SPK) emerged in 1970 at the University of Heidelberg as an antipsychiatry group arguing that capitalism was quite literally the source of society's ills. The group's founder, Dr. Wolfgang Huber, had worked as an assistant lecturer in the university's psychiatric and neurological clinic since 1964 and was told in early 1970 he no longer had a position after increasing conflict with colleagues and his superiors. Huber and a number of patients occupied the administration offices and went on a hunger strike. The group published leaflets and held teach-ins before the situation escalated, a member committed suicide in April, and the apartments of other members were raided in connection with the search for the RAF in June 1971. The SPK disbanded in July 1971 (it was succeeded by the IZRU) and Huber was sent to prison in 1972 for involvement with a criminal group and the production of explosives and false identifications.[93]

The intersection of the SPK with the RAF on a personnel level is significant. The Special Commission investigating the Baader-Meinhof Group found evidence linking Huber to the RAF in a safe house, RAF members Gerhard Müller and Carmen Roll were members of the SPK, and there were even reports that Müller, who was arrested with Meinhof, first met her in the SPK.[94] The SPK also proved a fertile recruiting ground, with former members of the patient collective dominating the ranks of the RAF's second generation, including the group that stormed the West German Embassy in Stockholm and killed two hostages in 1975.[95] On July 12, 1971, the SPK distanced itself from the main-stream leftist scene, joining the RAF on its radical periphery. The statement it released was typewritten and prefaced with a quotation from Mao, thus con-forming to the standard for a RAF text. A day later a leaflet appeared with SPK crossed out and replaced with RAF, and while years later in the *info* Meinhof writes of this being a mere print error, she does so in the context of describing the self-conception of the SPK (shortly before its demise) as the "propagandists of the RAF" (*propagandisten der raf*).[96] In fact, a leaflet described as "the last to be distributed by the members of the former SPK" cites the RAF directly when outlining the program of the antipsychiatry group's successor, the IZRU.[97] Like-wise, the RAF made the SPK catchphrase "make your illness your weapon" (*aus der Krankheit eine Waffe*) a slogan of its own during the prison hunger strikes.

The connections go deeper than mere formatting and a broad anticapitalist affinity. The enlightenment program of the RAF—"capitalism has made you unhappy, you just don't realize it"—was easily married with that of the SPK—"capitalism has made you sick, you just don't realize it." A report from October 23, 1973, on material found in Meinhof's cell describes an *info* in which Ensslin suggests the group incorporate the SPK philosophy.[98] In an example of the influence of the SPK on the RAF, Meinhof metaphorically links the wounded society to the wounded individual body in a speech she wrote for Astrid Proll to deliver in court.[99] It would be misleading to conflate the two organizations, but the medical/political discourse of the RAF had its precursor in the SPK. Central to the newly medicalized political program was the hunger strike. The starving body and its treatment enabled RAF prisoners to literally embody their rhetoric and construct their own bodies as loci for both Nazi resistance and anticolonial struggle.

In her third treatise, *Black September*, Meinhof describes the brutal murders of Israeli athletes during the Munich Olympic Games in September 1972 as hav-ing "documented courage and power," and now the violence of self-starvation enabled the performative documentation of the prisoners' claim of Nazi victim-hood.[100] Presenting the postwar Federal Republic as a continuation of the fascist Third Reich was a mainstay of RAF rhetoric, the group conceived of themselves as a belated resistance movement, and self-starvation was a key element in the conception of prisoners as Nazi victims. The self-fulfilling prophecy of visually and physically aligning themselves—that is, their bodies—with concentration camp prisoners in the Third Reich was very much consistent with their own private conception of their identity and their experience. In May 1973, Mein-hof wrote in the *info* that "the political concept for the death wing, cologne, is, i say quite clearly: gas. my auschwitz fantasies were real in there."[101] She writes of Nazi experimentation and torture, a mood maintained in her poetic description of isolation and "the feeling that your skin is being pulled off."[102]

Ensslin, too, framed the prison experience in terms of Nazi atrocities: "Difference death wing to isolation: Auschwitz to Buchenwald. The difference is simple: more survive Buchenwald than Auschwitz . . . The only thing that can surprise us in here, to be very clear about it, is that we haven't received a lethal injection. But nothing else."[103] Externally the starving prisoner provided a powerful image that could evoke Nazi atrocities to match the private "fantasies" of RAF prisoners.

The starved body drew on the economy of images in West Germany in the 1970s. Photographs of Nazi atrocities were central to denazification and the Allies' effort to reeducate the German population in the immediate postwar period. Images were pasted on windows and in public places in West Germany, allowing Germans to bear witness to the treatment of Nazi prisoners, some for the first time. From the end of the 1940s, however, such imagery faded from public consciousness and years of "visual amnesia" set in. Habbo Knoch writes of this amnesia as having nothing to do with an absence of images or photos; instead, it is indicative of the cultural "re-coding" (*umkodieren*) of such images, which he traces from their role in Nazi wartime propaganda and later their function as part of the Allies' postwar reeducation efforts through to their "reemergence" as symbols of political resistance in the protest scene of the 1970s. The reemergence of this imagery in the late 1960s represents, then, one such recoding rather than a rediscovery.[104] The broad range of images was pared down to representations of concentration camps, particularly Auschwitz (at the expense of other Nazi war crimes), so it is not surprising to see images of starving terrorists emerging in the midst of a new wave of Holocaust imagery. The emaciated body of Holger Meins was such an image.

Meins's death in 1974 during the third hunger strike allowed the fantasies of RAF victimhood to appear in the public realm. This image owes its iconic status among sympathizers and members of the second generation to its ability to draw on the historical imagery of the Nazi period. This association was no coincidence, as RAF lawyers Groenewold and Croissant had actively promoted it, and it is highly probable that Groenewold sourced and released the autopsy photo.[105] Nor was it lost on protestors who often explicitly spelled it out, reproducing the image at protest after protest.[106] Birgit Hogefeld, a member of the third generation of the RAF, even spoke of this image as being "one of the central factors [in her becoming a terrorist] because this emaciated person had so much in common with the concentration camp prisoners."[107] A member of the Second of June Movement, Inge Viett, described the intense feeling in the group that led to the murder of Günter von Drenkmann as stemming from the association of Meins with the dead in Buchenwald, Auschwitz, and the other concentration camps, and Hans-Joachim Klein confessed to having an autopsy photo of Meins with him at all times so as not to let the hate subside.[108]

Veneration of dead members among members and supporters was nothing new. Before Meins's death, Petra Schelm (shot July 1971), Georg von Rauch (shot December 1971), and Thomas Weisbecker (shot March 1972) were celebrated in RAF texts, and attacks were carried out by commandos carrying Schelm's and Weisbecker's names. In the context of prison protest, and in response to his mother's pleas to stop his 1979 hunger strike, RAF prisoner Gert Schneider confirmed that if "someone dies, then the name for the next commando is clear."[109] Two years after Schneider's comments, in April 1981, RAF member Sigurd Debus did die in a Hamburg prison as a result of 68 days of self-starvation. Debus became a figurehead for the prison campaign, but his martyrdom could not eclipse the sanctification of Meins, which was founded in the visual overlap with concentration camp victims.

It was not just the process of starving, however, that fed the discursive analogy between RAF prisoner and Nazi victim. The hunger strike also drew a response from the prison authorities, which would feed back into this discourse. It is indicative of the impossible situation the authorities found themselves in that the construction of force-feeding (the official response to hunger) would reinforce evocations of the recent history of Nazi medicine, experimentation, and a technicized intrusion on the body that had been established in the earliest phase of the RAF incarceration. A committee leaflet signed by doctors in the context of the "scintigraphy campaign" of late 1973 places the forced examination of Meinhof directly in the "tradition of NS-medicine of German fascism."[110] Scintigraphy is a diagnostic technique in which radioisotopes are injected into the patient in order to produce a two-dimensional image and was used to form part of a psychiatric diagnosis. In April 1973 the attorney general charged Professor H. Witter with the task of determining whether Meinhof could be considered criminally responsible for her actions between June 1970 and her arrest. Since Meinhof refused to release her doctor from the restraints of doctor–patient confidentiality, thus making her records unavailable, Witter recommended an X-ray of her skull, scintigraphy of her brain, and the use of electroencephalography, among other diagnostic tools.[111]

The campaign against the treatment of prisoners and the diagnostic methods (the concern was not scintigraphy itself, but rather the forced anesthetization and the associated risk of death) created an understanding of prison medicine as allowing sensory deprivation of and experimentation on prisoners using modern technologies. As part of the campaign, the prison holding Meinhof, Cologne-Ossendorf, was referred to as the "new Klingelpütz."[112] Meinhof also wrote *info* entries that began with the date and her location: Klingelpütz.[113] Cologne-Ossendorf prison was built in 1969, but its nickname drew on the name of the prison it replaced, the Klingelpütz Prison, which served as a Nazi execution site during World War II. The new prison retained the nickname, and with it the National Socialist connotations. Today a memorial to Nazi victims stands on the site of the former prison.

The scintigraphy and forced examination campaigns played out in the context of the second hunger strike, during which prisoners were force-fed. At this early stage, the issue of force-feeding was kept out of the mainstream media, which undermined an explicit RAF strategy. Heading into this second strike, the prisoners worked on the assumption that everyone being "on the hose" (*am Schlauch*) would engender public support for the RAF, but they failed to take into account the lack of reporting.[114] The image of a prisoner "on the hose" was, however, part of the alternative media reports, and in this forum it became part of a broad discourse on the technicized intrusion on the unwilling patient, with analogous links to Nazi medical practice.[115] *Red Aid* wrote of the "spirit of Hitler's concentration camps," and it was this spirit Meinhof described in her declaration for the third hunger strike, printed in the same issue: "Isolation is the old tool of Imperialism with new technology, final solution through liquidation of minorities, which back then were declared not worthy of living, today (in the terminology of the pigs) not worthy of basic rights."[116] This alludes to not only a Nazi past but also an imperialist present, as National Socialist medicine became interchangeable with "imperialist science" (*imperialistische wissenschaft*).[117]

The notion of "imperialism" was already a long-standing RAF preoccupation. In Meinhof's early RAF texts, "imperialism" was vague and referred mainly to U.S. actions in Vietnam and "anti-imperialism" was interchangeable with "anti-Americanism."[118] In prison, "imperialism" was also framed in terms of the body and medicine. A 110-page committee booklet from January 1974 placed the treatment of prisoners in the context of a worldwide network of torture research. The cover of the booklet showed images of the torture methods, and an anonymous insider wrote of research being conducted at the University of Hamburg, as well as at Fort Knox (Kentucky), in Prague, and in London.[119] Research into sensory deprivation, torture, and brainwashing was under way around the world. Programs were already in place in the United States during World War II and intensified in the 1950s. Brainwashing and reprogramming had become research interests for government-funded programs, not least of all because of the treatment of U.S. soldiers captured during the Korean War. The Soviet Union also developed expertise in sensory deprivation as part of its space program.[120]

In West Germany, research into torture was already being conducted under the guidance of Professor Johann M. Burchard at the Psychiatric Division of the Hamburg-Eppendorf University Clinic in 1967, where a *camera silens* (a completely dark and soundproof room used as an instrument of both torture and research into the effects of sensory deprivation) was constructed. The German Research Foundation also funded the research project "Special Research Area 115"

(*Sonderforschungsbereich 115*) an interdisciplinary project that included studies conducting research using the *camera silens*.[121] In his 1973 *Kursbuch* article, Teuns made the direct link between such torture research and the prison conditions suffered by RAF prisoners. Sensory deprivation, in particular, became an important linking association between torture research and the RAF experience—so much so that in a letter from January 6, 1974, Meinhof complained that "the hamburg committee let the camera silens be stolen from them by the KSV [Communist Student Union]."[122] It was this link that was placed firmly within an international context of research cooperation by a committee insider at the beginning of 1974.[123]

In this sense, a medicalized language of intervention on the unwilling body was used to evoke a cultural memory of the Nazi past but also to develop a discourse of a worldwide imperialist medicine and an associated anti-imperialism and anticolonialism. Meinhof combined medicalized politics and the colonization metaphor describing a viral colonialism and the colonized individual: "the colonized person *heals* himself of the thousand wounds (the sickness), by chasing out the colonial master at gunpoint, he fights for his LIFE (spk: the antithesis of sickness is life)."[124] She expanded her notion of individual colonization in 1974 in the *info*:

> if colonization was a conquest, in which the existing social (economic, political, cultural and communication) structures were destroyed, that is: the natives were denied them, and made subordinate to a regime—colonial regime/imperialism—, in which they don't participate,
> in which they only ever appear as things—
> then the colonized individual is a deprived individual, and the deprivation process in isolation is the same as what billions have suffered, endured in their colonization—and which caused an endless number to perish.[125]

She used Frantz Fanon's description of colonialism as a systematic negation of the other and the theme of deprivation to frame the body of the individual prisoner as a site for anticolonialist struggle. Meinhof allowed RAF members to embody their long-held affinity with the peoples of the third and colonized worlds, not by bringing the fires of Vietnam to West German streets, but by raining imperialism onto the prisoner body.

The colonization metaphor also extended to the brain. Meinhof wrote in the *info* of "colonized brains," and a campaign soon evolved around the slogan "liberate the colonized consciousness."[126] The distinction between the terms "personality," "consciousness," and "brain" had by then been steadily eroded (by both the authorities and the prisoners), with the meanings collapsing to the diagnosable—that is, the physical, measurable body. Such a collapse meant that brain X-ray, scintigraphy, psychological deterioration due to prison conditions, "psychiatric exploration," as well as "bodily intrusions to get blood and urine samples," cavity searches, and the act of forcing a feeding tube down the throat of a prisoner were able to exist on the same metaphorical plane: all represented an attack on the physical integrity of the prisoner body.[127]

The hunger and torture campaigns were the mechanisms the RAF used to repackage its rhetoric and reshape the discourse of terrorism. In prison, hunger was used to sanctify the internal hierarchy and discipline of the group, while externally Meinhof refashioned the RAF struggle from one expressed in terms of ideologies to a medicalized politics capable of countering a mainstream, scientific discourse of terrorism. The strikes allowed RAF prisoners to inscribe onto their bodies their conception of a belated Nazi resistance and anticolonialist struggle. This self-starvation in turn reinvigorated the RAF. It performed a brand of terrorism that gave life to the organization, which was at least on its knees after the arrests of 1972. Without it, the story of West German terrorism could well have petered out in the mid-1970s. Of course it did not, and in their final years in prison, the RAF leadership group developed a set of discursive strategies that operated parallel to—and occasionally in combination with—the hunger strikes. These strategies gathered around the Stammheim trial, and they similarly repackaged established RAF positions for a new forum and new audiences. In this context, the judicial system, and the witness stand, proved just as effective as the *info* and the *out-fo*.

CHAPTER 4

Show, Trial, and Error

that's the question: w h o will use the publicity that Stammheim has for their own ends: them or us, the federal prosecutors for the implementation of their strategy of extermination against the urban guerilla on the terrain of the judiciary or us.[1]

—Entry in the *info* from 1975 or 1976

A RAF lawyer wrote in the *info* that he would respond to a summons for prisoners to appear in a Berlin trial by demanding an end to isolation and an end to the "show trials."[2] Berlin was a show trial, as was Zweibrücken before it and Frankfurt after it, just not in the sense intended by the lawyer. The trial in Stammheim, however, was the biggest show in town. The Stuttgart suburb of Stammheim has become synonymous with the RAF. It is shorthand for the debate over prison conditions, it will be forever linked with the deaths of the leading RAF figures, and from May 21, 1975, to April 28, 1977, it was the site of the most expensive trial in the history of the Federal Republic. This trial, in particular, provided a stage for both the West German judiciary and the RAF prisoners to communicate with their respective audiences beyond the courtroom. It offered the state the chance to perform due process and reframe the terrorist threat as mere criminality, while for Meinhof and the RAF it offered an opportunity to again repackage the group's terrorism, this time in terms of human rights and international law. Having reshaped its message for the prison context via self-starvation, the group developed two main performative strategies for the courtroom: the constructions of the "political prisoner" and the "prisoner of war" (POW). Both sets of strategies must, however, be seen in the context of the numerous proceedings that came before Stammheim, during which both sides honed their tactics through a process of trial and error.

The West German authorities set the tone for the Stammheim trial with the construction of a specifically designed courthouse. The windowless structure next to the Stammheim Prison cost approximately 12 million German marks to build. The interior walls were bare concrete, the heating and ventilation pipes were exposed, and there were enough yellow, plastic chairs inside to seat two hundred, with eighty reserved for the press. Outside the courthouse, a two-and-a-half-meter-high fence, a line of *cheval-de-frise*, and an additional two-meter-high wall surrounded the complex, and steel netting was erected on the roof to protect it from explosive devices. Once the trial began, police helicopters patrolled the air space above the Stammheim courthouse, armed soldiers were stationed on the roof, mounted police patrolled the perimeter, and mobile teams of policemen were positioned in front of the building in civilian cars. Visitors to the trial passed through the first of numerous security checks four hundred meters before the building.

The structure has retrospectively been described as a "memorial in steel and concrete" built in honor of the terrorists while they were still alive.[3] This is in line with contemporaneous concerns that the Stammheim courtroom represented the already "set-in-concrete conviction" of the accused.[4] The same concerns were also raised before the sitting judges, when on the twenty-fourth day of the trial, RAF lawyer Rupert von Plottnitz requested the proceedings be shifted from Stammheim to Stuttgart's Regional Court or Higher Regional Court. He concluded his lengthy request by arguing "it is ridiculous to speak of a presumption of innocence . . . In this context, it is absolutely appropriate to speak of the pre-formulation of a guilty verdict, which in the form of this building was long ago cast in concrete."[5] Meinhof also wrote an extended and private meditation on the design of the Stammheim courthouse in which she describes it as embodying state interests:

> the architecture of this trial bunker looks like the american embassy in saigon. this corresponds with the situation—even if the connections are complicated . . . the architecture of this concrete fortress reproduces the particular relationship between german and us imperialism, the specific situation of the revolution in germany with its history of defeats and the role west german imperialism has in the chain of us imperialism . . . the architecture of this concrete fortress, the deployment of the police and the federal border guard, the identification checks and body searches, the automobile searches, the character of this trial as an exception—3 years of preparation via pure propaganda, and 3 years in the death wing and total social isolation in order to exhibit us here as broken people, destroyed fighters.[6]

In this text she places the design of the courtroom on a similar level of importance as the three years she and the remaining RAF leaders spent in prison.

In addition to the courtroom, a legislative fortress was prepared for the trial with amendments to the Code of Criminal Procedure (*Strafprozessordnung*, StPO) rushed through the West German parliament in late 1974. "Lex RAF" came into force on January 1, 1975, and was aimed primarily at inhibiting the activities of the RAF defense team. During the numerous trials of RAF members in the years leading up to Stammheim, the role of the defense lawyer became the subject of debate, particularly in the tabloid press. The discussion centered on the line between advocating for alleged terrorists and supporting terrorism. The underlying suggestion was that RAF lawyers were abusing their position and rights as defense counsel, and the targeted legislative changes of 1975 sought to restrict their role.[7]

Changes to section 137 saw the number of lawyers chosen by the defendants limited to three to allay concerns that unwieldy teams of lawyers would interrupt and slow the proceedings.[8] Amendments to section 138a meant a lawyer was to be excluded from proceedings if he or she were strongly suspected of

1. being involved in the act at the centre of the investigation,
2. abusing prison contact with the accused to commit criminal offenses or significantly compromise the security of a penal facility, or
3. committing an act that, in the case of a conviction of the accused, would constitute being an accessory after the fact, obstruction of punishment or the receiving or handling of stolen goods.[9]

There were precedents for the expulsion of individual lawyers—RAF lawyer Eberhard Becker was expelled from a trial involving the Social Patients' Collective (*Sozialistisches Patientenkollektiv*, SPK) in 1971, for example—but on February 14, 1973, the Federal Constitutional Court ruled that the practice had no legal basis. Thus section 138a gave the practice solid legal ground for the first time.[10] One consequence of this change was that Baader began the trial without a single lawyer of his choice after Klaus Croissant and Hans-Christian Ströbele were excluded and Siegfried Haag was arrested. The arrest came at what Siegfried Buback described as a "tactically convenient point in time."[11] Section 146 was amended to prohibit lawyers from defending more than one defendant. When coupled with the new legal construct of the "criminal association" (*kriminelle Vereinigung*; see section 129 of the criminal code), it meant the RAF could not be defended collectively but could be tried collectively.[12] This development made linking individuals to specific crimes less of a burden for the prosecution and ensured, for example, that Meinhof faced court over the murder of police officer Norbert Schmidt, a crime committed by Gerhard Müller.[13]

Exhaustive preparation was by no means limited to the prosecution. For its part the RAF was adamant that "all proceedings against RAF prisoners are o n e trial," and it went into Stammheim with a set of model strategies honed during the numerous trials involving its members from 1972 to 1975.[14] This consciously uniform approach to legal proceedings and court appearances throughout the country included challenging the authority of the court or judge, switching defense lawyers, submitting endless petitions, disruptive behavior, and arguing its members were not fit to stand trial.

The tactic of not recognizing the authority of the court stretches back to before the formation of the RAF. The closing comments to the arson trial of 1969—subsequently published under the title "Before such a Judiciary, we won't Defend Ourselves"—made it clear the defendants Andreas Baader, Gudrun Ensslin, Thorwald Proll, and Horst Söhnlein did not acknowledge the legitimacy of the process.[15] This statement was intended at once as a playful demonstration of self-determination and a denial of the legitimacy of the proceedings. The refusal to engage with the process was a constant throughout later RAF trials and is evident in the 1975 assumption made by RAF lawyer that beyond the broader defense strategies of challenging the authority of the court, no discussion would be entered into regarding the specific charges. The strategy of disruption also remained from the arson trial, but the pranks of 1969 designed to make "authoritative structures fall over themselves" developed along two main paths: petitions and behavior.[16]

In an issue of the *Red Aid* magazine that was confiscated from a package intended for Meinhof, an article appeared that set out "how one gives investigating judges stomach ulcers."[17] The text outlined the twin strategies of compiling complaints, including advice on which paragraphs of the constitution to reference, which articles of the relevant human rights conventions to cite, and provocative behavior in the courtroom. Endless submissions to the court by the defense dominated, in particular, the first forty days of the Stammheim trial, with petitions repeatedly filed calling for the recusal of one or all of the judges on grounds of bias, the reinstatement of excluded defense lawyers, or the examination of the accused by doctors of their choice.

Part of the RAF policy of courtroom behavior included attempts to frustrate the process with silence. In early July 1973, a newsletter compiled by RAF lawyer Kurt Groenewold gave notice of the tactic: "Several are meant to testify, at the court's request, at Asdonk's trial. Nothing will be said."[18] As the article in *Red Aid* suggests, this was common advice not limited solely to the RAF. Other publications, such as a booklet produced by a cooperative of Berlin youth centers, offered the same advice on how to behave during searches, arrests, observations, and questioning: "1. Provide personal details only . . . 2. Apart from that, do not make any other statements! Every word could be used against you" and, most important, "SAY NOTHING."[19] The next step was to get a lawyer, preferably from the list provided, which was topped by the lawyer collective of

Klaus Eschen (RAF lawyer), Horst Mahler (lawyer and former RAF member), Ströbele (RAF lawyer), and Henning Spangenberg (RAF lawyer).

Groenewold's strategy for Berlin was adhered to and none of the RAF members called as witnesses said anything on the stand. As a result, Meinhof was fined three hundred German marks by the Regional Court in Berlin for refusing to answer questions.[20] This tactic manifested in the Stammheim trial in the refusal of all the accused to participate in the *Vernehmung zur Person*, a procedural step during which the accused is required to give his or her name, date of birth, place of birth, marital status, nationality, occupation, and address, and answer background questions. Whereas Thorwald Proll in 1969 had responded by giving his birth year as the year of the French Revolution, Meinhof in 1975 simply refused to answer the question and asked to leave the courtroom. She eventually called the judge an "asshole," provoking her expulsion from the building.[21] This additional strategy of verbal abuse and provocation was a conscious effort to force the judges to remove them from the court. A more serious concern for the state, however, was the tactic of the accused removing their own defense lawyers.

Switching from one lawyer to the next, and often back again, was both an emotional reaction and a defense strategy. The RAF leaders demanded full compliance from their legal representatives, revealing at times their bitingly cynical view of their lawyers as "part of the [judicial] machine."[22] They were adamant that "we define our relationship to the lawyers according to the criteria of the proletarian alliance politics . . . we define it according to our interests."[23] Beyond an internal power struggle and the ambivalence of the prisoners, adjusting the defense team was also a means to slow the legal process. In a newsletter on a Groenewold letterhead dated June 16, 1973, the plan is discussed with regard to the trial of Astrid Proll to rotate the lawyers on the legal team. This would, so the plan goes, force the judges to continually readjust to new defense counsel.[24] It was not only the judges who had to adjust, as each new counsel required time to get up to speed with the proceedings to date. Federal prosecutors were wary of the maneuvering of legal counsel as a trial strategy as early as the beginning of 1974 and cited Meinhof's and Ensslin's already established pattern of behavior as the basis for their concerns.[25] This strategy was still evident during the Stammheim trial. Meinhof, for example, wrote to the Higher Regional Court of Stuttgart to officially remove lawyer Michael Oberwinder from her defense team on March 11, 1976, only to reverse her decision three days later.[26]

To counteract this strategy, the prisoners were assigned legal counsel (*Pflichtverteidiger*), or as the RAF called them, enforced lawyers (*Zwangsverteidiger*), to ensure a degree of continuity in the defense team. Each prisoner was assigned three lawyers in addition to those of their choice and a further assigned lawyer at the beginning of the trial. It is not surprising that RAF members refused to acknowledge or cooperate with the counsels assigned to them. Meinhof expressed the views of the group in court: "it is simple. This enforced defense is an instrument of the Federal Prosecution."[27]

Another method of disrupting and slowing a trial was exploiting the effects of the numerous hunger strikes by arguing that they were unfit to stand trial. While the assigned counsel addressed—on the level of legal technicality at least—the inability of a trial to proceed smoothly without a coherent defense team, the RAF worked on exploiting the impossibility of conducting a trial without defendants. In an *info* dated June 16, 1973, Groenewold discusses the issue of fitness to stand trial (*Verhandlungsfähigkeit*) under the subheading "hunger strike," writing that "in the case of ASDONK, she underwent detailed examinations: blood/urine. She was declared *sick*, that means the trial was cancelled, no free time or visits etc."[28] It was important to note, he continued, that if a defendant refuses to attend a trial then the court can proceed in their absence, but "if someone is sick and therefore cannot come, the court cannot proceed, if someone is sick for longer than 10 days, the trial shuts down."[29] While the hunger strikes were not embarked on as a legal strategy, the potential advantage of the failing health of the prisoners was recognized early on. Similarly, the prosecution feared that provisions for considering a prisoner's fitness to stand trial could be "abused by defendants to hinder the continuation of the proceedings against them by consciously causing themselves to be unfit to stand trial."[30] This led to an impasse over the health of the defendants and the legitimacy of the associated medical examinations that became the major stalemate of the first forty days of the trial.

These first weeks and months were dominated by contrasting medical opinions that attempted to establish whether the prisoners' failing health was caused by the prison conditions or the hunger strikes, and whether or not it meant they were unfit to stand trial. The defense was denied the opportunity to have the prisoners examined by doctors of their choice, and the prisoners refused to cooperate with the prison doctors, making many of the medical conclusions drawn in theses first weeks highly speculative.[31] The context for Professor Joachim Rauschke's professional opinion, for example, was the three-and-a-half days he was present at the trial during which Meinhof said nothing.[32] The decisive moment came on the thirty-ninth day of the trial. The session lasted three minutes, long enough for the judge to announce that the expert medical witnesses had returned their reports and the court would retire to consider them.[33] The following day the court conceded the accused were not fit to stand trial, but argued, on the basis of the new formulation of section 231a of the StPO passed as part of the "Lex RAF" bundle of amendments, that the trial could continue in their absence, as they contributed to their condition:

The trial shall proceed in the absence of the defendants.

    Reasons:

    The defendants are unfit to stand trial for the purpose of § 231a of the StPO.* The provisions of §231a of the StPO are designed to ensure a defendant does not hinder proceedings by knowingly contributing to his or her lack of fitness to stand trial . . . The senate has no doubt that the hunger strikes are at least a contributing factor to the present state of the defendants' health.[34]

This would prove pivotal, as subsequent to the ruling, attendance of the RAF prisoners, who up until then had been present at all sessions except when expelled from the courtroom, was negligible. Sessions rarely began with them present, and when they did appear it was often for short periods of time. Of the 68 sitting days between this decision and Meinhof's death, she was present at the beginning of 6 (remaining present for differing amounts of time, occasionally only minutes), she drifted in and out for 10, and she did not appear for 52 (of which she was excluded by the court for 30).

Both the prosecution and the RAF and its defense team went into the long anticipated Stammheim trial armed with carefully considered strategies that had been refined by trial and error during legal clashes throughout the early 1970s. Legislative changes excluded RAF lawyers from proceedings, outlawed collective defense while trying the defendants as a "criminal organization," and allowed the court to nullify the issue of fitness to stand trial by proceeding in the absence of the defendants. These changes remain part of the Federal Republic criminal code, but have not been used since. For its part, the RAF took into the Stammheim trial an established and unified strategy that included silence, numerous changes in their legal team, and arguing they were unfit to stand trial. But of all the strategies developed for and employed during the Stammheim trial, arguably the most important for both sides was the recognition of the performative potential to use the proceedings as a show.

Show Trial

In 1962 Vera Brühne attained nationwide infamy after being charged with a double murder. Hysteria whipped up by the tabloid press surrounded the trial of the attractive, middle-class Brühne, with the image of a calculating, blonde femme fatale pitted against the then prevailing ideal of the woman as mother and housewife. Doubts about Brühne's guilt, or at the very least the legality of the conviction, still remain, and at the time Meinhof wrote, "The dignity of the individual ceases to exist before a German court; beyond the chalk circle, starting from the public gallery and to the last rural, urban, social and anti-social corners, the first day of proceedings sees the constitutional state founded on the rule of law suspended and public opinion set in."[35] Meinhof's article was at once a condemnation of the role of the popular press in shaping the public opinion that carried such a dubious conviction and recognition of the importance of the court of public opinion. Later, and when on trial herself, the public reception of the proceedings presented not only a threat but also an opportunity. In fact, the ability of the Stammheim trial, and the reporting of it, to shape public opinion was arguably the primary focus of the proceedings. The courtroom provided the RAF and the Federal Criminal Police Office (*Bundeskriminalamt*, BKA) the opportunity to perform in a public forum with both sides actively courting the media. Behind what at times seemed the mere pretense of a criminal trial, both sides talked past each other and to their respective audiences, employing focused strategies of public engagement and discourse management.

The federal prosecutor took steps to influence the reception of the trial even before it began. In November 1974 the police conducted "Operation Winter's Journey" (*Aktion Winterreise*). This nationwide search for 23 suspects saw hundreds of offices and apartments searched and people arrested, and leftist bookshops, publishers, and communes left in ruins, but it resulted in no charges. The head of the BKA, Horst Herold, later conceded the operation was an end unto itself, saying that large operations were almost never great successes, but they made a measurable and positive impression on the population.[36] Minister of the Interior, Werner Maihofer, released the "Documentation of the Activities of Anarchist Violent Criminals in the Federal Republic of Germany" (*Dokumentation über Aktivitäten anarchistischer Gewalttäter in der Bundesrepublik Deutschland*) to coincide with "Operation Winter's Journey." This bundle of 29 documents found in RAF cells and apartments in Frankfurt, Hamburg, and Bremen—also known as the *Maihofer-Dokumentation*—was highly influential in terms of reporting on radio, television, and in the print press both domestically and abroad.[37] Beyond providing the press with imagery and information, accusations of direct influence were leveled at sitting judges and the federal prosecutor.

During the trial, judges drew accusations from lawyer Otto Schily that they were attempting to steer the reception of the proceedings after Judge Eberhard Foth wrote to the *Stuttgarter Zeitung* condemning the newspaper's reporting of the trial, and Judge Theodor Prinzing reportedly regularly telephoned the *Südwestfunk* radio station.[38] A petition from August 1975 against all sitting judges argued that the influence went the other way as well, with Prinzing repeatedly referring to the reception of the trial in the courtroom as well as in his judgments.[39] Ulf Stuberger, the self-proclaimed sole journalist to attend every session of the Stammheim trial, also wrote of the federal prosecutor selectively passing on information to reporters considered sympathetic to the state. He described a "secret meeting" between the director of public prosecutions and editors of the major media outlets at which, according to Stuberger's sources,

Attorney General Buback expressed his "particular desire" (*dringender Wunsch*) for reporting on the RAF to refer to the Baader-Meinhof Gang (*Bande*) instead of the Baader-Meinhof Group (*Gruppe*). Further prescribed terminologies became apparent to him and his colleagues only later, as their work was consistently edited.[40] This targeted use of language emerged in the months leading up to the trial and two years after the 1972 *Baader-Meinhof-Report* had identified that the state lacked a "coherent, political language for a rapid response."[41] The authorities clearly understood the communicative value of the Stammheim trial, and the defendants, too, built their approach around the performativity of the proceedings.

By 1975 the RAF already had a track record in using the judicial system as a forum for its political statements. This strategy emerged as early as the 1969 arson trial of Baader and Ensslin. The declaration of responsibility and elucidation of the political motivations did not accompany the act, but were announced weeks later and from the witness stand by Ensslin. In addition, the defendants had their statement published in the alternative pamphlet series *Voltaire*. Later the RAF trials of the early 1970s were used to announce RAF hunger strikes and distribute copies of the hunger strike declarations. On September 13, 1974, Meinhof used the court in Berlin to present a declaration on the liberation of Baader. In the subsequent break in proceedings her lawyer, Hans-Christian Ströbele, distributed copies of the declaration to representatives of the press.[42] With regard to the trial of Astrid Proll in Frankfurt, Meinhof admonished lawyers Ströbele, Ulrich Preuß, and Groenewold for missing the chance to use the trial to continue the established "isolation" and "torture" arguments:

> do you have your heads up your ass, or what's going on!???!
>   you had the possibility in frankfurt to really make some noise—the chance to launch one hell of an attack on the torture of isolation—and the cologne death wing—where astrid has been tortured, to the bone, to the core,—wait—and you don't take it. you just carry on litigating.[43]

When not delivering or distributing statements during court appearances, Meinhof was preparing speeches for others, most notably the "Main Contradiction Paper" (*Hauptwiderspruch-Paper*).[44] This statement was read by Astrid Proll at her Frankfurt trial on October 2, 1974, and a version of it was, according to official reports on the *info* discussions of late 1973, intended to be published as the group's fourth treatise.[45]

The effort in Stammheim was, if anything, even more focused. Correspondence between prisoners and lawyers reveals a structured media campaign waged via the reporting of the trial as central to their strategic response, and the planning began early. Baader wrote in June 1974 that "it is by no means clear that a case will even be made in stgt [Stuttgart]. we only have an interest in this event if we can turn it . . . but again, we will not c o o p e r a t e in trials that don't transport anything, that don't create publicity. they'll only get the statement and after that no defense lawyers + no accused."[46] The primary interest of the prisoners in the proceedings was not the chance it offered to launch a defense, but clearly its ability to provide a public forum. The "turning" of the trial was clearly not to take place at the level of the law with the legal "terrain" conceded to the prosecution and the "legal shit" (*jurscheiss*) deemed "unimportant" (*unwichtig*): "we know that from the 4 months of experience here. it [the legal stuff] doesn't help you get a perspective, it only annoys you. petitions are o n l y a vehicle and a lever, nothing more. because it's just the way it is that the function and therefore the structure of the judicial rituals, the paragraph-jungle, is to produce oppression. that means: you cannot turn it. the state has the power on that terrain and only a rat like b could think of suggesting that the balance of power could be changed by judicial tricks and maneuvers."[47] If the RAF were to turn the trial, it would be done on the terrain of public perception. Having been asked by her own lawyers to limit her argument to legal issues Meinhof wrote that "whether a defense with legal arguments will get up also depends—but increasingly in the second and third instance on the legal level of the arguments. if anything in this respect can still be achieved—is primarily a question of power. that is, power mediated by that which takes place with respect to publicity."[48] Meinhof in particular acknowledged the strategy's audience beyond the confines of the courtroom. She was adamant that "our line is clear: everything we do, we do with respect to proletarian and international publicity. everything . . . you say: a published brief is always better received when it is limited to legal arguments—by whom?"[49]

A discussion piece by a RAF lawyer found in Groenewold's office in 1975 reveals this focus on the "show," describing a "dramaturgic defense framework" (*dramaturgischer Verteidigungsrahmen*) designed not to engage with the charges, but instead, seeking to reveal what the RAF understood to be the broader political dimension and social contexts.[50] Two major threads of this strategy were framing the trial as a political—as opposed to a criminal—trial, and arguing the West German guerrilla was part of a wider international conflict. Central to these were, in turn, the constructions of the "political prisoner" and the "prisoner of war."[51]

Political Prisoner Status

In a television appearance to coincide with the beginning of the trial, Judge Prinzing declared this was no political trial, it was, instead, a "normal criminal case" (*normaler Straffall*).[52] For the prisoners, however, the trial was undoubtedly political. In a statement supporting her latest recusal motion from July 1975, Meinhof triumphantly described the Stammheim trial as "the first political trial in the Federal Republic since 1945."[53] Moreover, *info* correspondence reveals she considered it to be the most important political trial that would set the scene for all political trials.[54]

Beyond their own conviction that Stammheim was a political trial, the RAF prisoners believed the idea of a "normal trial" (*normales Strafverfahren*) to be part of a cynical collection of tactics designed to "eliminate" (*ausschalten*) a political defense. They saw it as an attempt to rob the proceedings, and by extension the deeds of the RAF, of the legitimacy the group sought to impose on them.[55] Prosecutors arguably sought to empty the trial of its political potency before it began by choosing to charge the RAF prisoners with forming a terrorist group. Individual charges for individual crimes had the potential to depoliticize the proceedings further still, but the burden of proof would have been far greater and RAF members could not have been tried as a group. The charge of forming a terrorist group did allow the authorities to avoid political crimes of high treason. A case for such charges could have easily been made given RAF texts, but they would have forced the political nature of the trial into the center of the proceedings.[56]

The prisoners own interpretations of the state strategy were based more on the official and constant emphasis in the media that this was a purely criminal trial. Judge Prinzing, for example, made comments to that effect before the trial began, and in July 1976 Justice Minister Hans-Jochen Vogel reiterated that the "proceedings [were] directed exclusively at the criminal activities and not their supposed political motivation."[57] Behind the scenes, Home Secretary Hans-Dietrich Genscher warned as early as 1971 against coupling the words "political" and "violence," preferring to speak of "violence" as "crime."[58] This idea of a nonpolitical trial very much informed the RAF defense:

> defense becomes political opposition against the politics of the federal prosecutor, the domestic strategy of the new fascism: counterinsurgency,
>   or
>   it is part of the project of the federal prosecution—by contributing to their deception—
>   their deception in the form of the feigned "normal trial."[59]

The strategy to counter this was equally clear: "the point here is to destroy the 'normal trial' . . . destruction of the normal trial is precisely n o t sabotage of the trial but exposure of the truth of these proceedings against us and with it the truth about the social democracy and with that the truth about the west german state as a function of us imperialism, a function of the main enemy of the peoples of the world."[60] To expose these truths, the group needed to reinforce the notion that this was a political, not a criminal trial. This included monitoring not only their own lawyers, who, after all, were still "part of the machine," to ensure they did not fall into the trap of "playing the role of the 'normal trial,'" but also the strategic use of the term "political prisoner."[61]

The RAF members clearly understood themselves to be political prisoners in the sense that theirs was a political organization and they were in prison. The term "political prisoner," however, was less straightforward. In the lead up to the trial the term and its merits were fiercely contested both within the RAF and among the group's sympathizers. A document found in Meinhof's cell in July 1973 outlined the Red Aid position on the meaning and use of the term "political prisoner":

> In normal usage the term "pG" [political prisoner] covers two groups: 1.) from the pigs' perspective, every offender who has transgressed §§ 80-109 k of the criminal code (treason, law of association etc.) and §§ 125-131 (breach of the public peace . . .) 2.) in liberal/traditionally leftist usage, every prisoner who is locked up for political reasons, that is, (is said to have) committed a crime due to political motivations . . . Under the guidance of RA [Red Aid] the term has been widened to include 3.) every prisonologist that understands prison as a ruling-class *political* tool of oppression and finally 4.) indeed all prisonologists who resist it, even if they're still politically "unconscious" . . . As a result, this had led to everyone understanding the term "pG" to mean something different, and even RA generally uses the term in the sense of 2.) (despite assertions to the contrary) Such a hazy term is not usable.[62]

Volker Speitel, a RAF member whose first contact with the radical leftist scene was via the Red Aid organization in 1972, described the definition of "political prisoner" as a central sticking point for the diverse group. Some thought all prisoners were political prisoners, others only wanted to support the RAF prisoners, "and others still, voted for the support of the revolutionary working class, whatever that meant."[63]

The Red Aid analysis was part of a wider debate at the time among a number of (also radical, but not militant) left-wing organizations on the usability of the term. A further document confiscated during the same search of Meinhof's cell and marked "FOR INTERNAL USE ONLY," described the discussion at a meeting of RAF lawyers and representatives of the committees, the Information Centre Red People's University (*Informationszentrum Rote Volksuniversität*, IZRU), Red Aid, the Communist Student Union (*Kommunistischer Studenverband*, KSV), and the Communist Party of Germany (*Kommunistische Partei Deutschlands*, KPD).[64] The catalyst for the discussion was a protest in February where RAF lawyers and other groups staged a four-day hunger strike in solidarity with striking prisoners in front of the Federal Court of Justice (*Bundesgerichtshof*, BGH). Disagreement among the protesters arose as to the relationship of the protest to the hunger strike campaign. One of the consequences was an at times heated debate over the meaning of "political prisoner." A summary of the meetings on May 5 and 6, 1973, is evidence of the confusion:

> All lawyers, with the exception of two, are for the slogan "*political* prisoners." Also for the concept pG are the IZRU and the KSV, although they both understand the term to mean different things.
>
> The Red Aids and former prisoners (Schiller, Herzog, Mauer) think this term is divisive and not of any use in prison.
>
> In contrast, the lawyers argue along the same lines as the prominent RAF prisoners.
>
> Although doubts have emerged as to whether the lawyers are correctly communicating the opinions of the prisoners.[65]

In summary, the IZRU did not want any discrimination between RAF and other prisoners and justified the term by arguing that all prisoners were political prisoners, not just those whose motivations for the crime were ostensibly "political."[66] The KPD, KSV, and Red Aid organizations, on the other hand, used the term in the sense of their "avant-garde and cadre theory." Despite this commonality, it was the IZRU, the KPD, and KSV that came to an agreement in May 1973 on the use of the term "political prisoner," leaving Red Aid isolated.[67]

These discussions took place in the context of the RAF hunger strikes, which aimed to mobilize entire prison populations. Categorizing some prisoners as "political" was divisive and made it more difficult for non-RAF prisoners to identify with the strikes. Meinhof's sister reported to the meeting participants that Meinhof saw this as a problem. The strikes had at that stage not developed a prison-wide following or inspired solidarity among prisoners.[68] The potentially problematic nature of the term within the penal system meant a compromise was necessary for internal purposes, such as the hunger strike declarations. In a draft hunger strike declaration from June 1974, Meinhof adopts a very broad, but not the broadest, definition. A "political prisoner," she wrote "is any prisoner who recognizes his position, who has recognized himself as the prisoner of the ruling class—of money, who offers resistance against the incarceration of extermination of the isolated prisoners and cretinizing treatment of all prisoners, and is therefore in solitary confinement or treatment with solitary confinement at any moment."[69] This compromise was reflected in a committee publication from October 1974:

To be a political prisoner means to stand opposed to the p o l i t i c a l class justice: the *Staatsschutz*.[70] To be a political prisoner in the FRG is to be a prisoner of the state that incriminates revolutionaries in the interests of the enemies of the people, the enemies of the RAF (Red Army Faction) . . .

Also political prisoners are those who as prisoners comprehend that the prison system's disciplinary instrument, institution of the permanent fascism against the sections of the people, is for the maintenance of the capitalist regime and behaves accordingly; those who have overcome the divisive, private attitude "keep your mouth shut—and nothing will happen to you—then you'll make it" as an expression of misery, oppression, unconsciousness and lean on other prisoners.

In the end, to be a political prisoner in the FRG means to be subject to a creeping execution, bloodless and externally untraceable torture by social isolation/ sensory deprivation.[71]

Inherent in these compromise positions is the attempt to allow the existing prison population access to one RAF definition of political prisoner status. Separate from such internal use, however, a different more exclusive use of "pG" featured prominently in the RAF's attempted co-option of the international legal process as part of its defense.

In 1973 RAF lawyers made an application on behalf of Meinhof, Baader, Meins, and Wolfgang Grundmann to the European Commission of Human Rights. The complaint centered around prison conditions and isolation suffered by "political prisoners," the exclusion of defense counsel, as well as the assertion that through these conditions the "authorities thus [had] created a status of political prisoners whose rights [were] reduced in comparison to other prisoners." Similar allegations had already been rejected by the Federal Court and the Constitutional Court in West Germany, now the commission was to rule on whether these decisions violated articles 3, 6, 8, and 10 of the European Convention on Human Rights.[72] The application was eventually declared inadmissible to the European Court of Human Rights and "with regard to the applicants' allegation that as 'political prisoners' they are being subjected to torture by isolation," the commission found that "all the applicants are charged with grave offences, including murder, attempted murder, robbery and membership of a criminal organization. The applicants are thus not in custody because of their political convictions but because they are suspected of offences dangerous to the community. For this reason they cannot be regarded as 'political prisoners.'"[73] For the RAF this was not an unexpected decision, but importantly, nor was it swift.

A newsletter from June 1973 reveals that the human rights complaints had been drafted despite a clear recognition that the Commission on Human Rights would no doubt find in favor of West German penal practice. The application would nevertheless provide fertile discursive ground for the RAF campaign, as the commission would take years to uphold the conditions, and in the meantime "human rights," as Groenewold argued, would be "our field of operation" (*unser Operationsfeld*) as opposed to the legal "terrain" of the prosecution.[74] In fact, the delay in reaching a decision was due largely to the RAF defense team.

After the federal government requested one extension on the date it was given to comment on the application, the applicants were invited to make a submission by December 10, 1974. This deadline passed before a further extension was requested and granted. On January 23, 1975, three days after the new deadline, a second extension was requested and granted. When nothing had been sent to the commission by February 28, 1975, the case proceeded without the observations of the applicants and a ruling was handed down on May 30, 1975.[75] By not making any submissions the lawyers ensured information provided by the West German government would provide the sole basis for any decision, denying the application any chance of success. Perhaps more importantly, it dragged out the period of time that a RAF human rights complaint was before the commission and that a decision on West German "political prisoners" was pending.

The term "political prisoner" was also central to the material produced in the context of the hunger strike, featuring prominently in Meinhof's declarations and, of course, the texts by the committees against torture. Meinhof also made it clear what she and the RAF expected from commentators in an open letter to the "WRITERS CONFERENCE IN FRANKFURT ON 15.11.1974":

> what we . . . expect from writers is that you actively report the goals of our hunger strike, not only in resolutions at your conference but afterwards in the media and publishing houses to which you have access—on radio, television, in newspapers, magazines; . . . that you
> 1. actively publish our hunger strike declaration— . . .
> 3. that you use the term POLITICAL PRISONER as that which it is: a battle cry.[76]

While important in shaping the public reception of the strikes, the term also spilled into the trial, not only because the first weeks of the trial were spent arguing the effects of the strikes, but also because the RAF saw the trial, like the strikes, as a political (not medical, not legal) event.

Despite being contentious among the prisoners, their lawyers, the committees, and other sympathetic groups responsible for maintaining a media presence for the RAF, the term "political prisoner" became important to the discursive construction of the Stammheim trial as a political event. The prisoners themselves had concerns that the term would prove divisive within the penal system and therefore unusable for garnering support for the strikes. Nevertheless, it was embraced outside the prison system, and it was central to the strategy developed to directly counter the perceived prosecution strategy of the "normal trial." It was a pseudolegal argument with a clear discursive goal as part of the broader RAF defense strategy. A similar element of the same strategy was the construction of "prisoner of war."

Project Prisoner of War

On May 4, 1976, Otto Schily moved to call General Michael S. Davison, the Commander of the U.S. Army in Europe, to testify that the RAF bombing of a U.S. Army base in Heidelberg had a discernable effect on military operations in Indochina by destroying computers that were used to coordinate the movement of troops and air raids. He also called Richard Nixon to attest to the numerous attacks on U.S. facilities on both U.S. and foreign soil contributed in a material way to the decision to retreat from Indochina and cease operations.[77] These potential witnesses were among a number of high-profile figures Schily sought to have called before the court in an attempt to frame the RAF bombing spree as part of an international conflict with its epicenter in Vietnam.[78] This strategy fit the RAF defense of ignoring the charges and seeking to operate in the forum of international law and international publicity. It presented a justification for the May bombing spree as "self-defense" and launched a project for "international recognition of the RAF" (*Internationale Anerkennung der RAF*). Central to this project was the construction of the RAF members as prisoners of war (POWs).

The use of the term POW was born of flagging public interest in the group's struggle. The imprisoned leaders were concerned that the lines of argument of the legal campaigns would water down the primacy of the armed struggle. They rejected the tired slogans of the committees as too wishy-washy (*seicht*) and the purely verbal cries to "build up the red army" as not enough to engender true integration. The compromise was a slogan tailored to further enshrine the RAF prisoners as the focus of the struggle and fill the need for a rhetoric appropriate for the courtroom: "prisoners of war" was settled on as the central pillar in a project for "international recognition of the RAF." Volker Speitel described the term POW as not only a catchphrase with which to thematize the prison conditions, but also one capable of expressing the content of the armed struggle. He wrote of this international recognition of the RAF as containing more "dynamite" than the second-generation members ever had in the underground.[79]

The discourse of the POW is not necessarily inconsistent with explicit requests made by Meinhof and others within the penal system to be treated as "normal prisoners" (*normalgefangene*), as the two served different functions. Much like the controversy surrounding the term "political prisoner," the campaign for normal treatment was geared toward securing solidarity with non-RAF prisoners and can easily be reconciled with the push for external POW status, as the goals and forums remain distinct and separate. The term must also be understood within the context of contemporaneous developments in international law and negotiations regarding its legal definition.

Toward the end of the 1960s, and in light of the changing nature of armed conflict since the end of World War II, there was an increasing international push to reform the four traditional criteria defining a "privileged combatant": operating under military command, wearing a fixed distinctive sign (or uniforms for regulars), carrying arms openly, and conducting military operations consistently with the laws and customs of war. It was felt there was a growing discrepancy between the legalities and reality of war and that these criteria imposed impossible obligations on "irregulars" in conflicts in which guerrilla tactics were used. What followed was a protracted negotiation within the United Nations (UN) over what constituted a "national liberation movement," who were "parties to a conflict" and the very definition of the term POW.[80] The RAF defense sought to pick up on these developments to create an international context for the group's activities.

The broader two-part strategy consisted of presenting the "international context of oppression" and countering it with the "international context of the guerrilla movement."[81] Piggybacking international law was central to the latter, and the RAF prisoners made this clear to their defense team: "we demand o n l y , that you defend the prisoners from the urban guerrilla within the p o l i t i c a l LINE of defense, that is with a human rights' perspective in an international context."[82] Meinhof in particular advocated this line of defense and was seemingly convinced that the legal negotiations occupying the UN General Assembly were prompted, in part, by the RAF:

> in addition—prisoners of war:
>   you simply have to transpose what the un [UN] has long since done, these definitions (partisans etc.) onto the specifics of this trial.
>   and we would *remind* assholes like pfaff that the development of these un [UN] initiatives was thanks in large part to *us*—at least in terms of western europe.
>   The un [UN] definition includes us too in this term "international [illegible]," not defined as self-interest or psychological, but as "committed to a cause." this is definitive.
>   this is expressed in the moynihan amendments.[83]

The negotiating history reveals, however, that the General Assembly instead had liberation groups in colonized African nations in mind. Article 1, for example, was amended to make the law governing international conflicts apply also to conflicts of "self-determination." The amendment was designed to encompass national wars of liberation against colonial, alien, and racist (CAR) regimes. The accepted interpretation of CAR was deliberately narrow to avoid encouraging secessionist movements, while still recognizing national liberation movements. It effectively limited the scope of the amendments to (predominantly) African liberation groups. This intention was also evident at the 1974 Diplomatic Conference, where "genuine" movements—that is, those recognized by their regional intergovernmental organizations—were invited to participate. The RAF was not among them, nor was any other European group.[84]

Nevertheless, the argument underpinned the entire RAF approach of ignoring the specific charges and arguing instead for an international context. The POW argument was also made explicitly in the courtroom. In a motion to hear evidence, RAF lawyer Axel Azzola argued the trial should be abandoned and the accused should be found not guilty—even if the accusations against them were found to be true—and taken into custody as POWs. The prisoners, he argued, found themselves at war with the imperialist forces of capital within the Federal Republic and in alliance with other liberation movements such as the Front National de Liberté (FNL) in Vietnam, the Palestine Liberation Organization (PLO), and the Irish Republican Army (IRA). This assertion framed the RAF as being at war with "the imperialism of international capital and its agents" and presented the argument that this form of warfare should fall under the Geneva Conventions despite there being no provision for it.[85] International law had, it was argued, lagged behind developments in modern warfare, and legal categories needed to be adapted to this new form of warfare: "A viable definition of what we understand war to be in terms of international law must accommodate this new mode of warfare. It can no longer depend on the customary, formal criterion that the parties to a conflict must be nation states."[86] The new form of conflict was national wars of liberation fought across borders and in an international context: "national" in the sense that the goal of oppressed peoples was the founding of independent nation states, and "international" because they attack the "imperialist world-system." Azzola named a number of examples, including the treatment and status of IRA prisoners.

Despite including the legal negotiations surrounding the term POW in the defense, this was less a legal, and more a discursive strategy that played not to the judges, but to the wider public beyond the courtroom. In a letter to her lawyer in December 1975, Meinhof wrote: "international publicity is only attainable through the trial and the defense—the point is not to appeal to committees from which we can only expect to be knocked back—the point is to develop a political initiative in the trial and out of the confrontations during the trial . . . there is a project: prisoner of war status . . . the tactic in the trial can only be: resistance . . . and that makes sense in stammheim and only in stammheim, because the publicity is here."[87] It was also explicitly conceded that a status of "POW" was itself not the immediate goal, rather it was primarily a means to an end:

> and struggle for prisoner of war status. of course, we couldn't care less about the status. it is the operator for mobilizing international publicity for our struggle against the incarceration of extermination.
> and indeed for the recognition under international law of s o c i a l l y revolutionary movements as parties to a conflict—
> it is the only possibility for conducting our defense on the level of the judiciary: international law.[88]

Even Meinhof's death was used to promote the argument that the RAF prisoners were prisoners of war.

The minutes of a meeting between lawyers after the press conference regarding her death on May 9, 1976, mention a further press conference scheduled for May 12 in Paris, at which they would demand the RAF prisoners be treated as POWs under the Geneva Conventions. The demand was to be made alongside the simple assertion that "the frg [Federal Republic of Germany] cannot be allowed to murder any more prisoners in its prisons."[89] Later that month, via the *info*, RAF lawyers discussed a complimentary publication. They planned to produce a text with the working title "guerrilla and prisoner of war status" (*guerilla und kriegsgefangenenstatus*) that was to include a foreword, a declaration, a number of submissions to halt proceedings, and a weighty documentation section. The "whole thing," the letter continued,

> should be released by a publisher or a cooperative of different publishers.
> texts should be placed between the individual documents that make it clear that the application of the geneva conventions on the treatment of prisoners of war is necessary to prevent the extermination of the prisoners under the cloak of the "normal criminal case."[90]

In this plan the discursive strategies came together.

The project for recognition as political prisoners and POWs also worked in combination with self-starvation. It outlived the trial context to become a central part of the prison campaigns of the 1980s. Demands for POW and political prisoner status joined the antitorture protests as pillars of the hunger strikes until 1989. RAF prisoners called for protection under the Geneva Conventions, changes to prison conditions, and consolidation of political prisoners into larger groups.[91] The campaign was used to express RAF solidarity with other terrorist organizations and their imprisoned members, as it sought ideological and practical cooperation with groups such as France's *Action Directe*, Belgium's *Cellules Communistes Combattantes*, Spain's *GRAPO*, and Italy's *Brigate Rosse*. In this sense, what began as a sometimes cynical use of the languages of human rights and international law to secure a trial audience subsequently solidified as a discursive framework for the RAF's internationalism and ultimately failed attempts to establish a "Western European front" (*westeuropäische Front*).[92] This ongoing role the terminology played in sustaining the group grew out of the functions it served in the trial.

In Stammheim, the term "political prisoner" and the "project prisoner of war status" were created discursive space in the courtroom for the RAF's established anti-imperialism and anti-Americanism. Far from introducing new themes into the trial, the construction of the RAF prisoners as POWs repackaged well-known lines of argument in a manner appropriate for the forum. The affinity with liberation groups and revolutionary struggles in the third world established in Meinhof's RAF texts was expressed in Stammheim via the campaign for POW status. The legal status itself was not the goal, rather the point was to communicate the analogy to a wider, hopefully international public. The remaking of the RAF struggle as discourses of "political prisoner" and "POW" is indicative of the Stammheim trial being a lot more than the mere execution of the legal process. The legal process seemed to do little more than provide the pretext for the much broader communication taking place during the protracted finale of the first generation that culminated in the prison deaths of the remaining RAF leaders.

CHAPTER 5

SUICIDE = MURDER = SUICIDE

The lack of a suicide note is pivotal. In my opinion, it is definitive evidence against suicide and is contrary to everything else we know about her . . . For Ulrike Meinhof to commit suicide without leaving a suicide note is impossible.[1]

—Dr. Meyer, in his report for the International Investigation Commission (IUK), 1979

Despite being heard tapping away on her typewriter until late into the night she died, Meinhof did not leave a suicide note. The absence of such a note, and with it a ready-made and definitive interpretation, has given rise to endless speculation about the circumstances of her death. The resulting theories surrounding her demise are perhaps the most enduring of the RAF legacies. At the same time, however, it is impossible to discuss her death without also addressing the deaths of Andreas Baader, Gudrun Ensslin, and Jan-Carl Raspe a little over a year later, because the reception of the events have tended toward a popular, vague conflation: the "Stammheim myth."[2] This bundle of theories merges a number of interpretative threads, such as suicide as a desperate act, suicide as a defiant or even saintly rebellion, suicide as murder staged as suicide, suicide as suicide staged as murder, and simply suicide *as* murder.[3] This pattern of interpretation was activated when Meinhof was found dead, and reactivated with the deaths of the remaining members of the RAF core. It also underpins much of the sustained interest in the group as well as the martyrdom of the key RAF figures that motivated sympathizers and members into the 1990s. Putting the events of May 9, 1976, and October 18, 1977, in their historical contexts makes clear the manner in which the reaction to them evolved. It also reveals the role Meinhof played in shaping the reception of her own demise. While not leaving a note, her writings helped define a discourse on suicide that gave limits and direction to interpretations of her death.

May 8–9, 1976: Event and Reception

In the days following May 9, 1976, angry crowds gathered in front of prisons and courthouses in Stammheim, Hamm, and Moabit. People took to the streets and scuffled with police in Berlin, Munich, and Frankfurt. Protests were held and German interests attacked in Italy, Spain, France, Denmark, and even South America, and crass congratulatory notes were published in newspapers. Meinhof was dead and the world was watching. What it saw develop was a struggle over the meaning of her death.

Hours after she was found hanging from her cell window, the German Press Agency released a report that read, "According to the findings of the Federal Prosecutor, there existed in the weeks prior to Ulrike Meinhof's suicide a 'certain tension' between the 41-year-old and the remaining accused in the Stuttgart anarchist trial."[4] Shortly after, *Die Welt* reported "fundamental differences" (*tiefgreifende Auseinandersetzungen*) between Meinhof and her coaccused, and Federal Prosecutor Felix Kaul spoke of a "certain alienation" (*gewisse Entfremdung*) between Meinhof and Baader.[5] The official version of events was born: a weary and ostracized Meinhof had fashioned a noose from strips torn from her blue, prison-issue towel and hanged herself after recognizing that Baader was "nothing more than a criminal" (*ein reiner Krimineller*).[6]

The testimony of Stammheim guards who monitored the common area where the prisoners were allowed to spend time together seemed to corroborate the findings of the federal prosecutor. In the weeks before her death, guards said, Baader had taken to screaming at Meinhof and tearing up and labeling as "shit" (*Scheiße*) texts she had labored over for days.[7] In the years since, insiders have also spoken of the "tension" present in Stammheim. In a 2002 interview Mahler spoke of Baader and Ensslin deliberately "destroying" Meinhof.[8] In addition, Peter-Jürgen Boock, who was at the time of Meinhof's death a RAF member and a central figure in the group's second generation, recalls Baader playing "referee" in disputes between Ensslin and Meinhof and invariably siding with Ensslin. He also recalls an *info* that suggested suicide was "the best thing [Meinhof] could do with her screwed up life."[9]

The medical evidence released was also consistent with the suicide described by the authorities. In their official autopsy, court-appointed experts Professors Joachim Rauschke and Hans-Joachim Mallach concluded that Meinhof's death was suicide by strangulation, without any other person being involved. Meinhof's sister and lawyers then consulted their own expert, Professor Werner Janssen, who conducted another autopsy before reporting, "According to the usable findings of the second autopsy Ms. Meinhof died from strangulation. According to the results from investigations available to date, there is not evidence of the involvement of another person."[10] Despite these findings, however, an alternate version of events emerged almost as immediately as the official line. On May 11, 1976, the first day of the Stammheim trial after Meinhof's death, Raspe made a statement in court:

> We believe that Ulrike was executed; we do not know how, but we know who did it, and we can identify the logic of the method . . . As an execution, the death of Ulrike means that the international conflict—Guerilla state—had to culminate in this execution according to conditions we know and will now talk about. Strategically: against the politics of the illegal groups in the Federal Republic for which Ulrike has a fundamental ideological function, the goal was, as with every state measure and reaction against the RAF since its founding, its physical and moral annihilation and with it the destruction of its politics.[11]

He goes on to describe the relationship between Meinhof and Baader as sibling-like, painting a very different picture of the inner dynamics of the group and questioning the possibility of a suicidal "tension."[12] Boock subsequently cast doubt on the sincerity of the reaction of the remaining RAF prisoners, insisting the shock and grief they displayed were an act. There was a significant discrepancy between the private and public conception of Meinhof's death in the RAF inner circle. Privately there seemed little doubt Meinhof had committed suicide. Boock later told the federal prosecutor that accounts of Meinhof's future plans revealed by the RAF served to give the public the impression she had not wanted to end her life.[13]

The idea that Meinhof was murdered because of her ideological significance and that her murder was staged as a suicide found a willing audience among the crowds of protesters that gathered in the immediate aftermath of her death. Numerous hypothetical scenarios emerged to flesh out the theory. One such scenario centered on revelations in 1977 that a second, unmonitored staircase existed with access to the seventh floor next to Meinhof's cell. A third, unidentified person arrived, so the theory goes, on the helicopter that Ensslin testified both she and Meinhof heard on the night of her death and gained access to Meinhof's cell via this secret staircase. In an indictment against the Federal Republic, the International Committee for the Defense of Political Prisoners (*Internationales Komitee zur Verteidigung politischer Gefangener*, IKVpG) in turn adopted a broad conspiracy theory, framing Meinhof's death in terms of international cooperation between various secret services and a global strategy of counterinsurgency.[14]

Perhaps the greatest role in perpetuating what was now the official counterversion of murder was the formation of an International Investigation Commission (*Internationale Untersuchungskommission*, IUK) in August 1976. Wienke Zitlaff, Meinhof's sister, was instrumental in drawing together a group of lawyers, psychologists, philosophers, sociologists, and human rights experts into a commission, which was "international" in as much as its members came from a number of Western European countries.[15] After some two years the IUK released its report, presenting an overall picture supporting the theory that Meinhof's death was a murder staged as a suicide. Importantly, it provided the counterversion with the scientific body of evidence it had lacked.

The commission built its case largely by attempting to discredit evidence offered by the authorities, including the motive, the criminal investigation, and the medical reports. The IUK argued the official motive for suicide was based on internal RAF communications from 1973 to 1975, which had been deliberately taken out of context and fed to the media. Not only, argued the IUK, did these texts in their proper context prove the opposite, but they refer to a time far removed from Meinhof's death, meaning they were of no explanatory use. The report used a number of contradictions—such as weights and descriptions—in the two autopsies and subsequent testimonies as well as a number of inconsistencies in the criminal investigation to imply the involvement of a third person. Among these inconsistencies were the length of the noose in relation to the available length of towel and the absence of fibers found on the only two cutting tools Meinhof had, a bread knife and a pair of scissors. In addition, the mattress and chair she stepped off to hang herself were not mentioned in the original reports, and a camel-hair blanket with Baader's name on it was missing, but a lightbulb was present in her lamp, which should not have been. Prison policy stipulated that lightbulbs were collected every evening and redistributed in the morning. Finally, Meinhof was found wearing different clothes than those Ensslin testified she was last seen wearing.[16]

It was primarily the medical evidence, however, that was used to create a scenario different from the suicide in the official documents. A "Dr. Meyer" (presumably Hans Joachim Meyer, a West German neuropsychiatrist and member of the commission) argued that the noose was loose enough to easily slip over the head of the victim. This in turn led him to draw the conclusion that the suicidal Meinhof would have had to actively hold her chin to her chest to affect strangulation and avoid falling out of the noose. When Meinhof lost consciousness she would have been unable to maintain this position and would have fallen to the ground. Therefore, Meyer reasoned, Meinhof could only have been found hanging had rigor mortis set in and held the body in position, meaning she would have had to have been already dead when she was hanged.[17]

A 1976 response to Meinhof's death by unnamed English doctors included in the IUK report also mentions a positive result for seminal fluid after tests were carried out on "suspicious stains" on the prisoner's underwear. This positive result was used to imply a sexual assault before the murder, despite the absence of sperm found on the underwear. The presence of various bacteria from excrement and urine, which would have broken down the sperm in hours, was used to explain this absence.[18] It has since been argued the test carried out was rather standard and tested for any of the enzymes in the large phosphatase group, which includes seminal fluid. The general nature of the test usually produces a positive result, and therefore, contrary to the commission's findings, a negative result would have been suspicious.[19]

Meinhof famously wrote in 1974 that "should it ever be said that I have committed suicide, it was murder—external, violent forces—or total resistance," combining the notion of murder with an antifascist martyrdom.[20] This third reception emerged to challenge the victim statuses implicit in the official and alternate versions of events. She wrote in grandiose terms of suicide as a subversive act in the *info*, describing it as the "final act of rebellion," and retrospective attempts to find a subversive commentary in her death have centered, in particular, on its timing.[21] Meinhof died during the night of Saturday, May 8, the anniversary of VE Day, marking the end of World War II, and she was found on the morning of Sunday, May 9, Mothers' Day. Both dates have subsequently been used to argue for Meinhof's antifascist martyrdom.

By aligning her suicide with the victory of the Allies over National Socialism, some see a personal liberation. Given that Meinhof argued the postwar Federal Republic was a continuation of the fascist Nazi regime, her suicide has been understood as her escape from fascism, analogous to the liberation of Europe on VE Day. Similarly, suicide on Mothers' Day has also been interpreted as a rejection of the idyll of the Nationalist Socialist mother, which was cultivated in the Third Reich in part by co-opting Mothers' Day. Making Meinhof a martyr to the RAF cause extrapolated a preexisting tendency evident in Meinhof's prison nickname. The RAF leadership adopted nicknames for their prison communication, all of which were taken from Melville's *Moby Dick* except for Meinhof's: Ensslin chose for Meinhof the name "Therese," after a sixteenth-century Spanish nun canonized shortly after her death.[22] The idea of Meinhof playing an active role in consciously staging her suicide has survived the decades since 1976 and was a central theme in, for example, Elfriede Jelinek's play *Ulrike Maria Stuart* (2006). The Meinhof figure in the play talks of her suicide as a photo opportunity. She relates how it was not easy to position herself correctly for the camera: the bed had to be moved, the mattress laid before the window, the chair put on top of the mattress, and strips carefully torn from her prison towel, tied together, and then around her neck. Director of the 2006 debut production, Nicolas Stemann, also had Meinhof aided in the preparation of her noose by her elderly self, further alluding to an interpretation of Meinhof's death as deliberately performative, as consciously myth- and legacy-making.[23]

The issue of murder also made a return, albeit in a different guise, when sympathizers equated suicide with murder. Only days after Meinhof's death,

Dr. Wilfried Rasch described the prison conditions in Stammheim as "promoting suicide" (*selbstmordfördernd*).[24] Professor Axel Azzola also laid the blame for her death at the feet of authorities, saying "there is no such thing as suicide, there are only beaters and the hunted."[25] This fit within the discourse on RAF deaths established in the aftermath of Holger Meins's 1974 death by starvation. The crowds that gathered then were recalled by those that formed after news of Meinhof's suicide hit the airwaves. Meins, who starved himself to death, had written in his will that "should I die in prison, it was murder. Despite what the pigs will say," and those on the streets were united in the conviction that Meins was murdered, with graffiti on buildings and churches promising "revenge for Holger."[26] It is this idea of murder that has left the starkest footprint. The sensationalism of the conspiracy theory involving cover-ups and government agents married the argument that even if Meinhof died alone and at her own hand, this suicide was murder. This reception, and the surprisingly effortless conflation of the two "murders," provided a general pattern that was again set in motion 18 months later when the remaining RAF prisoners on level seven of Stammheim were found dead.

October 18, 1977: Event and Reception

At 7:41 on the morning of October 18, 1977, prison guards brought Raspe his breakfast. He normally waited by the door, but on this morning guards saw him sitting on his bed, bleeding from his left temple, but still breathing and moaning. Two paramedics arrived minutes later and Raspe was rushed to hospital, where, despite the efforts of surgeons, he died from a pistol shot to the head. After Raspe had first been moved from his cell, prison staff raced down the hall to find Baader sprawled across the floor of his cell, his head resting in a pool of blood. He was already dead from a gunshot wound to the head. Ensslin was also found dead, hanging from her cell window by a length of loudspeaker cable. The paramedics reached Irmgard Möller last, and found her lying on her bed. They rolled her onto her back, pulled back her blanket, and lifted her jumper to find four stab wounds to her chest and a bloody, serrated knife lying next to her. Möller was rushed to the hospital and survived. The events of this morning and the deaths of the remaining members of the first-generation leadership group must be understood against the background of the attempted liberation of the RAF prisoners through the kidnapping of a leading industrialist and the hijacking of Lufthansa flight LH 181.

Thoughts of escape had occupied the RAF prisoners since their capture, with the 1977 hijacking the last in a long line of attempts. A 1972 search of Meinhof's cell, only months after her arrest, turned up a hand-drawn—albeit incorrect—floor plan of the Cologne-Ossendorf prison.[27] Similarly, in 1972, in response to a complaint by RAF lawyer Heinrich Hannover that books he had intended for Meinhof had not been passed on, prison authorities described encoded messages about liberation attempts being smuggled out of prison.[28] In early 1974, and following the arrest of "anarchist criminals" (*anarchistische Gewalttäter*), police uncovered an escape plan involving four to five kilograms of explosives, fuses, detonator caps, and a small saw being smuggled to Baader in the spine of a *Leitz*-brand lever arch file.[29] Three sheets of paper were also found in Baader's trashcan in early 1975 that revealed a conversation between Baader, Ensslin, Meinhof, and Carmen Roll regarding flight times and the "stuff from wednesday" (*zeug vom mittwoch*). Police assumed the stuff from Wednesday related the newspaper reports from March 5 on the kidnapping of Christian Democratic Union (*Christlich Demokratische Union*, CDU) politician Peter Lorenz.[30]

Lorenz was taken hostage by the Second of June Movement and the ransom demanded was the release of six prisoners, including Horst Mahler, but not Baader, Meinhof, Ensslin, Raspe, or Möller. Mahler refused the exchange, but the five remaining prisoners were flown out of the Federal Republic by the government to Yemen, and Lorenz was subsequently released. The sole consolation for the leadership group of the RAF was a message from the kidnappers: "To our comrades in prison: we would like to get more of you out, but are not in a position to do so at the moment."[31]

The success of the Lorenz operation no doubt inspired the 1977 operation codenamed "Big Break Out" (*Big Raushole*), the September 5 kidnapping of Hanns-Martin Schleyer. Schleyer was the president of the Confederation of German Employers' Associations and the Federation of German Industries, and he was targeted because of his involvement with the Schutzstaffel (SS) in the Third Reich. The meticulously planned operation claimed the lives of Schleyer's driver and the two police officers assigned to protect him since the murder of banker Jürgen Ponto in a failed kidnap attempt. The following day, the Schleyer kidnappers dropped a letter addressed to the federal government in the letterbox of a Protestant dean in Wiesbaden demanding Baader, Ensslin, Raspe, Möller, and seven other prisoners be released, flown to a country of their choice, and each given DM 100,000. On this occasion the government did not agree to the demands and a standoff ensued that would outlive the RAF prisoners.

On October 13, and with the Schleyer saga entering its thirty-eighth day, the stakes were raised. A Lufthansa flight from Palma de Mallorca was hijacked by a group of four Palestinians demanding the release of the RAF prisoners in Stammheim. The plane with its 86 passengers and 5 crew members was rerouted and landed in Mogadishu four days later after stopping to refuel in Rome, Cyprus, Bahrain, Dubai, and Aden. In the early hours of October 18, the RAF prisoners in Stammheim heard reports of a special unit of the West

German Federal Police storming the Boeing, killing three of the hijackers and freeing all the hostages. Upon hearing the news of this latest failed attempt to liberate them, the RAF prisoners took their own lives, which in turn cost Schleyer his. The RAF captors murdered him when they heard the news of the Stammheim suicides, and then notified the press as to the location of his body: the trunk of a green Audi in Mulhouse, France.

The failed liberation must also be seen in the context of the RAF trial, in which the group had also run out of options. Having played all their cards—few of them legal, most of them performative—in the courtroom, the RAF prisoners were becoming aware that they were to spend the rest of their lives in prison, and consequently increasingly desperate. The view of the suicides as a last desperate act is supported by revelations by Boock—who along with Birgitte Mohnhaupt smuggled the weapons used in the suicide into Stammheim—that the RAF leaders told members on the outside only three days before the kidnapping of Schleyer: "free us or we'll take our destiny into our own hands." It was obvious to the RAF members in the underground, says Boock, that meant collective suicide.[32]

As with Meinhof's death, a counterversion of events emerged almost immediately. On January 16, 1978, having recovered from her injuries, Möller testified before a parliamentary inquiry that none of the prisoners had considered committing suicide.[33] Regarding her own injuries, Möller told the inquiry, "I did not attempt or intend to attempt suicide, nor was there any agreement to that affect in place."[34] As the sole surviving eyewitness to events, her account was crucial:

At around 5am I heard banging and squeaking.
These noises were very soft and dull, as if something had fallen over or a cabinet was being moved. I didn't immediately recognize the bangs as shots . . .
Afterwards I went back to sleep. Suddenly I was out, I lost consciousness, it all happened very quickly.
The last thing I remember was an intense noise in my head. I didn't see anyone and didn't notice anyone come in.
I then woke up in the corridor on a stretcher as a doubled-over, whimpering mess, freezing cold, wet through with blood and I heard voices—satisfied, spiteful: Baader and Ensslin are cold.[35]

RAF lawyers Otto Schily (later Minister for the Interior), Hans-Christian Ströbele (later a Greens' politician), and Karl-Heinz Weidenhammer added their voices to the murder theory, although all three have since distanced themselves from this view. Möller, however, has steadfastly maintained her story, while alluding to an ever-widening conspiracy theory that includes the federal government, North Atlantic Treaty Organization (NATO), high-level links between

Washington and Bonn, and a U.S. Central Intelligence Agency (CIA) model of staging murders as suicides.[36] Supporters also managed to highlight various inconsistencies in testimonies as evidence of a cover-up. For example, the two guards who found Raspe differed in their recollections of where exactly the firearm lay: in his open hand or underneath it.[37]

Although the counterversion of murder staged as suicide took root in sympathetic sections of the public and was encouraged by the RAF, there is evidence to suggest that despite being a useful propaganda tool, it was not believed within the inner RAF circles. Second-generation RAF members Monika Helbing and Susanne Albrecht, who at the time of the Stammheim deaths were holed up in Baghdad as part of a group monitoring the Mogadishu operation, recall the explicit understanding within the group that it was not murder staged as suicide, but suicide staged as murder. Both women have spoken of the key role Birgitte Mohnhaupt played in presenting the Stammheim deaths as a "suicide action" designed to further the RAF project.[38] Now leader of the RAF, Mohnhaupt was no doubt battling to maintain morale and admonished the group: "Can you really only see them as victims? It was an operation, do you understand, an operation! You can stop blubbering, you assholes!"[39] This followed the pattern of the reception of Meinhof's death with the victim status being flipped on its head, initially within the group and gradually beyond it.

What began as a sympathetic revision to give the dead RAF leaders some agency and a legacy has become a counterargument to the murder theory used by detractors. It has seen historical details interpreted as clues planted by the prisoners to give the impression of murder. For example, Baader fired two bullets—one into the mattress, one into the wall—laying the casings next to him before firing the third shot, and he had laced conversations in the weeks prior to the mass suicide with loaded statements. On September 13 he told Alfred Klaus, head of the antiterrorism unit: "the federal government can choose to either kill the prisoners or at some stage release them."[40] Similarly, on October 7 he noted that "none of us intends to commit suicide. If we are found dead here, we have been murdered as part of the traditional judicial and political measures of this policy."[41] Such comments are reminiscent of Meinhof's reported comment to her sister: "If you hear that I've killed myself, you can be sure it was murder."[42] But whereas Meinhof's words were used to argue against suicide, Baader's have also been cited to argue for the group's active and conscious involvement in the staging of their suicides as murders.

The question of "murder" has since made a late return to the debate. Far from accusing guards of pulling the triggers, tying the noose, or taking to Möller with a knife, the issue of state culpability has reemerged in the context of possible prevention of the suicides. The reactions of the guards upon finding Baader suggest they were fully aware the prisoners had access to firearms:

"Look, what a mess, there's the other pistol."[43] Moreover, given the listening devices in the prisoners' cells, it can be argued the prison authorities must have known something of the planned suicide. Surveillance of the prisoners was constant throughout their incarceration, but intensified with heightened security needs, such as the kidnapping of Schleyer. Did the authorities, who were eavesdropping on the group and seemed to be aware of the existence of the tools of suicide, know or suspect anything? If so, how is their inaction to be interpreted? The debate surrounding the 1977 deaths followed the broad pattern established in the aftermath of Meinhof's death.

Former RAF member Volker Speitel is rather cynical about the "Stammheim myth." When writing in the context of the "RAF book," a collection of texts and photos produced by the second generation, he noted that "with the supposed murder of the prisoners the Left has finally got their hands on a theme in which they themselves don't believe: the openly fascist state."[44] The cries of murder could not be reconciled, he continues, with the book they have in their hands featuring smuggled photos. After all, the Minox camera was smuggled into Stammheim as a test for the subsequent transportation of the guns. "Particularly clever people," Speitel writes with some sarcasm, "point out that a Minox Camera [that was used to take the photos] is only half the size of a gun."[45] While the construction of the events in Stammheim has developed a life of its own, it was allowed to develop by the discursive groundwork that had been laid over the decade prior. Central to this groundwork was the work of Meinhof.

"Self"-Killing: A Discourse of Suicide

The strands of interpretation presented here as broadly contemporaneous and discrete are, in fact, far from self-contained theories. Biographer Mario Krebs, for example, incorporated a number of them in his portrayal of Meinhof. He went to great lengths to establish Meinhof's antifascist pedigree, using her VE Day suicide to underscore a greatly exaggerated family history of resistance in World War II, and later outlined the IUK case of murder before concluding that given the prison conditions, "there is no such thing as suicide behind bars."[46] This is representative of the process of amalgamation evident in the "Stammheim myth," a conspiracy theory that has survived on a combination of sensational murder accusations and the interpretation of suicide as murder.

The success of this bundle of interpretations is not surprising given the model that existed for comprehending RAF deaths. Just as previous deaths, most notably that of Holger Meins, which the group framed as an execution, helped define the context in which Meinhof's death was understood, the events of May 1976 in turn shaped the understanding of the events of October 1977. Meinhof, in particular, had laid the foundation for the Stammheim myth in the years prior to the actual events. While it can only be inappropriately specu-lative to assign Meinhof's suicide a symbolic meaning, suggest she intended one, or argue she deliberately sought to influence its subsequent interpretation, Meinhof's writings did contribute to an overarching discourse of suicide that prepared the ground for the reception of her death.

When commenting on the potentiality of Meinhof's suicide being the result of a concentrated effort by authorities to destroy her, the IUK used quotation marks to write of "'self'-murder" (*"Selbst"-Mord*).[47] This sarcastic annotation used to imply the primacy of societal responsibility over that of the individual was not new. Meinhof had already adopted it years earlier, writing in a draft text from July 1974:

> The rulers know that this violent reduction of the human to a wage-slave and consuming animal as a pre-requisite for their continued accumulation of capi-tal in the metropolis FRG produces a monstrous impoverishment that expresses itself in:
>   hundreds of thousands of "suicide" attempts—including 15 000 "suicides," that 120 000 people are permanently cooped up in lunatic asylums,
>   in 600 000 "schizophrenics."[48]

In the same draft she frames mental illness and suicide as constructs of a system in which capital is not only mutually exclusive with, but actively destroys, human dignity. In a 1974 text signed by "the raf prisoners," suicide is framed as one of the symptoms of capitalism as part of an explanation for the absent revolutionary subject: "the problem in the metropoles is that although the system is politically and economically ripe for abolition, the revolutionary forces among the people are still too weak—there is more resignation, lethargy, depression, agony, more sick people and suicides, more people that lay down and die because one cannot live in this system any more than one can stand up and fight."[49] By this stage, such con-structions of suicide, or "self"-murder, were well established in Meinhof's writing.

In her second treatise, *Serve the People* (*Dem Volk dienen*), Meinhof opened with a quotation from Mao followed immediately by a similar case for the lethal force of capitalism:

> 20 000 people die every year—because the shareholders in the automobile indus-try only allow production for profit and don't consider the technical safety of their cars or the road design.
>   5 000 people die every year—at the workplace or on way to or from work, because the owners of the means of production are only concerned with their profits and not one accidental death more or less.
>   12 000 people commit suicide every year, because they don't want to die in the service of capital they'd prefer to end it all themselves.

> 1 000 children are murdered every year, because houses that are too small only
> exist so landlords can pocket high rents.
> They call death in the service of the exploiters a natural death. They call the
> refusal to die in the service of the exploiters an "unnatural death."[50]

By constructing capitalism as a destructive force that denies free will, she divested
the individual of responsibility for not only for suicide but child mortality, as
well as car and workplace accidents. This picked up a theme established earlier
in a cassette recording of Meinhof played at a Red Aid teach-in while the group
was still at large. In this recorded statement Meinhof established the unhealthy
effects of capitalism as well as the mutual exclusivity of capitalist profit and
worker well-being.[51]

Later, in *Serve the People*, Meinhof addressed poverty in West Germany. In a
level of statistical detail reminiscent of her radio work, she described the miser-
able situation of West Germany's poorest: 3 percent of the population unable
to work due to mental illness, 600,000 in poorhouses, 50,000 adults in prison,
50,000 youths raised in state care, 0.7 m2 allocated per mental patient in psychiatric institutions, and so on.[52] She pointed to a lack of infrastructure and
opportunity as the causes of social problems, among them suicide: "There is not
enough of anything in the *Märkische Viertel*: playgrounds, means of transportation, schools, cheap places to shop, doctors, lawyers. A breeding ground for
poverty, child abuse, suicide, gang crime, embitterment, misery. The *Märkisches
Viertel* is our social future . . . The television says, 'the Federal Republic is not
Latin America,' the poor in the Federal Republic have only themselves to blame
for their criminality, there are not many poor people—the evidence offered.
The Springer press prints this stuff. Fascist material."[53] In this same section, she
laments the imprisonment of the members of the Socialist Patients' Collective
(*Sozialistisches Patientenkollektiv*, SPK) because the organization had so logically
outlined the relationship between capitalism and sickness.

In the years before her death, Meinhof's "lethal world" (*tötende Welt*) resembled very closely the worldview of the SPK.[54] The SPK argued that capitalism
not only caused, but also had a vested interest in promoting, sickness. The calls
of "suicide equals murder equals suicide" that resounded among sympathizers
after Meinhof's death were a revival of the SPK slogan from the texts it distributed and the graffiti it sprayed around the cities in 1971. Meinhof adopted
from the SPK its manner of expressing its worldview of the causal relationship
between capitalism and illness by appropriating the slogan "make your sickness a weapon," and the quotation marks around "self"-murder. SPK newsletters numbers 35 and 37 from April 1971 described the then recent "suicide"
(*"Selbst"mord*) of a member "M." "M" was made worthless, the newsletters said,
by a system that blamed the unemployed, the sick, and the criminal for their

own predicaments and understood "material poverty and social ostracism [as] lethal, tools of murder of the capitalist society."⁵⁵ The adoption of SPK modes of expression was hardly surprising given the compatibility of the group's mission with Meinhof's earlier work.

The view of societal responsibility expressed in Meinhof's RAF texts is completely consistent with the stance she took as a journalist in her work with *konkret* and in her narrated dramatizations for radio. In a 1968 *konkret* article, in the aftermath of the police shooting of a young protester, she decried an overwhelming discourse of the innocence of the system in the dominant press: "It is only a small step from a faith in the futility and the inexplicability of Benno Ohnesorg's death, from a faith in the innocence of the system to saying the murdered and not the murderer is guilty."⁵⁶ Much of Meinhof's journalistic work served to highlight the role of society in marginalizing and isolating certain demographics, and the responsibility it must therefore assume for the antisocial and criminal behavior of groups such as exploited workers, particularly working women, as well as youths, particularly girls, in institutional care.

In her 1965 radio feature *Danger on the Assembly Line* (*Gefahr am Fließband*) she describes a dynamic that she would later frame as a lethal capitalist logic. This early work reveals her prolific use of statistics to bolster her argument, which can also be seen in *Serve the People*. While denouncing the business mentality that prioritizes profits over worker safety, her argument against it is at this stage still framed in terms of economic common sense: instead of only costing money, increased safety standards increase productivity, decrease waste, and save money. She also wrote extensively on the position of women in economically miraculous West Germany. There existed a major wage differential, despite formal safeguards in the constitution that ensured women equal pay for equal work. Two radio features in early 1967 tackled this problem, *Women Are Cheaper* (*Frauen sind billiger*) and *Half Weib—Half Person* (*Halb Weib—halb Mensch*).⁵⁷ For Meinhof, differences in pay were symptomatic of a society that still afforded women no personal freedom, a point emphasized by the narrator of *Women Are Cheaper*: "Today it is no longer biological but social restraints that prevent women from becoming aware of her opportunities, from realizing them . . . The idyll of the little housewife at the stove was almost seamlessly replaced with the idyll of the little housewife at the conveyor belt."⁵⁸ The argument presented in these radio pieces was subsequently reproduced in her 1968 *konkret* article "Women's Business" (*Frauenkram*).⁵⁹

By far Meinhof's most long-standing and most well-known research interest was the institutional care of youths, especially girls. She wrote an article on remedial schools in West Germany that was spread between two 1969 issues of *konkret*. A series of two articles with the title "Stupid—because they're poor" (*Doof—weil arm*) combined secondary research with interviews and investigated institutional failings she considered symptomatic of a broader social failure to integrate troubled students and young people from poor families. It was, she wrote, "an environment that acts criminally towards them, [that] makes them criminal," and contrary to the conventional wisdom, she continued, "their learning disabilities are a product of their poverty," not the other way around.[60]

Similarly her 1965 radio feature *Cast Out or Cared for* (*Ausgestossen oder aufgehoben*) investigated whether West German society gave children from welfare homes a chance.[61] Her 1966 *konkret* article "Flight from a girls' home" (*Flucht aus dem Mädchenheim*) not only reproduced the attack on an antiquated welfare system but retold the story of "Margarete M."[62] Margarete had a long history of being cared for by the state. She was shunted between institutions and families before going missing at 16. She was last seen drunk, high on meth, and wearing nothing but a fur coat, a bra, underwear, and high heels, which were too big for her. In addition to the alcohol abuse and delinquency bred by a society ignoring this "economically and commercially uninteresting" (*ökonomisch und kommerziell uninteressant*) demographic, Meinhof described in further features the violence, exploitation, criminal behavior, and prostitution experienced by girls from state homes.[63] The environment of the homes described in the features *Guxhagen—Girls in Care* (*Guxhagen—Mädchen in Fürsorgeerziehung*) and *Bambule* is authoritarian.[64] Meinhof also calls it sadomasochistic. There are no training opportunities and the girls are isolated from a society that understands poverty and criminality as the result of personal inclination.

The common social determinist undertone was not out of place at the time. In fact, Meinhof's research fit snuggly in with the broad Leftist scene, the women's movement, and the calls to reform authoritarian universities. Her line in *Bambule* that "violence produces counter-violence, pressure counter-pressure" (*Gewalt produziert Gegengewalt, Druck Gegendruck*) was used not only for the specific example of delinquent girls but also in the broader context of the escalating protests of the student movement. Nor were Meinhof's criticisms misdirected. There existed very real inequities and very fundamental problems, and tellingly, much progress has subsequently been made in these areas. However, what her early research also reveals is the basis for the discourse of social determinism that is maintained in her underground and prison texts, and explicitly includes the act of suicide. It made a major contribution to the "fertile ground" on which the "Stammheim myth" fell and thrived.[65]

The deaths of the Stammheim prisoners later became a fundamental and irreproachable part of the second- and third-generation RAF identity. The underlying anger it produced within the group helped motivate violence and sustain its confrontation with the West German state. It was not until the fall of the Berlin Wall that Stammheim stopped performing this function. With German reunification, former members of the RAF who had found a haven in

East Germany in the early 1980s were arrested. Their testimony undermined the notion that the Stammheim prisoners were murdered, piercing the cocoon of the inner RAF where the Stammheim myth had been vigorously protected.[66] Attempts were later made to fill this hole with the state "execution" of Wolfgang Grams in 1993.[67] The exemplar of the RAF logic of martyrdom that can be seen in the cases of Meins, Sigurd Debus, and Grams remained Stammheim. It may have been discredited as a foundational narrative within the group, but it continued to survive, embedded in popular consciousness. In 1996, for example, ex-RAF prisoner Monika Berberich received hearty applause from the thousands who gathered in the auditorium of the Technical University in Berlin to mark the twentieth anniversary of Meinhof's death when she affirmed that she was "still absolutely convinced that she was murdered."[68] This martyrdom endured the 1998 dissolution of the RAF to remain one of the most persistent and divisive of the group's legacies.

CONCLUSION

Voices and Echoes

everyone (except you of course) knows that YOU WERE ARE WILL BE THE VOICE.[1]

—Ensslin to Meinhof in a 1973 prison letter

Ulrike Meinhof struggled to find her voice. While courting attention in the student protest scene in the late 1950s, and rising to be a spokesperson for the student movement in the 1960s, she harbored doubts about her ability to convey her message. In 1970 she entered the underground at the height of her journalistic powers, transforming her renown as a writer, radio commentator, television personality, and filmmaker into an equal measure of infamy. Uncertainty continued to dog Meinhof as the Red Army Faction's (RAF's) underground and prison scribe. However, the voice she was increasingly unsure of in private, nonetheless reverberated publicly.[2] Her fame had rested on being able to capture the mood of protest, and in the underground her words and actions performed what became the RAF brand of terrorism. After her arrest, Meinhof managed to reinvent RAF rhetoric for a prison context and subsequently for a trial audience. She was able to inspire a new generation of RAF members from her cell and ensure West German terrorism did not peter out in the mid-1970s. Her voice also echoed long after her death, as she prepared the discursive foundation for the RAF violence of the 1980s and 1990s, as well as much of the RAF myth of the twenty-first century.

Gudrun Ensslin's prison reassurances both confirm Meinhof's central role as the RAF's mouthpiece and betray her insecurities. Doubts about her ability to communicate what she wanted to communicate emerged as she made a name for herself as a journalist. Her concerns that the capitalist media was able to crowd out dissent and subversion were emblematic of a wider student movement campaign against media magnate Axel Springer. The campaign raged against what it saw as the pitfalls of media monopolization and the potential for the manipulation of debate. The protestors had a tangible example of this manipulation with the shooting of Rudi Dutschke, and the anti-Springer campaign reached its high point with the blockades of Springer's publishing houses that followed. As the movement against Springer wound down in the late 1960s, however, Meinhof's frustrations ratcheted up, and she applied her critique of the media to her own writing.

Meinhof had already extended the logic of manipulation to journalistic writing. Her columns for *konkret* increasingly tackled the reporting of the news, highlighting the performative power of the media. She became frustrated with how the mainstream media were able to shape public debate and saw no room for an alternative message within the structures of professional journalism. When she turned her critique to her own work, in particular the genre of the column, she found it wanting. She found that what she produced was subject to the same capitalist forces, the same structural violence, that absorbed and nullified protest in mainstream reporting. This realization led to a series of attempts to "redemocratize" her journalistic efforts, such as through collective and anonymous authorship, as well as work in radio and film. Meinhof's frustration also contributed to her leaving *konkret*. None of her attempts to rediscover her platform was ultimately successful. Instead, the crisis deepened.

In the underground and later in prison, the logic of a manipulative and broken communication remained. The focus, however, shrank to language and words themselves. Similar experiments were made to break the down the structural violence that so troubled her in the context of the media and journalism. However, these experiments too were largely unsuccessful. In the end, for Meinhof, language was beholden to the same capitalist forces that squeezed out subversion in the monopolized mass media. Words could no longer be trusted to convey meaning, and they became the frontline for her personal struggle with communication. The trajectory of this struggle straddles her time as a journalist and a terrorist, and it confirms that actions did not trump words in the formation of the RAF. A mounting frustration with the means of communication went hand in hand with a creeping justification of violence, but it did not see Meinhof give up on language. She persisted with the written word in the underground, where what she wrote shaped the group's external image, internal dynamic, and intertwined with images and acts of physical violence to constitute RAF terrorism.

Given their panicked entrance into the underground, the RAF and its visual identity emerged while on the run. The first statements made by the group reveal the beginnings of a media practice that made concessions to the logic of the mainstream media. A name was settled on, a logo designed, and the group quickly identified its audiences and forums, tailoring its texts accordingly. Adapting the RAF message to the structures of the capitalist media may have been contrary to Meinhof's underlying desire to rewrite the rules of language, writing, and journalism, but it was a necessary pragmatic choice for a group with no real underground infrastructure other than a handful of typewriters and access to the postal system. Thus Meinhof used what was available to communicate while the RAF was on the run from police and launching a series of attacks.

Meinhof's words accompanied the bombing spree of 1972. In many ways the declarations rode the spectacle of the bombs to reach an audience. The violence created a story, and Meinhof's texts sent to broadcasters and newspapers delivered the RAF's interpretation of that story. The bombs also carried with them a symbolic value. The group targeted police stations, a judge, and U.S. military bases, giving expression to well-established antagonisms and underscoring these themes in the accompanying texts. More importantly, however, the words and violence of the bombing spree worked together to perform RAF terror within a mainstream narrative of war.

By the time of the attacks in May 1972, a rhetoric of war had long been central to the protest scene in West Germany. The student movement framed the situation in the Federal Republic of the 1960s by merging the idea of lingering German fascism with the global politics of the Vietnam War. This collage was also a constant theme in Meinhof's texts, and it became fundamental to the identity of RAF members, who considered themselves soldiers in an army fighting in a worldwide revolution. A mainstream narrative of war gathered around the conflict in Vietnam, but it remained separate from the discourse of terrorism, with politicians and the mainstream media avoiding the use of a language of war to describe domestic incidents. The two only merged with the RAF bombs. The violence of the 1972 spree was able to insert local acts of terrorism into the visual narrative of a foreign war. Given recent technological advances, the Vietnam War was experienced almost in real time via television and photographs. A vocabulary of images defined the West German experience of Vietnam, and the RAF bombings ensured their violence overlapped with that experience. The bombs, in combination with Meinhof's words, successfully imposed the RAF model of interpretation onto the mainstream media by bringing together the discourses of terror and war.

The implications of the uptake of the radical narrative of war were significant. Accepting the RAF declaration of war re-created the strict dichotomy of terrorist thinking. It also provided the self-conception of the RAF as an army of soldiers with an external source of legitimacy. Such confirmation also proved capable of sparking a resurgence of support, which had been at perhaps its lowest ebb in the immediate aftermath of the Hamburg bombing. It drew new members into the underground, and it paralleled the escalation in violence in the mid to late 1970s. The language of war was never as pronounced

after 1977, but the declarations and bombings ensured it was the dominant discursive framework during the most violent period of West German
terrorism.

Meinhof's treatises were composed for a more sympathetic audience. The
lengthy texts outlined the RAF's preferred strategy and its positions on specific issues and incidents. What these seemingly theoretical texts more con-
vincingly established was a terrorist morality. Ideological mainstays appeared
in the treatises as more of a visual than a textual element. They were removed
from any context and remained separate from the body of the text as prefacing
quotations. Rather than outline a theoretical position, this "picturesque" ideology was used to support themes of sacrifice, loyalty, treachery, martyrdom, and
glorious violence that helped bind the group in its increasing isolation. These
psychological drivers remained important to the internal group dynamic long
after the worldview articulated by Meinhof was formally revised in the early
1980s. While the specific ideological vocabulary used in the treatises eventually
fell out of favor, the moral program it nurtured was of great importance in the
underground, and particularly in prison.

With the leadership in prison, RAF rhetoric needed to be adjusted to the
new situation. Hunger strikes became the vehicle for these adjustments, as self-
starvation helped maintain a group identity and produced RAF victimhood
in terms of the prison experience. These notions of hunger were carried by
complex networks with discrete internal and external audiences. The network
within the penal system facilitated a sacralization of self-starvation among RAF
prisoners. It helped maintain a group identity and enabled prisoners to wage
the RAF struggle as "holy hunger," bringing the revolution from the streets into
their cells. For the group's audience beyond the prison walls, however, hunger
formed part of a countermedicalization of terror.

RAF leaders saw in the mainstream press and prison routine an attempt to
diagnose and dismiss their political message as an illness. Doctors were called on
to identify and explain terrorism, constructing terrorists as unstable or insane.
Not only was Meinhof's personal and well-known medical history a large part
of this medicalization, she also led the campaign to confront it within the same
discourse of science. Via the hunger strikes, she expressed RAF rhetoric in terms
of medicine, placing the confrontation between the state and the RAF in the
prisoner's body. The strikes aligned starving prisoners with concentration camp
victims and framed force-fed prisoners as victims of imperialist torture. They
allowed the RAF to inhabit the twin victim statuses of its anti-imperialism and
antifascism, and grew into the centerpiece of a growing public campaign of
support. The significance of this remodeled struggle, personified by imprisoned
members, was its ability to mobilize a new wave of RAF terrorists. The effects

of prolonged self-starvation on the prisoners' health were also exploited as a stalling tactic during the Stammheim trial.

The group took advantage of the prisoners' deteriorating health as part of a suite of strategies that aimed at frustrating the proceedings via provocation, silence, or choking the court with procedural submissions. The debate about the condition of the inmates was part of this approach, and competing medical experts slowed progress during the first weeks to a standstill. The ability to take advantage of the prisoners' deteriorating health in this manner was removed when the court ruled—relying on laws freshly passed for the trial—that it could proceed in the absence of defendants. The abuse of judges and histrionic monologues, particularly by Andreas Baader and Ensslin, remained features of the trial, but the group also developed performative strategies to make use of the stage and the audience it had in Stammheim. Meinhof again led the remodeling of RAF terrorism for a new forum by expressing the group's anti-imperialism and internationalism in terms of human rights and international legal conventions.

The first pillar of this strategy was to frame the accused as political prisoners. The use of the term needed to be tightly managed because it was employed differently beyond prison walls than within. In the context of the penal system, the term was avoided. RAF prisoners sought to break down any distinctions that could prevent normal prisoners from identifying with them and their prison protests. Externally, and particularly for the trial, the term "political prisoner" was actively employed to negate the idea of Stammheim as being a normal criminal trial. It also underpinned applications made to the European Commission of Human Rights on behalf of the "political prisoners" of Stammheim. The applications were never intended to be successful. They were instead an attempt to use the application process to hijack the language of international law and human rights. The second pillar of the group's strategy similarly looked to make use of international conventions.

The project during the trial to construct the accused as prisoners of war (POWs) was part of an attempt to secure international recognition. The use of the term POW was a calculated choice, made to revive waning interest and enshrine the RAF as a genuine part of a worldwide struggle. The strategy appealed to the Geneva Conventions and sought to piggyback the contemporaneous debate about the definition of a "privileged combatant." The publicity, however, and not the status itself, was the goal. Just as the use of "political prisoner" was an often-cynical attempt to counter the construction of the RAF as mere criminals, the project to attain POW status was an equally cynical use of legal conventions to insert the group into an international context of legitimate resistance. The prison campaigns and the Stammheim trial dominated the incarceration of the RAF founders, and with it the final years of their lives, they also outlived the leading first-generation figures and continued to shape RAF terrorism beyond 1977.

The violence of the German Autumn represented a significant blow to the RAF on many fronts.[3] The events in Mogadishu signaled the conclusive defeat of the urban guerilla strategy, and the brutality of the Hanns-Martin Schleyer murder, in particular, cost the group any possibility of broad-based sympathy.[4] Not only was the group increasingly isolated, but the Stammheim deaths left the remains of the group without focus. The fundamental operational goal of the second generation had been the liberation of the first, and for many, a sense of purpose perished with the imprisoned leaders. It also led to some members dropping out and finding new homes in East Germany. However, these setbacks did not bring an end to RAF violence. After taking a couple of years to regroup, a series of bomb attacks, assassination attempts, and targeted killings punctuated the 1980s and spilled over into the 1990s.[5] A lot of what survived of the RAF in late 1977 beyond a handful of radicals, and what underpinned the doggedness of the group, were the discursive frameworks set up by Meinhof during the incarceration of the first generation.

In the aftermath of 1977, the prison campaign evolved into a stand-alone prison movement, attracting prisoners not previously involved with the RAF and paralleling the group's acts of violence on the outside.[6] The hunger strikes and antitorture slogans combined with the language of political imprisonment and human rights, as well as calls for consolidation and POW status, to continue to perform RAF victimhood and international solidarity, helping to create and sustain a sympathetic base of supporters. This "legal arm" remained capable of mobilizing leftist activists, and it hand-delivered radicalized sympathizers to the illegal and underground tiers of the RAF.[7] It also served as a link between the illegals and the prisoners who still had a role in directing, or were still consulted about, external operations.[8] In some measure, then, the performative frameworks from the first-generation strikes and the Stammheim trial gave direction and resources to the violence that came after them. Having saved the group in the mid-1970s, they survived the German Autumn, as well as changes in structure, strategy, theoretical position, and personnel, to sustain the RAF through the 1980s.[9] Another important contributing factor to the persistence of the RAF after 1977 was the martyrdom of the first-generation leaders.

Meinhof's death in 1976 was the subject of intense debate with competing interpretations immediately vying for attention. The same pattern of interpretation that pitted variations of murder against variations of suicide was again set in motion with the deaths of the remaining leading figures in 1977. The Stammheim myth emerged as a mix—resilient, but not necessarily internally logical—of conspiracy theories and rival explanations that often overlapped. The strength of the Stammheim myth rests in part on the preprepared model for understanding the RAF deaths. That is to say, Meinhof played a role in the reception of her own death by having set the discursive parameters for the Stammheim myth in her writing. The logic that "suicide is murder is suicide" that allows the enduring legacy of Stammheim to be so malleable had long been established in Meinhof's journalism, RAF texts, and prison writings by the time she was found dead.

In the wake of the prison deaths, the Stammheim myth became a fundamental part of the RAF identity. It remained an integral and irreproachable part of the group's worldview, and the anger it inspired helped bind the second and third generations.[10] It was not until German reunification that the Stammheim myth was undermined internally. Former RAF members, who had found haven in the former German Democratic Republic and were arrested soon after the demise of the East German state, openly questioned the murder theory and confirmed a suicide plan. The logic of martyrdom was so central to the group that members attempted to reactivate it internally with the 1993 death of Wolfgang Grams. While the idea of state-sanctioned murder as an effective internal narrative had been sabotaged, the Stammheim deaths nonetheless remained the standard for RAF victimhood in popular culture. As the epitome of RAF suffering, the Stammheim myth endured the fall of the Berlin Wall, the de-escalation of 1992, and even the group's own dissolution.[11]

What remained of the RAF in 1998 consigned the group to history: "Almost twenty-eight years ago, on May 14, 1970, the RAF was born in a liberation operation: today, we end this project."[12] The ground had shifted under the group and historical circumstances had marched by it. Much of what persisted into the new century was conspiracy theories and vague victimhood that rested on the logic of the Stammheim myth. These remains have contributed to the making of not only the RAF legend but also the Meinhof legend. Her victim status has proven resilient and is founded on either being driven to suicide or being murdered, which, within the logic of Stammheim, can be the same thing. She has become an icon, routinely venerated as a martyr of the Left.[13] The impact of Meinhof's work and her shaping of her own death has rippled through the decades, and it remains at the core of her own polemical place in German memory.

The importance of Meinhof's voice that Ensslin confirms in her prison letter and the timelessness that she implies can both be found in the performativity of Meinhof's words and deeds. Having lent the group her name, her face, her fame, and then her notoriety, Meinhof used them to make and remake RAF terrorism. She set in place discursive frameworks and strategies that at various times revived and consistently sustained the group. Her work was central to the terrorist identity that bound the group's members, it attracted new support, and it inspired waves of young people to enter the terrorist underground. It had, in short, deadly consequences. The violence of the 1970s is hard to imagine, and the attacks in subsequent decades would have been at least less likely without Meinhof. In her models of victimhood and martyrdom, her influence has also continued into a new century. Despite her insecurities and her behind-the-scenes battle to find her voice, Meinhof engaged in a very public, and often violent, struggle to communicate. She spoke, wrote, and acted with a voice that had resounding consequences and a long echo.

Notes

Preface

1. Ulrike Marie Meinhof, "Offener Brief an Farah Diba," *konkret* 6 (1967), 21–22.
2. Archival sources uncovered in 2009 revealed Kurras's involvement with the East German secret police, the *Stasi*, and his membership in the Socialist Unity Party of Germany (*Sozialistische Einheitspartei Deutschlands*, or SED). There is no suggestion that the shooting was ordered by East Germany, but Kurras's allegiances have proved corrective to the reception of the events of June 2. However, none of this changes the central place Ohnesorg's death holds in the narrative of the APO, the radicalization of the protest scene, and the debate on violence.
3. "Protest gegen die Gleichgültigkeit, mit der die Menschen dem Völkermord in Vietnam zusehen," as cited in Stefan Aust, *Der Baader Meinhof Komplex* (Munich: Wilhelm Goldmann Verlag, 1998), 75.
4. Ulrike Marie Meinhof, "Warenhausbrandstiftung," *konkret* 14 (1968), 5.
5. Ulrike Marie Meinhof, "Vom Protest zum Widerstand," *konkret* 5 (1968), 5.

Introduction

1. Johann Wolfgang von Goethe, *The Sufferings of Young Werther*, trans. Harry Steinhauer (New York: W. W. Norton, 1970), 95–96.
2. "*Leichensache, Eilt sehr!*" "keine tatrelevanten Spuren, Hinweise oder Aufzeichnungen," and "Auf dem Tisch fällt lediglich auf, daß dort u.a. das Buch mit dem Titel 'Philosophische Grammatik' von Ludwig Wittgenstein liegt. Von dem Buch sind die Leseseiten 84/85 aufgeschlagen," Hamburg Institute for Social Research (HIS), File (F) Me,U/016,001. All quoted sections of primary source material in this book have been reproduced as faithfully as possible. The orthography, spelling, grammar, and use of emphasis of the original have been retained, and all translations are the author's own unless otherwise specified. The original German is provided in brackets, for individual words and short phrases, or here in the notes, for longer sections.
3. Wittgenstein's assertion that "*Die Grenzen meiner Sprache* bedeuten die Grenzen meiner Welt" appeared not in *Philospische Grammatik* but in his *Tractatus*, which also appears on RAF reading lists. Sarah Colvin uses the presence of Wittgenstein's work on Meinhof's desk and in the RAF reading lists to underline the centrality of language to the understanding of Meinhof; see Sarah Colvin, *Ulrike Meinhof*

and West German Terrorism: Language, Violence, and Identity (New York: Camden House, 2009), 2–4.

4. See Andreas Musolff, *Krieg gegen die Öffentlichkeit. Terrorismus und politischer Sprachgebrauch* (Opladen: Westdeutscher Verlag, 1996), 9; and Mark Juergensmeyer, *Terror in the Mind of God: The Global Rise of Religious Violence* (London: University of California Press, 2000), 124. This assumption also underpins work in anthropology on violence as ritual, performance, and performative; see, for example, Anton Blok, "The Enigma of Senseless Violence," in *Meanings of Violence: A Cross Cultural Perspective*, ed. Göran Aijmer and Jon Abbink (New York: Berg, 2000), 23–38.

5. In the context of West German terrorism and the RAF, Klaus Weinhauer and Jörg Requate called for the implementation of a model that approaches terrorism as communicative when introducing their 2006 edited collection; see Klaus Weinhauer and Jörg Requate, "Einleitung: Die Herausforderung des 'Linksterrorismus,'" in *Terrorismus in der Bundesrepublik. Medien, Staat und Subkulturen in den 1970er Jahren*, ed. Klaus Weinhauer, Jörg Requate, and Heinz-Gerhard Haupt (Frankfurt am Main: Campus Verlag, 2006), 16. Similarly, in 2008, Nicole Colin, Beatrice De Graaf, Jacco Pekelder, and Joachim Umlauf prefaced their edited collection with a call for an understanding of terrorism as a "social construction that only comes into being via a process of communication between the 'terrorists' and the rest of the society" (*eine soziale Konstruktion, die erst durch einen Kommunikationsprozess zwischen den 'Terroristen' und dem Rest der Gesellschaft entsteht*); see Nicole Colin et al., "Einleitung: 'Terrorismus' als soziale Konstruktion," in *Der 'Deutsche Herbst' und die RAF in Politik, Medien und Kunst. Nationale und internationale Perspektiven*, ed. Nicole Colin et al. (Bielefeld: Transcript Verlag, 2008), 9.

6. As cited in Uwe Schütte, "Was ist und zu welchem Ende studieren wir den 'Kunst-Terrorismus'? Einige vorläufige Überlegungen zum Verhältnis von Kultur, Gewalt und Politik im 20. Jahrhundert und darüber hinaus," in *Mythos Terrorismus. Vom Deutschen Herbst zum 11. September*, ed. Matteo Galli and Heinz-Peter Preusser (Heidelberg: Universitätsverlag Winter, 2006), 191.

7. In the specific context of the RAF, the idea of terrorism as theater has picked up on not only the group's own sense of theatricality but also the overlap of the artistic avant-garde and the self-proclaimed political avant-garde on the fringes of the West German protest movement; see Arthur J. Sabatini, "Terrorismus und Performance," *Kunstforum International* 117 (1992): 147–50; Sara Hakemi, "'Burn, baby, burn!' Die andere Vorgeschichte der RAF," in *Zur Vorstellung des Terrors: Die RAF*, ed. Klaus Biesenbach (Göttingen: Steidl Verlag, 2005); Sarah Hakemi, "Terrorismus und Avantgarde," in *Die RAF und der linke Terrorismus*, vol. 1, ed. Wolfgang Kraushaar (Hamburg: Hamburger Edition, 2006); Thomas Hecken, *Avantgarde und Terrorismus. Rhetorik der Intensität und Programme der Revolte von den Futuristen bis zur RAF* (Bielefeld: Transcript Verlag, 2006); and Schütte, "Was ist und zu welchem Ende studieren wir den 'Kunst-Terrorismus'?"

8. Brian Jenkins, *International Terrorism: A New Mode of Conflict* (Los Angeles: Crescent Publications, 1975), 4.

9. Peter Waldmann, *Terrorismus. Provokation der Macht* (Hamburg: Murmann Verlag, 2005). Waldmann's book first appeared in 1998. See also Walter Laqueur,

Terrorism (London: Wiendenfeld and Nicolson, 1977); Alex P. Schmid and Janny de Graaf, *Violence as Communication: Insurgent Terrorism and the Western News Media* (London: Sage Publications, 1982); and Gabriel Weimann and Conrad Winn, *The Theatre of Terror: Mass Media and International Terrorism* (New York: Longman, 1994).

10. In his 2006 study of the RAF and West German terrorism, Andreas Elter explicitly adopts Waldmann's model, but not without qualification. Waldmann emphasized the primacy of the symbolic and the communicative, whereas Elter asserts that terrorist violence *can* be a communication strategy, but is often primarily still directed toward killing people; see Andreas Elter, "Die RAF und die Medien. Ein Fallbeispiel für terroristische Kommunikation," in *Die RAF und der linke Terrorismus*, ed. Wolfgang Kraushaar (Hamburg: Hamburger Edition, 2006), 1060.

11. Juergensmeyer, *Terror in the Mind of God*, 121–47.

12. "wörter, begriffe sind aktionen. aktionen sind begriffe," prison text by Ensslin as cited in Pieter Bakker Schut (ed.), *das info: briefe von gefangenen aus der raf aus der diskussion 1973–1977* (Plambeck: Neuer Malik Verlag, 1987), 14.

13. See J. L. Austin, *How to Do Things with Words* (Oxford: Clarendon Press, 1975). Austin first outlined performative utterances in a series of lectures in 1955.

14. Judith Butler, *Bodies That Matter: On the Discursive Limits of "Sex"* (New York: Routledge, 1993), 2.

15. Judith Butler, *Excitable Speech: A Politics of the Performative* (New York: Routledge, 1997), 51–52. Butler earlier outlined her idea of performativity in her important book *Gender Trouble* first published in 1990; see particularly Judith Butler, *Gender Trouble: Feminism and the Subversion of Identity* (New York: Routledge, 2008), 175–93.

16. Beatrice de Graaf and Bob de Graaff, for example, draw on Austin and Butler to write of the performativity of counterterrorism and the role of discourses of terrorism in creating the reality of terrorism; see Beatrice de Graaf and Bob de Graaff, "Bringing Politics Back In: The Introduction of the 'Performative Power' of Counterterrorism," *Critical Studies on Terrorism* 3(2) (2010): 267. The "linguistic turn" is a disciplinary focus on language as active in the construction of reality and our understanding of reality. From the 1970s, this shift worked its way from philosophy and linguistics, via the traditions of structuralism and poststructuralism, to the humanities more generally, including the writing of history. For more, see Michael Roberts, "Postmodernism and the Linguistic Turn," in *Making History: An introduction to the History and Practices of a Discipline*, ed. Peter Lambert and Phillipp Schofield (New York: Routledge, 2004).

17. Laqueur summarizes many of the historical difficulties in trying to define terrorism in *No End to War: Terrorism in the Twenty-First Century* (New York: Continuum, 2003), 232–38.

18. Andrea Musolff, "Bürgerkriegs-Szenarios und ihre Folgen. Die Terrorismusdebatte in der Bundesrepublik 1970–1993," in *Die RAF und der linke Terrorismus*, ed. Wolfgang Kraushaar (Hamburg: Hamburger Edition, 2006), 1183. Musolff's position is outlined in detail in his book *Krieg gegen die Öffentlichkeit* and the article "Terrorismus im öffentlichen Diskurs der BRD: Seine Deutung als Kriegsgeschehen und die Folgen," in *Terrorismus in der Bundesrepublik. Medien, Staat und*

Subkulturen in den 1970er Jahren, ed. Klaus Weinhauer, Jörg Requate, and Heinz-Gerhard Haupt (Frankfurt: Campus Verlag, 2006), 302–19.

19. Colvin, *Ulrike Meinhof and West German Terrorism*. For another dedicated linguistic study of the RAF, see Olaf Gätje, *Der Gruppenstil der RAF im 'Info'-System. Eine soziostilistische Untersuchung aus systematischer Perspektive* (Berlin: Walter de Gruyter, 2008). Gätje's sociolinguistic study of the RAF's prison communication network, the *info*, uses the idea of "style" as a medium by which a meaning based in communicative convention is transmitted.

20. Klaus Weinhauer and Jörg Requate, "Einleitung: Die Herausforderung des 'Linksterrorismus,'" 9, and Wolfgang Kraushaar, "Mythos RAF. Im Spannungsfeld von terroristischer Herausforderung und populistischer Bedrohungsphantasie," in *Die RAF und der linke Terrorismus*, ed. Wolfgang Kraushaar (Hamburg: Hamburger Edition, 2006), 1206.

21. Kraushaar, "Mythos RAF," 1208–9.

22. Rolf Sachsse, "Pentagramm hinter deutscher Maschinenpistole unter Russisch Brot. Zur Semiosphäre der Erinnerung an die Rote Armee Fraktion," in *Der "Deutsche Herbst" und die RAF in Politik, Medien und Kunst. Nationale und internationale Perspektiven*, ed. Nicole Colin et al. (Bielefeld: Transcript Verlag, 2008), 132.

23. Heinz-Peter Preußer, "Warum *Mythos* Terrorismus? Versuch einer Begriffsklärung," in *Mythos Terrorismus. Vom Deutschen Herbst zum 11. September*, ed. Matteo Galli and Heinz-Peter Preußer (Heidelberg: Universitätsverlag Winter, 2006), 70.

24. Susan Sontag, *On Photography* (New York: Anchor Books, 1990), 167, and *Regarding the Pain of Others* (New York: Picador, 2004), 88–89. For more on the evolution of the visual narrative in the historiography of the RAF, see Leith Passmore, "Another New Illustrated History: The Visual Turns in the Memory of West German Terrorism," *EDGE* 1(1) (2009), under "Article 2."

25. Sontag, *Regarding the Pain of Others*, 85–86.

26. Sontag writes of photography reviving a "primitive" sense of images as extensions of real things, as "physically distinct, manifestations of the same energy or spirit"; see Sontag, *On Photography*, 155–58. Roland Barthes also notes this relationship to the real as the unique quality of the photographic image, that "every photograph is somehow co-natural [co-substantial in Sontag's analysis] with its referent"; see Roland Barthes, *Camera Lucida* (New York: Hill and Wang, 1981), 76–77.

27. This link became established wisdom by the mid-1980s; see Susan L. Carruthers, *The Media at War: Communication and Conflict in the Twentieth Century* (London: MacMillan, 2000), 168–69.

28. For comments about filmic language of the attacks of September 2001, see Begoña Aretxaga, "Terror as a Thrill: First Thoughts on the 'War on Terrorism,'" *Anthropological Quarterly* 75(1) (2001): 140; and *Performance Studies: An Introduction*, ed. Richard Schechner (New York: Routledge, 2002), 265–69. In the context of their use of imagery, Bernd Weisbrod describes 1970s terrorists as the "first media-savvy militants"; see Bernd Weisbrod, "Terrorism as Performance: The Assassinations of Walther Rathenau and Hanns-Martin Schleyer," in *Control of Violence: Historical and International Perspectives on Violence in Modern Societies*, ed. Wilhelm Heitmeyer et al. (New York: Springer, 2011), 376.

29. "Kommunikation mit den Linken [lief] immer noch über das Wort" and "Die Macht der Bilder haben wir nie wirklich zu nutzen versucht," as cited in Petra Terhoeven, "Opferbilder—Täterbilder. Die Fotographie als Medium linksterroristischer Selbstermächtigung in Deutschland und Italien während der 70er Jahre", *Geschichte in Wissenschaft und Unterricht* 58(7/8) (2007): 390.

30. Terhoeven champions bringing the pictorial turn to the study of left-wing West German terrorism; see Terhoeven, "Opferbilder—Täterbilder," 380. For detail on the "pictorial turn," or "iconic" or "visual turn," see W. J. T. Mitchell, *Picture Theory: Essays on Verbal and Visual Representation* (Chicago: University of Chicago Press, 1994), 11–34.

31. Terhoeven, "Opferbilder—Täterbilder," 392–95. For analysis of the ongoing importance of the photos of Meins's dead body, see Carrie Collenberg, "Dead Holger," in *Baader-Meinhof Returns: History and Cultural Memory of German Left-Wing Terrorism*, ed. Gerrit-Jan Berendse and Ingo Cornils (New York: Rodopi, 2008), 65–81.

32. Martin Steinseifer, "Terrorismus als Medienereignis im Herbst 1977: Strategien, Dynamiken, Darstellungen, Deutungen," in *Terrorismus in der Bundesrepublik. Medien, Staat und Subkulturen in den 1970er Jahren*, ed. Klaus Weinhauer, Jörg Requate and Heinz-Gerhard Haupt (Frankfurt: Campus, 2006), 376. See also Martin Steinseifer, "'Fotos wie Brandwunden'?—Überlegungen zur deontischen Bedeutung von Pressefotografien am Beispiel von Hanns Martin Schleyer als Opfer der Roten Armee Fraktion," in *Brisante Semantik. Neuere Konzepte und Froschungsergebnisse einer kulturwissenschaftlichen Linguistik*, ed. Dietrich Busse, Thomas Niehr, and Thomas Wengeler (Tübingen: Max Niemeyer Verlag, 2005), 269–90.

33. Weisbrod, "Terrorism as Performance," 377.

34. Ibid., 366–67.

35. Ibid., 386.

36. Allen Feldman, *Formations of Violence: The Narrative of the Body and Political Terror in Northern Ireland* (Chicago: University of Chicago Press, 1991), 1–27. Feldman's work is representative of a body of mainly anthological work that has developed an approach to violence—not simply terrorist violence—as ritualistic and performative; see Blok, "The Enigma of Senseless Violence" and Göran Aijmer, "The Idiom of Violence in Imagery and Discourse," in *Meanings of Violence: A Cross Cultural Perspective*, ed. Göran Aijmer and Jon Abbink (New York: Berg, 2000), 1–21; and Joel Rhodes, *The Voice of Violence: Performative Violence as Protest in the Vietnam Era* (Praeger, Westport: 2001).

37. Juergensmeyer, *Terror in the Mind of God*, 125.

38. Wilfried Rasch cites the incomprehensibility, even "absurdity," of German terrorism—at first sight—as being behind the assumption that "psychological and psychopathological conditions of the offenders" were at the heart of the violence; see Wilfried Rasch, "Psychological Dimensions of Political Terrorism in the Federal Republic of Germany," *International Journal of Law and Psychiatry* 2 (1979): 79.

39. As cited in Bettina Röhl, "Warum ging Ulrike Meinhof in den Untergrund? Das Hirn der RAF," *Rheinische Post*, November 9, 2002.

132 • Notes

40. Colvin, *Ulrike Meinhof and West German Terrorism*, 189–90; and Sarah Colvin, "Ulrike Meinhof as Woman and Terrorist: Cultural Discourses of Violence and Virtue," in *Baader-Meinhof Returns. History and Cultural Memory of German Left-Wing Terrorism*, ed. Gerrit-Jan Berendse and Ingo Cornils (New York: Rodopi, 2008), 84–85.

41. Gerhard Schmidtchen, "Terroristische Karrieren," in *Lebenslaufanalysen*, ed. Herbert Jäger, Gerhard Schmidtchen, and Lieselotte Süllwold (Opladen: Westdeuscher Verlag, 1981), 29–31 and 66; and Iring Fetscher, Herfried Münkler, and Hannelore Ludwig, "Ideologien der Terroristen in der Bundesrepublik Deutschland," in *Analysen zum Terrorismus. Ideologien und Strategien*, ed. Federal Ministry of the Interior (Opladen: Westdeutscher Verlag, 1981), 58.

42. The author of one particular study concedes in his own introduction that such efforts lack any great explanatory significance; see Schmidtchen, "Terroristische Karrieren," 15.

43. Rasch, "Psychological Dimensions of Political Terrorism," 80. Ken Heskin reached similar conclusions in his work on sectarian violence in Ireland; see Ken Heskin, "The Psychology of Terrorism in Ireland," in *Terrorism in Ireland*, ed. Yonah Alexander and Alan O'Day (New York: St. Martin's Press, 1984), 88–105.

44. Jeff Victoroff, "The Mind of the Terrorist: A Review and Critique of Psychological Approaches," *Journal of Conflict Resolution* 49(1) (2005): 31; Arie W. Kruglanski and Shira Fishman, "The Psychology of Terrorism: 'Syndrome' Versus 'Tool' Perspectives," *Terrorism and Political Violence* 18 (2006): 194. For an overview of work from the 1960s to 1980s based on the assumption of abnormality that is couched in a revival of such theories in the aftermath of the attacks in New York, see Charles L. Ruby, "Are Terrorists Mentally Deranged?," *Analyses of Social Issues and Public Policy* 2(1) (2002): 16–18. Similarly, in 2005, John Horgan argued for both the "normality" assumption and a place for psychology in a broader interdisciplinary approach to terrorism while lamenting what he sees as the reemergence of the 1970s notion of "abnormality" in terrorism research since September 11, 2001; see John Horgan, *The Psychology of Terrorism* (New York: Routledge, 2005), 65–78.

45. Studies in the 1980s noted Meinhof's Protestant upbringing as contributing to an intransigent terrorist morality, but stopped short of arguing for a direct causal link to terrorism; see Fetscher, Münkler, and Ludwig, "Ideologien der Terroristen," 58; and Günter Rohrmoser and Jörg Fröhlich, "Ideologische Ursachen des Terrorismus," in *Analysen zum Terrorismus. Ideologien and Strategien*, ed. Federal Ministry of the Interior (Opladen: Westdeutscher Verlag, 1981), 315. More recently, however, Jörg Herrmann presented both Ensslin's and Meinhof's Protestantism as at least a causal cofactor in their respective radicalizations; see Jörg Herrmann, "Ulrike Meinhof und Gudrun Ensslin—Vom Protestantismus zum Terrorismus," in *Zur Vorstellung des Terrors: Die RAF*, ed. Klaus Biesenbach (Göttingen: Steidl Verlag, 2005), 113; and Hermann, "'Unsere Söhne und Töchter.' Protestantismus und RAF-Terrorismus in den 1970er Jahren," in *Die RAF und der linke Terrorismus*, ed. Wolfgang Kraushaar (Hamburg: Hamburger Edition, 2006), 651–52.

46. Sarah Colvin traces the narrative of virtue and saintliness in the telling of the Meinhof story; see Sarah Colvin, "Witch, Amazon, or Joan of Arc? Ulrike Meinhof's

Defenders, or How to Legitimize a Violent Woman," in *Women and Death 2: War-like Women in the German Literary and Cultural Imagination Since 1500*, ed. Sarah Colvin and Helen Watanabe-O'Kelly (New York: Camden House, 2009), 251–57; and Colvin, "Ulrike Meinhof as Woman and Terrorist," 95–96. For major biographical accounts, see Mario Krebs, *Ulrike Meinhof. Ein Leben im Widerspruch* (Reinbeck bei Hamburg: Rowohlt Taschenbuch Verlag, 1988); Stefan Aust, *Der Baader Meinhof Komplex* (Munich: Wilhelm Goldmann Verlag, 1998); and Alois Prinz, *Lieber wütend als traurig. Die Lebensgeschichte der Ulrike Meinhof* (Berlin: Suhrkamp, 2005).

47. Colvin, "Witch, Amazon, or Joan of Arc?" 251.
48. Ibid., 251; and Colvin, "Ulrike Meinhof as Woman and Terrorist," 95.
49. Colvin, "Witch, Amazon, or Joan of Arc?" 255.
50. Krebs, *Ulrike Meinhof*, 16; Aust, *Der Baader Meinhof Komplex*, 31–35; and Prinz, *Lieber wütend als traurig*, 28.
51. Bettina Röhl's colossal work presents a biographical account of her parents, Klaus Rainer Röhl and Ulrike Meinhof, during the 1960s. Röhl uncovers their links to the East German regime and its financial support for the magazine *konkret*. She is also particularly scathing of her mother's cold-blooded and flippant instrumentalization of issues such as the emergency laws, the Eichmann trial, and the Holocaust as catalysts for attacks against the West German government; see Bettina Röhl, *So macht Kommunismus Spaß. Ulrike Meinhof, Klaus Rainer Röhl und die Akte KONKRET* (Hamburg: Europäische Verlagsanstalt, 2006). Kristin Wesemann seeks a more scientific approach to outline Meinhof's political beliefs, including her committed communism; see Kristin Wesemann, *Ulrike Meinhof. Kommunistin, Journalistin, Terroristin—eine politische Biographie* (Baden-Baden: Nomos, 2007). Jutta Ditfurth does not employ the gendered narratives of previous accounts, but her work is nonetheless an attempt to rehabilitate the terrorist as she lays blame for Meinhof's evolution with West German society, not Meinhof herself; see Jutta Ditfurth, *Ulrike Meinhof. Die Biographie* (Berlin: Ullstein, 2007). Preece presents these biographies as part of what he calls the "biographical turn" in RAF history. This turn refers to the spike in biographies in the mid-2000s, particularly around the thirtieth anniversary of the German Autumn, that dealt with figures associated with the RAF in some way; see Julian Preece, "The Lives of the RAF Revisited: The Biographical Turn," *Memory Studies* 3(2) (2010): 151–63.
52. Röhl, *So macht Kommunismus Spaß*, 135–36. Ditfurth also confirms Riemeck's Nazi past, undermining the familial background of resistance; see Ditfurth, *Ulrike Meinhof*, 35.
53. For detailed accounts of the gendered narratives of West German terrorism as a stubborn reactivation of nineteenth-century criminology, see Colvin, *Ulrike Meinhof and West German Terrorism*, 189–99; Colvin, "Witch, Amazon, or Joan of Arc?" 257–61; and Colvin, "Ulrike Meinhof as Woman and Terrorist," 86–92. The understanding of the female suicide bomber in the West after September 11, 2001, has similarly relied heavily on gendered stereotypes. In contrast to her male counterpart, the female suicide bomber is assumed to be emotional, irrational, perhaps hormonal, or somehow masculine or unfeminine, and her motivations are assumed to be personal or domestic rather than ideological; see Terri Toles

Patkin, "Explosive Baggage: Female Palestinian Suicide Bombers and the Rhetoric of Emotion," *Women and Language* 27(2) (2004): 79–88; Dan Berkowitz, "Suicide Bombers as Women Warriors: Making News through Mythical Archetypes," *Journalism and Mass Communication Quarterly* 82(3) (2005): 607–22; Brigitte L. Nacos, "The Portrayal of Female Terrorists in the Media: Similar Framing Patterns in the News Coverage of Women in Politics and in Terrorism," *Studies in Conflict & Terrorism* 28 (2005): 435–51; and Cindy D. Ness, "In the Name of the Cause: Women's Work in Secular and Religious Terrorism," *Studies in Conflict & Terrorism* 28 (2005): 353–73.

54. As cited in Colvin, *Ulrike Meinhof and West German Terrorism*, 195.

55. Ensslin is described as more manly than the male RAF members in *Der Baader Meinhof Report. Dokumente—Analysen—Zusammenhänge. Aus den Akten des Bundeskriminalamtes, der "Sonderkommission, Bonn" und dem Bundesamt für Verfassungsschutz* (Mainz: v. Hase & Koehler Verlag, 1972), 34. Also cited in Colvin, *Ulrike Meinhof and West German Terrorism*, 191.

56. Female homosexuality and bisexuality have been noted as associative and causal factors behind women entering the terrorist underground; see Herbert Jäger, Gerhard Schmidtchen, and Lieselotte Süllwold (ed.), *Lebenslaufanalysen* (Opladen: Westdeutscher Verlag, 1981), 107. The *Baader Meinhof Report* wrote of "pastor's daughter" (*Pfarrerstochter*) Ensslin's first kiss and that she was still a virgin at 22. One page later Ensslin is "long since no 'pastor's daughter' anymore" (*schon lange kein "Pfarrerstochter" mehr*), as the report describes her threesomes with her first lover. In contrast to Ensslin, Meinhof "messed around" (*gab sich . . . ab*) from a very early age, despite not having the "strong sexual appeal that Ensslin undoubtedly possessed" (*starke sexuelle Ausstrahlung wie die letztere sie ganz fraglos besitzt*); see *Der Baader Meinhof Report*, 33–34.

57. Clare Bielby, "Remembering the Red Army Faction," *Memory Studies* 3(2), 2010: 141–42. Bielby argues that many of the gendered narratives of West German terrorism were still in place thirty years later.

58. Preece argues that the incident has been used to condemn Meinhof, or simply ignored by her rehabilitators; see Preece, "The Lives of the RAF Revisited," 157.

59. Colvin, "Ulrike Meinhof as Woman and Terrorist," 96; and Colvin, "Witch, Amazon, or Joan of Arc?" 259.

Chapter 1

1. "mann—war das finster—ich KONNTE nich schreiben—nich im kopp aber aufm papier war ALLES nur noch müll, hack," see German Federal Archive (GFA), Holding (H) 362, File (F) 3369: XI/20.

2. Colvin writes of Meinhof's battle with language in her final prison years, see Sarah Colvin, *Ulrike Meinhof and West German Terrorism: Language, Violence, and Identity* (New York: Camden House, 2009), 165–72; and Colvin, "'Wenn deine Identität Kampf ist': violence, gendered language and identity in the writing of Ulrike Marie Meinhof," in *Violence, Culture and Identity: Essays on German and Austrian Literature, Politics and Society*, ed. Helen Chambers (Bern: Peter Lang, 2006).

3. The magazine *konkret* was originally called the *Studentenkurier*. For detailed accounts of Meinhof's introduction to *konkret* as well as the magazine's East German financiers, see Bettina Röhl, *So macht Kommunismus Spaß. Ulrike Meinhof, Klaus Rainer Röhl und die Akte KONKRET* (Hamburg: Europäische Verlagsanstalt, 2006); Jutta Ditfurth, *Ulrike Meinhof. Die Biographie* (Berlin: Ullstein, 2007); and Kristin Wesemann, *Ulrike Meinhof. Kommunistin, Journalistin, Terroristin—eine politische Biographie* (Baden-Baden: Nomos, 2007).

4. Klaus Rainer Röhl as cited in Wesemann, *Ulrike Meinhof*, 144.

5. Röhl, *So macht Kommunismus Spaß*, 252.

6. Wesemann, *Ulrike Meinhof*, 158–59.

7. "[a]uch der Artikel 48 WRV setzte Grundrechte außer Kraft," see Ulrike Marie Meinhof, "Notstand? Notstand!" *konkret* 18 (1960): 1.

8. "Deutschland 1960—jeder Dritte vergleicht es mit dem Deutschland von 1933," see ibid.

9. "Wie wir unsere Eltern nach Hitler fragen, so werden wir eines Tages nach Herrn Strauß gefragt werden," see Ulrike Marie Meinhof, "Hitler in Euch," *konkret* 10 (1961): 8.

10. For the article, see Ulrike Marie Meinhof, "Ein Mann mit guten Manieren. Ein Tag Karl-Wolff-Prozess," *konkret* 9 (1964).

11. See Robert Neumann, "Ein Lübke zuviel?" *konkret* 7 (1966): 15–21 and "Baute Lübke KZs?" *konkret* 12 (1966):14–15.

12. Röhl, *So macht Kommunismus Spaß*, 493.

13. For work on state-run homes for delinquent girls, see, for example, the radio features *Ausgestossen oder aufgehoben: Heimkinder in der Bundesrepublik* (Abendstudio, 1965), *Guxhagen—Mädchen in Fürsorgeerziehung. Ein Heim in Essen* (Abendstudio, 1969), and *Bambule: Fürsorgeerziehung aus der Sicht von drei ehemaligen Berliner Heimmädchen* (Abendstudio, 1969), as well as articles such as "Flucht aus dem Mädchenheim," *konkret* 9 (1966): 18–23. For work on workers, see, for example, "Kranker Mann, was nun?" *konkret* 7 (1963): 7–9, and the radio feature *Gefahr vom Fließband: Arbeitsunfälle, beobachtet und kritisch beschrieben* (Abendstudio, 1965). For work on foreign workers, see, for example, a television reportage for *Panorama* on guest workers produced in October 1965 and the column "Kuli oder Kollege. Gastarbeiter in Deutschland," *konkret* 11 (1966): 22–27. For work on women, see, for example, "Frauenkram," *konkret* 7 (1968): 24–27, 52. For work on women workers, see the radio features *Frauen sind billiger: Ein Bericht über Frauenarbeit in der Bundesrepublik* (Abendstudio, 1967) and *Halb Weib—halb Mensch: Ein Diskussionsbeitrag zur Situation der Frau zwischen Familie und Erwerbstätigkeit* (Abendstudio, 1967). For work on the poor, see, for example, "Früchte der Knappheit," *konkret* 8 (1963): 13–15; "Doof—weil arm. Hilfsschulkinder," *konkret* 5 (1969): 38–42; and "Doof—weil arm. Hilfsschulkinder, 2. Teil," *konkret* 6 (1969): 34–37.

14. "Erst wenn über die Landesgrenzen hinaus eine Sache zum Skandal geworden ist, wenn es um das Ansehen der Bundesrepublik im befreundeten Ausland geht, gewinnen Opfer und Gegner des Faschismus politisches Terrain," see Ulrike Marie Meinhof, "Zum neuen Jahr," *konkret* 1 (1963): 4.

15. "die zurückgebliebene Körpergestalt des Oskar [ist] ein Symbol für die Situation des avantgardistischen Schriftstellers in der kapitalistischen Gesellschaft— damit scheint gemeint: allseitig beengt, unfähig sich auszuwachsen, abgedrängt in Bereiche der Skurrilität und Perversion," as cited in Röhl, *So macht Kommunismus Spaß*, 318.

16. Jürgen Seifert said of Meinhof in her early days as chief editor of *konkret* that "she wanted to have an effect, really have an effect" (*sie wollte wirken, unbedingt wirken*), and Renate Riemeck recalls Meinhof as having the impression that *konkret* was "a platform from which she could have an effect" (*eine Plattform, auf der sie wirken konnte*); see Röhl, *So macht Kommunismus Spaß*, 329–30. In addition, director Eberhard Itzenplitz recalls that during their work together on her film *Bambule*, Meinhof "understood very quickly that effect is the final and only criterion in all dramatic arts" (*begriff sehr bald, daß Wirkung das letzte und einzige Kriterium aller szenischen Künste ist*); see Eberhard Itzenplitz, "Über die Filmarbeit mit Ulrike Meinhof," in *Bambule. Fürsorge—Sorge für wen?* (Berlin: Verlag Klaus Wagenbach, 2002), 114.

17. "was das Ding erstmal einbringen muss: / 1. Information über Basisorganisationen und zwar über alle, die veröffentlichen: Zeitungen, theor. Organe, Programmdiskussion, Flugblätter . . . / 2. Presseauswertung (zentral in diesem Büro und über *ein* Ausschnittsbüro) die Stichworte etwa RAF, Polizeiorganisation, BGS, Organisation, Antiterror, Geheimdienste, Guerilla - kommt aber noch mehr - Groenewold finanziert das u. in seinem Büro wird das brauchbare Zeug rausgesucht . . . und vervielfältigt von da an die Anwaltsbüros zu den Gefangenen," see GFA, H 362, F 3132.

18. "Zellendurchsuchung 16.7.73" in GFA, H 362, F 3369: VII/1a.

19. "Politische Impulse, wie sie von den Studenten am Beispiel des Schah-Besuches ausgingen, am Beispiel der Berliner Gegenuniversität, der Vietnamdemonstrationen, der Proteste gegen die Polizei und den Berliner Bürgermeister Albertz, wie sie vom Kongreß *Notstand der Demokratie* ausgingen und von den Notstandsbeschlüssen des Deutschen Gewerkschaftsbundes, erreichen bereits heute nur noch einen kleinen Teil der Öffentlichkeit, einen Ausschnitt der Bevölkerung, haben nur kleine Chancen überhaupt zur Kenntnis genommen zu werden, zur Diskussion gestellt zu werden," see Ulrike Marie Meinhof, "Enteignet Springer!" *konkret* 9 (1967): 2–3.

20. "zielt freilich auf einen Demokratiebegriff, den Augstein nicht im Sinn und Springer nicht im BILD hat: Er zielt darauf, Meinungs- und Pressefreiheit statt Manipulation der öffentlichen Meinung zur Aufhebung der Manipulation zu benutzen; statt Informationen zu lenken und zu blockieren, Informationen zu verbreiten; statt politische Meinung einzupeitschen, kritisches Bewußtsein auszubilden; statt das Volk einzuschläfern, es aufzuwecken; statt es sich verblöden und 'rekeln' zu lassen, es zu emanzipieren," see Meinhof, "Enteignet Springer!" 3.

21. Wolfgang Kraushaar, "Kleinkrieg gegen einen Großverleger. Von der Anti-Springer-Kampagne der APO zu den Brand- und Bombenanschlägen der RAF," in *Die RAF und der linke Terrorismus*, ed. Wolfgang Kraushaar (Hamburg: Hamburger Edition, 2006), 1081–82.

22. Max Horkheimer and Theodor W. Adorno, "The Culture Industry: Enlightenment as Mass Deception," in *The Dialectic of Enlightenment: Philosophical Fragments*, ed. Gunzelin Schmid Noerr, trans. Edmund Jephcott (Stanford: Stanford University Press, 2002), 95–96, 125–26.

23. The philosophical prerequisite for Enzensberger was, as it was for Adorno, the Enlightenment; see Hans Magnus Enzensberger, *Bewußtseins-Industrie* (Frankfurt am Main: Suhrkamp Verlag, 1962), 10–14.

24. Ulrike Marie Meinhof, "Springer-Fernsehen." *konkret* 4 (1965): 3.

25. Matteo Galli, " 'Mit dem Einkaufswagen durch den Geschichts-Supermarkt'? Zu einigen Bestandteilen des so genannten Mythos RAF in den Künsten: Entstehung, Entwicklung und Neukontextualisierung," in *Mythos Terrorismus. Vom Deutschen Herbst zum 11. September*, ed. Matteo Galli and Heinz-Peter Preusser (Heidelberg: Universitätsverlag Winter, 2006), 102. Though the original has disappeared, a remake was produced in 2000 with two important changes: the packet of matches that were to light the Molotov cocktail and that originally lay on Regis Debray's *Revolution in the Revolution?* (1967) now lay on Naomi Klein's *No Logo!* (2001), and the *Springerhaus* of 1968 was replaced with a Nike store; see Gerd Conradt, "Nicht oder Sein—Ikonen der Zeitgeschichte," in *Zur Vorstellung des Terrors: Die RAF*, ed. Klaus Biesenbach (Göttingen: Steidl Verlag, 2005), 132.

26. Peter Schneider, "BILD macht dumm," *konkret* 3 (1968): 15; and Kraushaar, "Kleinkrieg gegen einen Großverleger," 1088.

27. Ensslin tried to distance the RAF from this attack during her trial by testifying the plan was Meinhof's and that the rest of the group knew nothing of it. This shook Meinhof, who did not return to the courtroom before she was found dead in her cell five days later. However, Gerhard Müller testified that while it was Meinhof's idea, she had sought and received the consent of Baader, Ensslin, Raspe, and Meins; see Kraushaar, "Kleinkrieg gegen einen Großverleger," 1105.

28. "daß seine Zeitungen die antikommunistische Hetze gegen die Neue Linke, gegen solidarische Aktionen der Arbeiterklasse wie Streiks, gegen die kommunistischen Parteien hier und in anderen Ländern einstellen; daß der Springerkonzern die Hetze gegen die Befreiungsbewegungen in der Dritten Welt einstellt, besonders gegen die arabischen Völker, die für die Befreiung Palästinas kämpfen; daß er seine propagandistische und materielle Unterstützung für den Zionismus—die imperialistische Politik der herrschenden Klasse Israels einstellt; daß die Springerpresse aufhört, über die ausländischen Arbeiter hier rassistische Lügenberichte zu verbreiten," see RAF, "Sprengstoffanschlag auf das Springer-Hochhaus in Hamburg," in *Rote Armee Fraktion. Texte und Materialien zur Geschichte der RAF*, ed. ID-Verlag (Berlin: ID-Verlag, 1997), 147.

29. See order in Hamburg Institute for Social Research (HIS), File (F) Me,U/012,006.

30. Diederichs's *Konzentration in den Massenmedien* was an empirical study of media concentration that offered a statistical overview of the Federal Republic's media landscape. The stated goal of the book was to produce a comprehensive resource with a set of comparable criteria for the diagnosis of concentration in the production side of the mass media. In his review of the literature, Diederichs noted Adorno and Horkheimer's notion of the "culture industry" and Enzensberger's "consciousness industry" as pillars, among others, of the theory. He also noted their

particular importance to the student movement and the anti-Springer campaign of the late 1960s, but the work as a whole deliberately steered away from any conclusion on political implications of the statistical results. Diederichs wrote of "monopoly" as overreaching the description of the current situation, he undercut terms such as "monologization" (*Monologisierung*) and "monotonization" (*Monotonisierung*), and described talk of "opinion-manipulation" (*Meinungs-manipulation*) as vague and sweeping. See Helmut H. Diederichs, *Konzentration in den Massenmedien: systematischer Überblick zur Situation in der BRD* (Munich: C. Hanser, 1973).

31. Müller's *Der Springer-Konzern* relied heavily on Habermas to address the "apparatusization" (*Apparatisierung*) of the public sphere and the role of journalists in that process. Müller argued that industrial societies require large apparatuses in the realm of communication to allow themselves to be understood. He addressed the concentration of the press when questioning how public opinion can be freely formed when these apparatuses are controlled by only a few. See Hans Dieter Müller, *Der Springer-Konzern: eine kritische Studie* (Munich: R. Piper & Co., 1968).

32. See order in GFA, H 362, F 3170.

33. In his *Kommunikationssoziologie*, Holzer worked within a framework that relied heavily on Adorno and Horkheimer's notion of the "culture industry," and asked whether, in the face of an increasing tendency toward oligopolization and monopolization in the capitalist economy, industrial freedoms were at all reconcilable with journalistic freedoms, and whether the idea of an informed citizen must remain a fiction because "informed democracy" and the capitalist production of information (that is, its dependence on income from advertising) were mutually exclusive. See Horst Holzer, *Kommunikationssoziologie* (Reinbeck bei Hamburg: Rowohlt, 1973).

34. Hund's introduction to *Kommunikationstopologie* was relatively cautionary and warned against what he argued was an unbalanced perspective espoused by Enzensberger as well as Adorno and Horkheimer. These critiques, Hund wrote, focused too heavily on the economic characteristics of the production of mass communication at the expense of the characteristics of its content. An overemphasis on the determination of form (over content), argued Hund, led to a misjudgment of the role of technical advances and, at its most pessimistic (Hund cited Adorno and Horkheimer as an example here), a rejection of processes of mass communication altogether. See Wulf D. Hund, ed., *Kommunikationstopologie: exemplarische Figuren gesellschaftlicher Nachrichtenvermittlung* (Frankfurt am Main: Europäische Verlagsanstalt, 1973).

35. Schmidt and Becker's *Reaktionen auf politische Vorgänge* was part of a series coedited by Adorno. It presented the results of surveys prepared and conducted by the Institute for Social Research (*Institut für Sozialforschung*) in Frankfurt am Main to gauge public opinion in the wake of the Eichmann trial, the *Spiegel* affair, and the metal workers' strike in Baden-Württemberg. Schmidt and Becker conceive of the mass media as holding and protecting a monopoly over public opinion in what is a framework based in Adorno's analysis. See Regina Schmidt and Egon Becker, *Reaktionen auf politische Vorgänge. Drei Meinungsstudien aus der Bundesrepublik* (Frankfurt am Main: Europäische Verlagsanstalt, 1967).

36. The order is cited in Andreas Elter, "Die RAF und die Medien. Ein Fallbeispiel für terroristische Kommunikation," in *Die RAF und der linke Terrorismus*, ed. Wolfgang Kraushaar (Hamburg: Hamburger Edition, 2006), 1069.
37. An *info* to Baader and Ensslin in HIS, F Me,U/008,001.
38. Ulrike Marie Meinhof, "Zum Kanzlerwechsel. Adenauer und die Volksmeinung," *konkret* 11 (1963): 8.
39. The letter in held in HIS, F SO 09/006,003.
40. See *infos* in HIS, F RA 02/005,005.
41. Ditfurth writes of Meinhof writing a number of essays in Riemeck's name and style when her foster mother was overwhelmed with work; see Ditfurth, *Ulrike Meinhof*, 161.
42. Holtkamp wrote an article in the style of the *Bild*, while Meinhof wrote one as Marion Gräfin von Dönhoff and parodied *Stern* columnist Sibylle; see Jürgen Holtkamp and Ulrike Marie Meinhof, "Ulbricht löst die DDR auf. Eine Presseparodie," *konkret* 12 (1964): 11–17.
43. "Das Konzept, wie Ulrike in Zukunft als Kolumnistin auftritt, mit festem Rahmen und Foto, hatten wir dem *stern* entlehnt, in dem eine gewisse Frau Sibylle sich regelmäßig verbreitete," Klaus Rainer Röhl as cited in Röhl, *So macht Kommunismus Spaß*, 423. Meinhof's picture first appears in issue 5 of 1965; see Ulrike Marie Meinhof, "Die Herausforderung und die Antwort," *konkret* 5 (1964): 5.
44. Jürgen Holtkamp, Ulrike Marie Meinhof, and Klaus Rainer Röhl, "Eine Presseparodie. Political fiction," *konkret* 12 (1966): 18–24.
45. "Wir wollten sie ursprünglich auf den 1. Juni 1968 verlegen, aber die politische Entwicklung, die der Spiegel in den letzten Wochen und Monaten genommen hat, zwang uns, den Termin auf den 1. Juli 67 vorzuverlegen, da sonst Gefahr besteht, daß die Zukunftsvision von der Wirklichkeit überholt wird," see Jürgen Holtkamp, Ulrike Marie Meinhof, and Klaus Rainer Röhl, "Political fiction: 'Spiegel' an Springer verkauft," *konkret* 6 (1967): 48.
46. "Aber auch Gesamtmetall dürfte es nicht entgangen sein, daß die Stunde Mehrarbeit in der Bundesrepublik im Zusammenhang mit den ausländischen Arbeitern diskutiert wird, daß weniger deutscher Fleiß als die Antipathie gegenüber den Ausländern als Bereitschaft zur Mehrarbeit zu Buche geschlagen ist," see Ulrike Marie Meinhof, "Lohnkampf," *konkret* 2 (1966): 2.
47. "Aber das Gericht hat alles Menschenmögliche getan, um zu verhindern, daß die Verhältnisse, die an Jürgen Bartschs Entwicklung Pate gestanden haben, zum Prozeßgegenstand werden," see Ulrike Marie Meinhof, "Jürgen Bartsch und die Gesellschaft," *konkret* 1 (1968): 2.
48. "Die bürgerliche Wohlständigkeit als Wert an sich," "Unschuld des Systems," "Die Ordnung ist in Ordnung, verwirrt sind die andern," and "Engagement, aber anders," see Ulrike Marie Meinhof, "Wasserwerfer—auch gegen Frauen," *konkret* 4 (1968): 38–39.
49. "Waffe einer riesigen Auflage," and "so vertritt er [*Der Spiegel*] die Interessen der Reichen hierzulande, wie der Schah von Persien sie dortzulande vertritt, der Spiegel—'bewusst oder unbewusst'—mit den Mitteln der Verdrehung, Verdrängung, Verwirrung (dafür kann man sich natürlich auch noch andere Worte einfallen lassen), der Schah mit den Mitteln eines Polizeistaates," see Ulrike Marie

Meinhof, "Spiegels Spiegelbilder. Ein sehr offener Brief an Rudolf Augstein," *konkret* 1 (1968): 49, 51. Meinhof had earlier written of the *Spiegel*'s attack on Nirumand's book as a pedantic challenge of dates and percentages that offered only the appearance of a critique; see Ulrike Marie Meinhof, "Der unaufhaltsame Aufstieg des 'Spiegel'—oder Der Fall Nirumand," *konkret* 12 (1967): 26.

50. Meinhof's criticism could be viewed less cynically had she not also worked with emotion, silences, omission, and half-truths in her work. Her columns displayed a deliberate aversion to shades of grey and an often-cynical instrumentalization of highly emotional subject matter. Bettina Röhl in particular is scathing of Meinhof's instrumentalization of issues such as the emergency laws, the Eichmann trial, and the Holocaust in her attacks on the CDU government; see Röhl, *So macht Kommunismus Spaß*, 336, 50–51, and 445, respectively.

51. "Die Untauglichkeit meiner Mittel bringt mich fast um," Meinhof as cited in Joachim Fest, *Begegnungen. Über nahe und ferne Freunde* (Reinbeck bei Hamburg: Rowohlt, 2004), 268.

52. "Gleichstellung von Unterdrückung und dem Protest gegen Unterdrückung," see Ulrike Marie Meinhof, "Gegen-Gewalt," *konkret* 2 (1968): 2.

53. "Sie haben begriffen, daß die feierlichen Formen und die anständige Ordnung nicht schmerzlos und ungebrochen Platz für kritische Inhalte und demokratische Diskussionen einräumt," see Meinhof, "Gegen-Gewalt," 3.

54. "Wir wollen keine Heiligen, wir verlangen nur, daß Widerstand geleistet wird und die Unterwerfung unter die Gesetze des Marktes nicht als freier Journalismus ausgegeben wird und die Kunst, Termine zu halten, nicht mit der Kunst, Wahrheit unter die Leute zu bringen, verwechselt wird, und Redaktionsdemokratie nicht Sand im Getriebe ist und Kolumnismusfreiheit als das erkannt wird, was sie ist: Ein Prestige-, ein Profitfaktor, ein Leserbetrug, ein Selbstbetrug, Personenkult," see Ulrike Marie Meinhof, "Kolumnismus," *konkret* 2 (1969): 2.

55. "Kolumnisten sind die Neger im State Department, die Frauen in der Bundesregierung, Feigenblatt, Alibi, Ausrede," see Meinhof, "Kolumnismus," 2.

56. Meinhof as cited in Ditfurth, *Ulrike Meinhof*, 252.

57. "Produkt kollektiver Schreibe" and "inhaltlich und formulativ genauer und verbindlicher," see Meinhof as cited in Ditfurth, *Ulrike Meinhof*, 253.

58. Wesemann, *Ulrike Meinhof*, 322.

59. GFA, H 362, F 3164: 83.

60. "Welt der Zeichen und Symbole," see Wesemann, *Ulrike Meinhof*, 325.

61. "Wir wollen keine Hörfunkfeatures herstellen, die für die öffentlichrechtlichen Sendeanstalten geeignet sind, sondern Features, bestimmt für die Agitationsarbeit in den Basisgruppen der Organisationen der Linken," as cited in Wesemann, *Ulrike Meinhof*, 325.

62. "die Lehrveranstaltung diene nicht der Ausbildung von Journalisten, die politisch gegen die Linke arbeiteten; die Ergebnisse dieser Lehrveranstaltung hätten der Agitationsarbeit zu dienen; die Teilnehmer der Lehrveranstaltung hätten Verbindung zur Roten Garde und zum Roten Spartakusbund aufzunehmen," as cited in "FREIE UNIVERSITÄT BERLIN 1948–1973—Hochschule im Umbruch Teil VI: Die ungeliebte Reform (1969–1973)," accessed March 11, 2011, http://fuberlin.tripod.com.

63. GFA, H 362, F 3164.
64. Stefan Aust, *Der Baader Meinhof Komplex* (Munich: Wilhelm Goldmann Verlag, 1998), 48.
65. Ulrike Marie Meinhof, "Napalm und Pudding," *konkret* 5 (1967): 2.
66. "Nicht Napalmbomben auf Frauen, Kinder und Greise abzuwerfen ist demnach kriminell, sondern dagegen zu protestieren," see Meinhof, "Napalm und Pudding," 2. "Was geht mich Vietnam an . . . ich habe Orgasmusschwierigkeiten," Kunzelmann as cited in Ditfurth, *Ulrike Meinhof*, 200–201.
67. "Protest ist, wenn ich sage, das und das paßt mir nicht. Widerstand ist, wenn ich dafür sorge, daß das und das, was mir nicht paßt, nicht länger geschieht. Protest ist, wenn ich sage, ich mache nicht mehr mit. Widerstand ist, wenn ich dafür sorge, daß alle andern auch nicht mehr mitmachen," see Ulrike Marie Meinhof, "Vom Protest zum Widerstand," *konkret* 5 (1968): 5.
68. "Das progressive Moment einer Warenhausbrandstiftung liegt nicht in der Vernichtung der Waren, es liegt in der Kriminalität der Tat, im Gesetzbruch," see Ulrike Marie Meinhof, "Warenhausbrandstiftung," *konkret* 14 (1968): 5. The English translation of the title is taken from Karin Bauer, ed. *Everybody Talks About the Weather . . . We Don't: The Writings of Ulrike Meinhof* (New York: Seven Stories, 2008), 244.
69. "Gegen Brandstiftung im allgemeinen spricht, daß dabei Menschen gefährdet sein könnten, die nicht gefährdet sein sollen," see Meinhof, "Warenhausbrandstiftung," 5.
70. Musolff, for example, sees this article as the point at which rhetorical radicalism was replaced with a "dynamic of increasingly brutal actions" (*Dynamik immer brutalerer Aktionen*). He draws a straight line from Meinhof's analysis of the arson attack to RAF terrorist violence; see Andreas Musolff, *Krieg gegen die Öffentlichkeit. Terrorismus und politischer Sprachgebrauch* (Opladen: Westdeutscher Verlag, 1996), 155. Colvin disagrees, arguing that in this article Meinhof still upheld the differentiation between violence against people and violence against things; see Colvin, *Ulrike Meinhof and West German Terrorism*, 43; and Colvin, " 'Wenn deine Identität Kampf ist,' " 290–91. Despite the perhaps unnecessary relative clause in the article that suggests Meinhof thought there were in fact some people that should be put in danger, there is anecdotal evidence that suggests Meinhof upheld this important distinction in October 1969. Biographer Ditfurth, for example, relates the story of Meinhof learning of a plan to bomb attack, to sabotage, and bring awareness to the construction of warships in West Germany for the Portuguese dictatorship, and her sole concern being whether or not the saboteurs could ensure that no people would be hurt in the attack; see Ditfurth, *Ulrike Meinhof*, 248.
71. " 'Natürlich kann geschossen werden.' Ulrike Meinhof über der Baader-Aktion," *Der Spiegel* 25 (1970): 75.
72. Colvin tracks Meinhof's role in a linguistic justification of violence; see Colvin, *Ulrike Meinhof and West German Terrorism*, 36–45. Despite recognizing the "irony in the enormous volume of words on paper produced by the group around Meinhof" (110) given the group's declared primacy of praxis, she frames the justification

of violence in terms of the logic that "language can be replaced with violence" (106).

73. "einen Mut und eine Kraft dokumentiert," see RAF, "Die Aktion des Schwarzen September in München," in *Rote Armee Fraktion. Texte und Materialien zur Geschichte der RAF*, ed. ID-Verlag (Berlin: ID-Verlag, 1997), 151.

74. "Die Sprache der Guerilla ist die Aktion, ihr werden Sie zuhören," see GFA, H 362, F 3441: 146.

75. "gegen den versuch der staatlichen propaganda, den anschlag im hamburger hauptbahnhof in die nähe der raf zu rücken, stellen wir fest: / die sprache dieser explosion ist die sprache der r e a k t i o n ," see HIS, F RA 02/005,005.

76. Colvin sees a lack of a "tangible adversary" in prison as the catalyst for Meinhof making language both her tool and her enemy; see Colvin, *Ulrike Meinhof and West German Terrorism*, 165–72; and Colvin, "'Wenn deine Identität Kampf ist,'" 296.

77. HIS, F RA 02/005,005 and F Me,U/009,003. Meinhof also wrote of RAF writings as "weapons" in a response in the *info* from July 1974 to Mahler's text *Neue Straßenverkehrsordnung*; see Pieter Bakker Schut, ed., *das info: briefe von gefangenen aus der raf aus der diskussion 1973–1977* (Plambeck: Neuer Malik Verlag, 1987), 107.

78. "revolutionäre theorie ist kritische theorie. wo wir sie formuliert haben, um sie zu veröffentlichen, haben wir sie als *waffe* bestimmt und immer bezogen auf klar umrissene probleme der praxis des kampfes aus der illegalität . . . die theoretischen schriften der raf waren . . . als waffen bestimmt, weil waffe alles ist, was dem bewaffneten kampf aus der illegalität nützt," Meinhof as cited in Colvin, "'Wenn deine Identität Kampf ist,'" 297.

79. "dein zentraler satz ist: 'jeder kampf muss unmissverständlich ein kampf für die interessen und bedürfnisse der massen sein'—ein nichtsagenderes, aufgeblaseneres wort als 'unmissverständlich' gibts überhaupt nicht—aber: wenn du vor lauter massenfetischismus oder meinswegen auch nochmal: kitsch die genossen nicht siehst, dann mach dich fett drauf, ein kader zu sein, aber du bist es nicht," see Bakker Schut, ed., *das info*, 23.

80. "noch ne theorie: beschwörungsformeln, mao runtergebetet," see ibid., 107.

81. "auf opportunistischen scheiss inhaltlich einzugehen, weil seine wurzeln nicht im wortgeklingel liegen, sondern in der verinnerlichten, innerlich akzeptierten selbstentfremdung, derjenige, was immer er schwatzt, als stimme des systems und seiner komplizenschaft aus bewusster oder unbewusster identifikation mit dem feind (wie auch immer vermittelt) rationalisiert," see ibid., 108.

82. See note 1 of this chapter.

83. "du musst vielleicht mal ticken—ich weiss es nicht—dass man mit worten nur was erreichen kann, wenn sie den begriff der wirklichen situation bringen, die, in der jeder im imperialismus ist; dass es sinnlos ist, mit worten agitieren zu wollen, da *nur* aufklärung agitiert, wahrheit," see Bakker Schut, ed., *das info*, 264.

84. Colvin, "'Wenn deine Identität Kampf ist'" 298.

85. "so gesagt: das proletariat wird zur klasse, indem es selbst handelt—was aber ein prozeß ist, der mit der formel: durch revolutionäre initiative der guerilla wird das prolet. zur klasse—so vereinfacht ausgedrückt wird, daß man das als phrase

empfindet. also so geht's mir. einfach zu verkürzt, formelhaft . . . verdammt—es gibt sachen, die werden erst dadurch wahr, daß man sie tut und nicht dadurch, daß man sie sagt," see HIS, F Me, U/012,001.

86. "einer meint, was er sagt. wenn er was anderes meint, soll er es sagen, soll er es sich erkämpfen, es sagen zu k ö n n e n , die worte, sätze, tatsachen, begriffe *finden*, also *suchen*," see Bakker Schut, ed., *das info*, 232. For the reference to hunting (*jagen*) terms see ibid., 233.

87. "anstrengung," and "[realität] auf den begriff bringen," see ibid., 264.

88. For more on taboo breaking in Meinhof's writing, see Colvin, " 'Wenn deine Identität Kampf ist,' " 292–94.

89. "klar ist irgendwie, daß die alte schreibe überhaupt nicht mehr geht und die neue ist noch nicht da," see HIS, F Me, U/015,006.

90. "es kommt bei dieser sorte schreibe nicht darauf an, alle möglichen einzelheiten, einzelgedanken an den mann zu bringen. es kommt bei ihr darauf an, identität zum ausdruck zu bringen. / mit tatsachen ist das auch so ne sache. sie werden unter der hand im nu zur ware—nämlich beweismittel, beleg, beispiel, shit. . . . / naja—die vertikale klassenanalyse. in dem lernprozeß, jedenfalls bei mir, war sie unheimlich wichtig, aber du—wozu? wozu klassenanalyse? es kann auch wieder nur ne ware werden," see HIS, F Me,U/015,006.

91. Shortly after, and in the face of a response to her ideas from Ensslin, Meinhof seems to withdraw her comments, writing that "was ich da vorn paar tagen gebramscht hab, dass tatsachen einem unter der hand zu geld werden, war dreck. erhob ich mein momentanes problem zur regel," see Bakker Schut, ed., *das info*, 163. This is, however, only a concession that the problem with language—and indeed, it remains a problem—may be peculiar to her situation.

92. Colvin argues Meinhof was not successful in developing a revolutionary approach to language or shifting the accepted rules of communication; see Colvin, " 'Wenn deine Identität Kampf ist' " 304.

Chapter 2

1. "Veröffentlicht das!" See German Federal Archive (GFA), Holding (H) 362, File (F) 3130: 26–32.

2. Meinhof's movements after the liberation of Baader and until around November 1971 are re-created in police files held in GFA, H 362, F 3164.

3. GFA, H 362, F 3168.

4. Baader, Meins, and Raspe were arrested together on June 1, Ensslin was arrested on June 7, and Meinhof was arrested with Gerhard Müller on June 15.

5. GFA, H 362, F 3168: 1–7, and F 3164.

6. GFA, H 362, F 3164: 100–101. Joachim Fest also recalls Meinhof being "not one for action" (*kein Aktionstyp*), see Joachim Fest, *Begegnungen. Über nahe und ferne Freunde* (Reinbeck bei Hamburg: Rowohlt, 2004), 268; and Jillian Becker cites Eva Rühmkorf's recollection of Meinhof telling her, "People like you and me may think about throwing stones at other people, but we wouldn't actually do it," see Jillian Becker, *Hitler's Children: The Story of the Baader-Meinhof Terrorist Gang* (London: Joseph, 1977), 154.

7. GFA, H 362, F 3424.
8. For Proll's comments, see an interview in *Baader-Meinhof: In Love with Terror*, dir. Ben Lewis (BBC4, 2002).
9. For the report on water pistols, see GFA, H 362, F 3164: 150.
10. For the book *Waffenkunde und Schießlehre für Jäger* and textbook *Lehrbuch über organische Chemie*, see GFA, H 362, F 3435: 16–19. For the annotated weapons magazine, see GFA, H 362, F 3409. The "Hübner" safe house was rented by a person claiming to be "Renate Hübner," who was identified by the landlord as Meinhof, see GFA, H 362, F 3352.
11. "aschblond nr 105," "lichtblond nr 100," "haar color crème," see a radioteletype regarding the renting of a bungalow by Meinhof in GFA, H 362, F 3409.
12. GFA, H 362, F 3424: C.
13. Bettina Röhl cites Klaus Rainer Röhl's recollection that Meinhof clearly enjoyed working undercover and taking part in clandestine meetings, see Bettina Röhl, *So macht Kommunismus Spaß. Ulrike Meinhof, Klaus Rainer Röhl und die Akte KONKRET* (Hamburg: Europäische Verlagsanstalt, 2006), 241.
14. "freute sich wie ein Schneekönig," see Heinrich Hannover, *Die Republik vor Gericht 1954–1995. Erinnerungen eines unbequemen Rechtsanwalts* (Berlin: Aufbau Taschenbuch Verlag, 2005), 387.
15. *Der Baader Meinhof Report. Dokumente—Analysen—Zusammenhänge. Aus den Akten des Bundeskriminalamtes, der "Sonderkommission, Bonn" und dem Bundesamt für Verfassungsschutz* (Mainz: v. Hase & Koehler Verlag, 1972), 47.
16. "Beide hatten—so richtig schön unauffällig—seltsame längliche Köfferchen auf dem Schoß, mit deren Inhalt notfalls die 'Bullen' im Schach gehalten werden sollten. Auch diesmal konnte ich die äußeren Umstände der Begegnung nicht ganz Ernst nehmen," see Hannover, *Die Republik vor Gericht*, 388.
17. GFA, H 362, F 3166: 208–9. Beate Sturm, who was a member of the RAF until 1971, also described how Baader's behavior in the underground was able to make "politically heroic ideas" (*politisch-heroischen Vorstellungen*) disappear and convince her they were now in a real crime thriller, see Beate Sturm, "Man kann nur zurück-brüllen" *Der Spiegel* 7 (1972): 57.
18. The distinction between genres of RAF texts outlined here has been imposed retrospectively. Despite the clear differences, the group did not explicitly categorize the texts it produced, nor does a standard categorization exist. This can lead to confusion. At a rally to mark the twentieth anniversary of Meinhof's death, for example, former RAF member Ali Jansen was asked a question about the first RAF "paper" (*papier*). From the question it was clear it was a reference to the first treatise, however, Jansen instead began to talk about the statement that appeared in *agit 883*, see "Veranstaltung zum 20. Todestag von Ulrike Meinhof am 3. Mai 1996 im Auditorium Maximum der TU Berlin," http://www.nadir.org/nadir/archiv/PolitischeStroemungen/Stadtguerilla+RAF/RAF/ulrike_meinhof/va20/va20podium.html (accessed March 13, 2011).
19. Colvin also excludes Mahler's effort from consideration as a RAF text, see Sarah Colvin, *Ulrike Meinhof and West German Terrorism: Language, Violence, and Identity* (New York: Camden House, 2009), 98–99.

20. For the text denouncing a fake declaration, see GFA, H 362, F 3130: 301. Official analysis of the typewriters used by the RAF in the underground is held in GFA, H 362, F 3130, and Hamburg Institute for Social Research (HIS), File (F) SO, 09/002, 005.
21. "BKA Bericht vom 12.5.72" in HIS, F SO 09/005,004.
22. "Soko Bericht vom 15.1.73" in HIS, F SO 09/005,005.
23. The copy in police files was recovered on August 7, 1972, from the Karl-Marx bookshop in Frankfurt, see GFA, H 362, F 3130: 232.
24. GFA, H 362, F 3369: XII/I.
25. For more detail on the evolution of the logo and its elements, see Rolf Sachsse, "Pentagramm hinter deutscher Maschinenpistole unter Russisch Brot. Zur Semiosphäre der Erinnerung an die Rote Armee Fraktion," in *Der 'Deutsche Herbst' und die RAF in Politik, Medien und Kunst. Nationale und internationale Perspektiven*, ed. Nicole Colin, Beatrice De Graaf, Jacco Pekelder and Joachim Umlauf (Bielefeld: Transcript Verlag, 2008), 135–39.
26. "Name: 'Die Rote Armee aufbauen'—also kein Name sondern ein Satz: Er beinhaltet, was wir tun. Er beinhaltet zugleich, was zu tun jetzt notwendig ist," as cited in "Baader/Meinhof. Bis irgendwohin," *Der Spiegel* 25 (1970): 73.
27. Sachsse, "Pentagramm hinter deutscher Maschinenpistole," 136.
28. Michael Hahn, "Land der Superpigs. Wie Agit 883 mit Black Panthers und Weathermen die 'zweite Front in den Metropolen' eröffnete," in *agit 883. Bewegung, Revolte, Underground in Westberlin 1969–1972*, ed. rotaprint 25 (Hamburg: Assoziation A, 2006), 141.
29. "Baader/Meinhof. Bis irgendwohin," 73. Aust also writes of Meinhof holing up with an American woman who was a member of the Black Panthers while separated from the group after the liberation of Baader, see Stefan Aust, *Der Baader Meinhof Komplex* (Munich: Wilhelm Goldmann Verlag, 1998), 29.
30. Michael Hahn argues the BPP logo was included by the editors, see Hahn, "Land der Superpigs," 148.
31. "intellektuellen Schwätzern, den Hosenscheißern, den Alles-besser-Wissern" and "potentiell revolutionären Teilen des Volkes," see "Die Rote Armee aufbauen" in *Rote Armee Fraktion. Texte und Materialien zur Geschichte der RAF*, ed. ID-Verlag (Berlin: ID-Verlag, 1997), 24.
32. "Veranstaltung zum 20. Todestag von Ulrike Meinhof."
33. "eine wichtige Sache, die die Linke betrifft," see "Baader/Meinhof. Bis irgendwohin," 72.
34. RAF, "Das Konzept Stadtguerilla," in *Rote Armee Fraktion. Texte und Materialien zur Geschichte der RAF*, ed. ID-Verlag (Berlin: ID-Verlag, 1997), 27.
35. The individual involvement in the bombings outlined here follows the testimony of one-time RAF member Gerhard Müller at the Stammheim trial, see Helmut Brunn and Thomas Kirn, *Rechtsanwälte, Linksanwälte* (Frankfurt am Main: Eichborn, 2004), 326–27.
36. The name of the "Commando 2nd of June" is a reference to 1967 death of Benno Ohnesorg.
37. Wolfgang Kraushaar, "Kleinkrieg gegen einen Großverleger. Von der Anti-Springer-Kampagne der APO zu den Brand- und Bombenanschlägen der RAF,"

in *Die RAF und der linke Terrorismus*, ed. Wolfgang Kraushaar (Hamburg: Hamburger Edition, 2006), 1105.

38. For a detailed account of the Hamburg bombing in the context of the group's ongoing dispute with the Springer publishing house, see ibid.
39. The name of the "Commando 15th of July" is a reference to the death of Petra Schelm, who, after evading a roadblock and a subsequent chase, was shot dead by police on July 15, 1971.
40. These dates are those stamped on the envelopes. In the case of *Der Spiegel*, this information is not available, however, the letter arrived on May 31, suggesting it was sent on May 30, see HIS, F SO 09/002,005: 469.
41. GFA, H 362, F 3130: 4, 30, 42, 93, and 233, as well as HIS, F SO, 09/006,007: 15.14 and F SO 09/002,005: 461–69.
42. Andreas Elter, *Propaganda der Tat. Die RAF und die Medien* (Frankfurt am Main: Suhrkamp Verlag, 2008), 123–25.
43. GFA, H 362, F 3130: 232.
44. Ibid.
45. HIS, F SO 09/006,007: 15.12
46. "Aus Gesprächen innerhalb der Gruppe weiß ich, daß Ulrike MEINHOF die nach dem Anschlag in Hamburg herausgegebene Erklärung, wie auch alle anderen Erklärungen nach Sprengstoffanschlägen, verfaßt hat," as cited in Kraushaar, "Kleinkrieg gegen einen Großverleger," 1105.
47. GFA, H 362, F 3130: 320.
48. The *Frankfurter Rundschau* did report the possibility that the text was a fake, but three days later on the front cover, see "Unklarheit über neue Terror-Drohungen," *Frankfurter Rundschau*, May 29, 1972.
49. "An die Nachrichtenredakteure der westdeutschen Presse" in GFA, H 362, F 3130: 245.
50. Petr Kropotkin, "The Spirit of Revolt," in *The Essential Kropotkin*, ed. Emile Capouya and Keitha Tompkins (London: MacMillan Press, 1976), 7.
51. The statement was printed on page 4 of the *Frankfurter Rundschau* from January 25, 1972.
52. Carlos Marighella, *Mini-Manual of the Urban Guerilla* (Montreal: Abraham Guillen Press & Arm The Spirit, 2002), 31.
53. "Verhältnis Massenarbeit—Stadtguerilla" and "Propaganda durch Flugblätter—sehr wichtig, ungeheuer wichtig," see notes found in Meinhof's cell on July 16, 1973, in GFA, H 362, F 3370: XVI/156.
54. Andreas Elter, "Die RAF und die Medien. Ein Fallbeispiel für terroristische Kommunikation," in *Die RAF und der linke Terrorismus*, ed. Wolfgang Kraushaar (Hamburg: Hamburger Edition, 2006), 1067. Waldmann makes a similar, more general, argument that terrorist acts fulfill the criteria of an "interesting" news story, see Peter Waldmann, *Terrorismus. Provokation der Macht* (Hamburg: Murmann Verlag, 2005), 83.
55. Elter, *Propaganda der Tat*, 125.
56. As cited in Andrew R. Carlson, *Anarchism in Germany* (Metuchen: Scarecrow Press, 1972), 252–53.
57. Waldmann, *Terrorismus. Provokation der Macht*, 40.

58. RAF, "Anschläge in Augsburg und München," in *Rote Armee Fraktion. Texte und Materialien zur Geschichte der RAF*, ed. ID-Verlag (Berlin: ID-Verlag, 1997), 145–46.

59. "Er hat den Mordversuch an Grashof, der den Bullen nicht gelungen ist, an dem wehrlosen Grashof wiederholt," see RAF, "Anschlag auf den BGH-Richter Buddenberg in Karlsruhe," in *Rote Armee Fraktion. Texte und Materialien zur Geschichte der RAF*, ed. ID-Verlag (Berlin: ID-Verlag, 1997), 146.

60. RAF, "Sprengstoffanschlag auf das Springer-Hochhaus in Hamburg," in *Rote Armee Fraktion. Texte und Materialien zur Geschichte der RAF*, ed. ID-Verlag (Berlin: ID-Verlag, 1997), 147.

61. "Für die Ausrottungsstrategen von Vietnam sollen Westdeutschland und Westberlin kein sicheres Hinterland mehr sein," see RAF, "Anschlag auf das Hauptquartier der US-Army in Frankfurt/Main," in *Rote Armee Fraktion. Texte und Materialien zur Geschichte der RAF*, ed. ID-Verlag (Berlin: ID-Verlag, 1997), 145.

62. "Der Anschlag wurde durchgeführt, nachdem General Daniel James . . . am Mittwoch in Washington erklärt hatte: 'Für die US-Luftwaffe bleibt bei Bombenangriffen künftig kein Ziel nördlich und südlich des 17. Breitengrades ausgenommen,'" see RAF, "Bombenanschlag auf das Hauptquartier der US-Army in Europa in Heidelberg. Erklärung vom 25. Mai 1972," in *Rote Armee Fraktion. Texte und Materialien zur Geschichte der RAF*, ed. ID-Verlag (Berlin: ID-Verlag, 1997), 147.

63. "Sprache der Explosion," see RAF, "Erklärung der RAF zum Bombenanschlag im Hamburger Hauptbahnhof," in *Rote Armee Fraktion. Texte und Materialien zur Geschichte der RAF*, ed. ID-Verlag (Berlin: ID-Verlag, 1997), 196. The statement denounced an attack on the Hamburg train station as not a RAF attack.

64. For extended work on the evolution of the war metaphor in the context of West German terrorism and counterterrorism, see Andreas Musolff, *Krieg gegen die Öffentlichkeit. Terrorismus und politischer Sprachgebrauch* (Opladen: Westdeutscher Verlag, 1996); Andreas Musolff, "Terrorismus im öffentlichen Diskurs der BRD: Seine Deutung als Kriegsgeschehen und die Folgen," in *Terrorismus in der Bundesrepublik. Medien, Staat und Subkulturen in den 1970er Jahren*, ed. Klaus Weinhauer, Jörg Requate, and Heinz-Gerhard Haupt (Frankfurt: Campus Verlag, 2006); and Andreas Musolff, "Bürgerkriegs-Szenarios und ihre Folgen. Die Terrorismusdebatte in der Bundesrepublik 1970–1993," in *Die RAF und der linke Terrorismus*, ed. Wolfgang Kraushaar (Hamburg: Hamburger Edition, 2006).

65. Wolfgang Kraushaar, "Der Vietcong als Mythos des bewaffneten Volksaufstandes," in *Die RAF und der linke Terrorismus*, ed. Wolfgang Kraushaar (Hamburg: Hamburger Edition, 2006), 766.

66. Wolfgang Kraushaar writes of it being irrefutable that the Vietcong served as a prototype of the guerilla and a fundamental *Identifikationsobjekt* for student rebellion, see ibid., 762. This is also true of the RAF, which, despite basing its model of the guerilla explicitly on South American theories, identified strongly with the Vietcong.

67. Musolff, "Terrorismus im öffentlichen Diskurs der BRD," 314–15.

68. Kraushaar, "Kleinkrieg gegen einen Großverleger," 1088–89.

69. Musolff has identified the timing of the emergence and role of the mainstream war narrative, see Musolff, "Bürgerkriegs-Szenarios und ihre Folgen," 1172–73; and Musolff, "Terrorismus im öffentlichen Diskurs der BRD," 308.

70. "die Verbrennung dreier amerikanischer Kosmonauten in ihrer Kapsel, die Selbstverbrennung des Saigoner Mönchs, die japanischen Selbstmord-Happenings, Godards Film 'Weekend,' ein Gedicht von Robert Sward—das sind jeweils ästhetische und reale Ereignisse, die substantiell austauschbar geworden sind, so sehr haben sich die ehemals gegensätzlichen Sphären von Kunst und Realität ineinander geschoben bis zur Deckungsgleichheit: Die Realität wird zunehmend stilisiert wahrgenommen, die Kunst fast nur noch als Realitätspartikel erträglich," see Karl Heinz Bohrer, "Surrealismus und Terror, oder die Aporien des Juste-milieu," in *Die gefährdete Phantasie, oder Surrealismus und Terror* (Munich: Carl Hanser Verlag, 1970), 34.

71. Kraushaar, "Der Vietcong als Mythos des bewaffneten Volksaufstandes," 751.

72. Ibid., 762–63.

73. Roland Barthes, *Image, Music, Text*, trans. Stephen Heath (London: Flamingo, 1984), 25.

74. W. J. T. Mitchell, *Picture Theory: Essays on Verbal and Visual Representation* (Chicago: University of Chicago Press, 1994), 94–98.

75. Jürgen Serke, "Terror in Deutschland. Die Bombenleger," *Stern* 24 (1972): 18–19.

76. Musolff, "Terrorismus im öffentlichen Diskurs der BRD," 314.

77. Heinrich Böll, "Will Ulrike Meinhof Gnade oder freies Geleit?" *Der Spiegel* 3 (1972): 54–56.

78. In the context of the "war on terror" waged in response to the attacks of 9/11, Joseba Zulaika wrote that the danger of "formally adopting the terrorists' own game . . . lies in reproducing it endlessly," see Joseba Zulaika, "The Self-Fulfilling Prophecies of Counterterrorism," *Radical History Review* 85 (2003): 198. Begoña Aretxaga made a similar observation in the immediate aftermath of the 9/11 attacks, writing that a "war against terrorism . . . mirrors the state of exception characteristic of insurgent violence, and in so doing it reproduces it ad infinitum," see Begoña Aretxaga, "Terror as a Thrill: First Thoughts on the 'War on Terrorism,'" *Anthropological Quarterly* 75(1) (2001): 149.

79. Musolff, "Bürgerkriegs-Szenarios und ihre Folgen," 1183. Colvin writes of the binary thinking of good and evil, black and white, as being the defining feature of the RAF's and the West German state's language of war, see Colvin, *Ulrike Meinhof and West German Terrorism*, 137–39.

80. Musolff argues that the emergence of second and third generations of the RAF can be seen in part as a result of the war metaphor and the external confirmation of the terrorists' self-image as soldiers in a war, see Musolff, "Terrorismus im öffentlichen Diskurs der BRD," 316. He also sees the longevity of the war metaphor in the RAF prisoners' claims for political prisoner and prisoner of war (POW) status, and the rights pertaining to those statuses (309). For more on the evolution and use of the terms "political prisoner" and "POW," see chapter 4.

81. Colvin agrees with Musolff that by engaging in the radical narrative of war, the West German state stoked support for the RAF at a time when it was increasingly

vulnerable due to its increasing isolation, see Colvin, *Ulrike Meinhof and West German Terrorism*, 140.

82. "marcuse gehört uns . . . also, der witz den ich z.b. darin sehe, daß man mit marcuse so umgeht, wie marcuse nat. selbst nicht mit sich umgeht," as cited in Iring Fetscher, Herfried Münkler, and Hannelore Ludwig, "Ideologien der Terroristen in der Bundesrepublik Deutschland," in *Analysen zum Terrorismus. Ideologien and Strategien*, ed. Federal Ministry of the Interior, *Analysen zum Terrorismus* (Opladen: Westdeutscher Verlag, 1981), 57.

83. Meinhof is assumed to be the author, given the content, style, and elocution of the text, see "Bericht vom 27. Mai 1972" in HIS, F KOK, 03/003: 3; and GFA, H 362, F 3377: 200. Butz Peters writes of a mail-out from a fake Bonn address, see Butz Peters, *RAF. Terrorismus in Deutschland* (Stuttgart: Deutsche Verlags-Anstalt, 1991), 128.

84. "Bericht vom 27. Mai 1972" in HIS, F KOK, 03/003: 2–3.

85. GFA, H 362, F 3377: 200. A "Soko B/M Vermerk" from November 15 concludes that it is the same author as that of *Urban Guerilla*, that is, Meinhof, see HIS, F SO 09/005,004: 2.

86. "BKA Bericht vom 12.5.72" in HIS, F SO 09/005,004: 1. For the article, see "Solange sie nicht die Fresse voll kriegen," *Der Spiegel* 8 (1972).

87. GFA, H 362, F 3130: 32, and F 3130: 39.

88. "BKA Bericht vom 12.5.72" in HIS, F SO 09/005,004: 1.

89. "Soko B/M Vermerk vom 12.11.73" in HIS, F SO 09/005,004: 1–2.

90. Ibid.

91. Ibid.: 1.

92. The *Sonderkommission* again cites stylistic consistency with the previous RAF texts as evidence of Meinhof's authorship, see "Soko Bericht vom 15.1.73" in HIS, F SO 09/005,005: 2; and "BKA Vermerk vom 25.10.1973" in F SO 09/005,005: 1.

93. "Soko Bericht vom 15.1.73" in HIS, F SO 09/005,005: 16–18.

94. Ibid.: 1–2; and "Soko Vermerk vom 22.11.73" in F SO 09/005,005: 1–2.

95. "Bericht vom 27. Mai 1972" in HIS, F KOK 03/003: 3.

96. See Walter Laqueur, *The New Terrorism and the Arms of Mass Destruction* (Oxford: Oxford University Press, 1999), 274; and Waldmann, *Terrorismus. Provokation der Macht*, 212.

97. Fetscher, Münkler, and Ludwig, "Ideologien der Terroristen," 75.

98. The radicalism of the late 1960s, Koenen argues, was far ahead of any theoretical firmness, see Gerd Koenen, "Armed Innocence, or 'Hitler's Children' Revisited," in *Baader-Meinhof Returns: History and Cultural Memory of German Left-Wing Terrorism*, ed. Gerrit-Jan Berendse and Ingo Cornils (Amsterdam: Rodopi, 2008), 25. Similarly, Charity Scribner describes the group's praxis as "essentially symbolic," its legacy as "heavy on style but light on political analysis," and the various ideological positions that made up the RAF as superficial and often inherently contradictory, see Charity Scribner, "Buildings on Fire: The Situationist International and the Red Army Faction," *Grey Room* 26 (2007): 32, 47.

99. Fetscher, Münkler, and Ludwig, "Ideologien der Terroristen," 179.

100. Ibid. For a study of the specific example of Meinhof, see Stefan T. Possony and L. Francis Bouchey, *International Terrorism: The Communist Connection. With a Case*

Study of West German Terrorist Ulrike Meinhof (Washington: American Council for World Freedom, 1978). Both of these studies were commissioned by Western governments: the Federal Republic of Germany and the United States, respectively.

101. Klaus Rainer Röhl conceded Meinhof's schooling in popular leftist theories of the day, including those of Marx, Lenin, and Brecht, came later than most and did not involve a direct engagement with the sources. Her Marxism was a type of neo-Marxism absorbed from the environment around her. Journalist Jillian Becker cited Meinhof's friend Monika Mitscherlich as saying that "[Meinhof] was not really a Socialist. Perhaps in her own mind she was. But she did not understand Marxism. I am sure she never read Marx," see Jillian Becker, *Hitler's Children: The Story of the Baader-Meinhof Terrorist Gang* (London: Joseph, 1977), 130. Colvin also cites prison correspondence in which Meinhof concedes that she had not read Marcuse, see Colvin, *Ulrike Meinhof and West German Terrorism*, 64.

102. "'besetzte Formeln' . . . aus den Tiefen der marxistischen Mottenkiste" and "Sprache des Protests," see Fest, *Begegnungen*, 253.

103. Günter Rohrmoser and Jörg Fröhlich, "Ideologische Ursachen des Terrorismus," in *Analysen zum Terrorismus. Ideologien und Strategien*, ed. Federal Ministry of the Interior (Opladen: Westdeutscher Verlag, 1981), 294.

104. Theo Ligthart, "avantgarde, 2000/2004," in *Zur Vorstellung des Terrors: Die RAF*, ed. Klaus Biesenbach (Göttingen: Steidl Verlag, 2005), 68. Stefan Reinecke describes this shift as one from history into style, see Stefan Reinecke, "Die RAF und die Politik der Zeichen," in *Zur Vorstellung des Terrors: Die RAF*, ed. Klaus Biesenbach (Göttingen: Steidl Verlag, 2005), 219.

105. Dick Hebdige, *Subculture: The Meaning of Style* (London: Methuen & Co, 1979), 3.

106. Roland Barthes, *Mythologies*, trans. Annette Lavers (London: Vintage, 2000), 114, 29.

107. Ibid., 125.

108. "Affinitäten wurden über formale Zusammenhänge hergestellt, dasselbe Aussehen, dieselbe Musik, dieselben Gewohnheiten, dieselben Schlagwörter und Parolen," see Volker Speitel, "'Wir wollten alles und gleichzeitig nichts,'" *Der Spiegel* 31 (1980): 37.

109. "der O-Ton der Guerilla [unterscheidet sich] von John-Wayne-Filmen und Räuber-und-Gendarm-Spiel nur noch dadurch, daß bei der RAF wirklich Blut aus zerfetzten Leichen fließt," see Volker Speitel, "'Wir wollten alles und gleichzeitig nichts' (III)," *Der Spiegel* 33 (1980): 34.

110. "Die Zitate von Mao, Lenin, Marx, Il Manifesto, von den Tupamaros oder woher auch immer, die sie als Belege für die Richtigkeit ihres Vorgehens anführen, dienen in ihrer ersten programmatischen Schrift über das 'Konzept Stadtguerilla' u. in dem 'Traktat über die Methode' fast ausschließlich nur als Mottos für die einzelnen behandelten Fragenkomplexe . . . Darüberhinaus gewinnt man den Eindruck, daß die zitierten, jeweils spezifischen Erfahrungen von Marx, Lenin, Madel oder beispielsweise auch Mao eher wie allgemeine Weisheiten benutzt, u. so auf die im Grunde eben doch ganz andere, völlig unzureichend erfaßte u. besondere Situation der BRD projiziert werden; mit anderen Worten, daß die eben erwähnte Handlungsanweisung von Mao Tsetung nicht beachtet oder zumindest nicht

immer eingehalten wurde. Damit reicht das Zitieren auch bei den RAF-Genossen oft sehr nahe an die Grenze des Dogmatismus," see "Über die RAF," *Gegenbaldrian. Ein deutsches Beunruhigungsmagazin* (1973): 3, as cited in the police report on material found during a search of Meinhof's prison cell in 1973, in GFA, H 362, F 3370: XVI/56-XVI/72.

111. Peters, *RAF. Terrorismus in Deutschland*, 138.

112. The intransigent moral program supported in the treatises by picturesque ideology is an example of how the RAF in many ways became what its members had hated. The texts revolved around themes of bravery, sacrifice, loyalty, and duty, themes that were not only nonideological, but, in the language of the time, distinctly fascist. The irony of aggressively employing psychological drivers that so echo the mechanics of Nazism is representative of a central paradox that weaves its way through RAF history. Most emblematic of this inherent contradiction is the manner in which the group raged against what it saw as lingering Nazism in the Federal Republic while celebrating the 1972 murder of Jews on German soil barely decades after the Holocaust. More than confirmation of intuitive inconsistencies in RAF logic, the transformation of leftist ideology into a moral imperative can be seen as a footnote to Habermas's 1967 cautionary tale of "leftist fascism" and the slide into dogmatism.

113. "Es hat keinen Zweck, den falschen Leuten das Richtige erklären zu wollen," see "Die Rote Armee aufbauen" 24.

114. "Ich beharre fest darauf, daß jemand, der keine Untersuchung angestellt hat, auch kein Mitspracherecht haben kann," see RAF, "Das Konzept Stadtguerilla," 27.

115. "Konkurrenzkampf von Intellektuellen, die sich vor einer imaginären Jury, die die Arbeiterklasse nicht sein kann, weil ihre Sprache schon deren Mitsprache ausschließt, den Rang um die bessere Marx-Rezeption ablaufen. Es ist ihnen peinlicher, bei einem falschen Marx-Zitat ertappt zu werden als bei einer Lüge, wenn von ihrer Praxis die Rede ist. Die Seitenzahlen, die sie in ihren Anmerkungen angeben, stimmen fast immer, die Mitgliederzahlen, die sie für ihre Organisationen angeben, stimmen fast nie," see ibid., 37–38.

116. RAF, "Die Aktion des Schwarzen September in München," in *Rote Armee Fraktion. Texte und Materialien zur Geschichte der RAF*, ed. ID-Verlag (Berlin: ID-Verlag, 1997), 159.

117. "Es werden Legionen von 'Marxisten' anrücken, die mit ganzen Batterien von Marx-Zitaten 'nachweisen' werden, daß der hier gezeigte Weg 'reines Abenteurertum,' 'Blanquismus,' 'Putschismus,' 'Anarchismus' sei. Nun gut. Die Ismen-Krämerei überlassen wir gern den Schriftgelehrten; wenn wir nur der Revolution in Deutschland einen Schritt näher kommen. 'Armer Marx und armer Engels, welcher Mißbrauch ist schon mit Zitaten aus ihren Werken getrieben worden!'" See Horst Mahler, "Über den bewaffneten Kampf in Westeuropa," in *Rote Armee Fraktion. Texte und Materialien zur Geschichte der RAF*, ed. ID-Verlag (Berlin: ID-Verlag, 1997), 101.

118. Oskar Negt, "Rede zum Angela-Davis-Kongress 1972. Im Zeichen der Gewalt," http://www.linksnet.de/artikel.php?id=374 (accessed March 24, 2011).

119. "Im gegenwärtigen Stadium der Geschichte kann niemand mehr bestreiten, daß eine bewaffnete Gruppe, so klein sie auch sein mag, bessere Aussichten hat, sich in

eine große Volksarmee zu verwandeln, als eine Gruppe, die sich darauf beschränkt, revolutionäre Lehrsätze zu verkünden," see RAF, "Dem Volk dienen. Stadtguerilla und Klassenkampf," in *Rote Armee Fraktion. Texte und Materialien zur Geschichte der RAF*, ed. ID-Verlag (Berlin: ID-Verlag, 1997), 116.

120. "der bewaffnete Kampf als 'die höchste Form des Marxismus-Leninismus' (Mao)," see RAF, "Das Konzept Stadtguerilla," 31.

121. "Wenn ihr allerdings wissen wollt, was die Kommunisten denken, dann seht auf ihre Hände und nicht auf ihren Mund," see ibid.

122. "Wer ein bestimmtes Ding oder einen Komplex von Dingen direkt kennen lernen will, muß persönlich am praktischen Kampf zur Veränderung der Wirklichkeit, zur Veränderung des Dinges oder des Komplexes von Dingen teilnehmen, denn nur so kommt er mit der Erscheinung der betreffenden Dinge in Berührung, und erst durch die persönliche Teilnahme am praktischen Kampf zur Veränderung der Wirklichkeit ist er imstande, das Wesen jenes Dinges bzw. jenes Komplexes von Dingen zu enthüllen und sie zu verstehen. / Aber der Marxismus legt der Theorie darum und nur darum ernste Bedeutung bei, weil sie die Anleitung zum Handeln sein kann. Wenn man über eine richtige Theorie verfügt, sie aber nur als etwas behandelt, worüber man einmal schwatzt, um es dann in die Schublade zu legen, was man jedoch keineswegs in die Praxis umsetzt, dann wird diese Theorie, so gut sie auch sein mag, bedeutungslos," see ibid., 36–37.

123. Fetscher, Münkler, and Ludwig, "Ideologien der Terroristen," 24, 54.

124. "Siegen heißt, prinzipiell akzeptieren, daß das Leben nicht das höchste Gut des Revolutionärs ist," see RAF, "Das Konzept Stadtguerilla," 39.

125. "An marxistischer Kritik und Selbstkritik hat sie sich zu orientieren, an sonst nichts. 'Wer keine Angst vor Vierteilung hat, wagt es, den Kaiser vom Pferd zu zerren,' sagt Mao dazu," see ibid., 43.

126. "Ohne den Rückzug in bürgerliche Berufe offen zu halten, ohne die Revolution nochmal an den Nagel im Reihenhaus hängen zu können, ohne also auch das zu wollen, also mit dem Pathos, das Blanqui ausgedrückt hat: 'Die Pflicht eines Revolutionärs ist, immer zu kämpfen, trotzdem zu kämpfen, bis zum Tod kämpfen,'" see ibid.

127. "In alten Zeiten gab es in China einen Schriftsteller namens Sima Tjiän. Dieser sagte einmal: 'Es stirbt allerdings ein jeder; aber der Tod des einen ist gewichtiger als der Tai-Berg, der Tod des anderen hat weniger Gewicht als Schwanenflaum,'" see RAF, "Dem Volk dienen," 112.

128. RAF member Petra Schelm was the group's first casualty when shot by police in July 1971, von Rauch belonged to the radical left scene before being shot by a plain-clothes officer in December 1971, and Weisbecker was shot by police in March 1972.

129. RAF, "Dem Volk dienen," 112.

130. "es ist die Frage, . . . ob es uns gelingen kann, die reaktionäre Militarisierung in ein revolutionäre umzuwandeln, ob es besser ist, 'sich einfach hinzulegen und zu sterben oder aufzustehen und Widerstand zu leisten,'" see ibid., 136.

131. "antiimperialistisch, anti-faschistisch und internationalistisch," see RAF, "Die Aktion des Schwarzen September in München," 151.

132. "Der Tod der arabischen Genossen wiegt schwerer als der Tai-Berg," see ibid., 177.

133. See the prison communiqué as cited in Pieter Bakker Schut, ed., *das info: briefe von gefangenen aus der raf aus der diskussion 1973–1977* (Plambeck: Neuer Malik Verlag, 1987), 185.
134. "Zwischen uns und dem Feind einen klaren Trennungsstrich ziehen!" See RAF, "Das Konzept Stadtguerilla," 27.
135. "Wenn wir vom Feind bekämpft werden, dann ist das gut; denn es ist ein Beweis, daß wir zwischen uns und dem Feind einen klaren Trennungsstrich gezogen haben. Wenn uns der Feind energisch entgegentritt, uns in den schwärzesten Farben malt und gar nichts bei uns gelten läßt, dann ist das noch besser; denn es zeugt davon, daß wir nicht nur zwischen uns und dem Feind eine klare Trennungslinie gezogen haben, sondern daß unsere Arbeit auch glänzende Erfolge gezeitigt hat," see ibid.
136. Ibid. 44.
137. "Somit muß man von seinem Wesen her; aus einer langen Perspektive, in strategischer Hinsicht den Imperialismus und alle Reaktionäre als das betrachten, was sie in Wirklichkeit sind: als Papiertiger. Darauf müssen wir unser strategisches Denken gründen. Andererseits sind sie aber wiederum lebendige, eisenharte, wirkliche Tiger; die Menschen fressen. Darauf müssen wir unser taktisches Denken gründen," see ibid., 40.
138. RAF, "Dem Volk dienen," 138.
139. "Verräter müssen aus den Reihen der Revolution ausgeschlossen werden. Toleranz gegenüber Verrätern produziert neuen Verrat," see ibid., 141.
140. "Wir müssen nach Möglichkeit unnötige Opfer vermeiden. Alle Menschen in den Reihen der Revolution müssen füreinander sorgen, müssen sich liebevoll zueinander verhalten, einander helfen," see ibid., 143.
141. See Alexander Straßner, "Die dritte Generation der RAF," in *Die RAF und der linke Terrorismus*, ed. Wolfgang Kraushaar (Hamburg: Hamburger Edition, 2006), 499; and Tobias Wunschik, "Aufstieg und Zerfall. Die zweite Generation der RAF," in *Die RAF und der linke Terrorismus*, ed. Wolfgang Kraushaar (Hamburg: Hamburger Edition, 2006), 475–76.
142. Straßner, "Die dritte Generation der RAF," 499. There had been a necessary strategic adjustment in the wake of the Stammheim deaths that in 1978 saw the second generation move away from breaking the group's leaders out of prison and deadly attacks, see Wunschik, "Aufstieg und Zerfall," 476.

Chapter 3

1. Franz Kafka, "A Hunger Artist," in *The Complete Stories*, ed. Nahum N. Glatzer (New York: Schocken Books, 1971), 270.
2. There was another hunger strike in 1994 from July 27 to August 3 with different demands and a different focus. The strike was limited from the outset, and the striking prisoners were seeking the release of an individual prisoner, Irmgard Möller, see RAF, "Hungerstreikerklärung vom 27. Juli 1994," in *Rote Armee Fraktion. Texte und Materialien zur Geschichte der RAF*, ed. ID-Verlag (Berlin: ID-Verlag, 1997), 498–99.
3. "Neun Hungerstreiks haben wir gemacht, zwei Gefangene sind darin gestorben, viele von uns haben Gesundheitsschäden. Jetzt muß schluß sein mit dieser

achtzehn Jahre langen Tortur," RAF, "Hungerstreikerklärung vom 1. Februar 1989," in *Rote Armee Fraktion. Texte und Materialien zur Geschichte der RAF*, ed. ID-Verlag (Berlin: ID-Verlag, 1997), 389.

4. Self-starvation can be approached as a performative act within a specific cultural context and placed within a history tracing the cultural currency of food abstinence from the food practices of medieval spirituality, through the demonic self-starvation of the Reformation, the eighteenth-century naturalization of hunger with the rise of empiricism, the spectacle of "hunger artists" and "living skeletons" of the late-nineteenth and early twentieth century, the emergence of a medicalized *anorexia nervosa* in the late-nineteenth century, to the particularly twentieth-century phenomenon of the political hunger strike. For broad histories of hunger, see Walter Vandereycken and Ron van Deth, *From Fasting Saints to Anorexic Girls: The History of Self-Starvation* (London: Athlone Press, 1996); and Joan Jacobs Brumberg, *Fasting Girls: The History of Anorexia Nervosa* (New York: Vintage Books, 2000). Bynum frames fasting—as male saints or female "miraculous maidens"—as central to spirituality of the medieval period, see Caroline Walker Bynum, *Holy Feast and Holy Fast: The Religious Significance of Food to Medieval Women* (Berkeley: University of California Press, 1987). In her study of anorexia, Ellmann writes of hunger as a form of speech and starving flesh as inscribed with social codes, see Maud Ellmann, *The Hunger Artists: Starving, Writing, and Imprisonment* (London: Virago Press, 1993). Like Ellmann, Feldman employs the metaphor of inscription from Kafka's *Penal Colony* to describe the enmeshing of the body with social codes and cultural discourses in his work on the political hunger strikes of the IRA, see Allen Feldman, *Formations of Violence: The Narrative of the Body and Political Terror in Northern Ireland* (Chicago: University of Chicago Press, 1991). Interestingly, Meinhof draws on the same Kafka metaphor when writing down comparisons and concepts that come to her when she thinks of her time in Cologne-Ossendorf Prison, see notes in Hamburg Institute for Social Research (HIS), File (F) Me,U/009,002. Feldman explicitly frames this encoding as not merely expressive of a given discourse, but as an affective process that can shape social and cultural reality. In her work on the dirty protests in Ireland, Aretxaga argues within a similar Foucauldian paradigm for an understanding of encoded and textualized bodies, see Begoña Aretxaga, "Dirty Protest: Symbolic Overdetermination and Gender in Northern Ireland Ethnic Violence," *Ethos* 23(2) (1995): 123–48.

5. "ab heute fresse ich nichts mehr, bis die Haftbedingungen geändert sind," as cited in Stefan Aust, *Der Baader Meinhof Komplex* (Munich: Wilhelm Goldmann Verlag, 1998), 281.

6. See documents relating to this individual protest in German Federal Archive (GFA), Holding (H) 362, File (F) 3155.

7. "In Berlin noch 7. Außerdem in Köln 4, Wittlich 1, Zweibrücken 2, Gotteszell 1 hungern noch! Außer den Berlinern werden alle mehr oder weniger regelmäßig künstlich ernährt. / Unterbrochen aus gesundheitlichen Gründen—unerträgliche Schmerzen—Kolik usw.—mit dem Willen wieder anzufangen, wenn es besser geht, haben Baader, Braun, Grundmann, Goergens, Mahler, Hoppe. Von den anderen weiß ich keine Einzelheiten. / Baader ist für Abbruch / 1. weil draußen

nichts wesentliches mehr läuft," see a prison "newsletter" dated June 16, 1973, in GFA, H 362, F 3370: XVI/21.

8. "Wir, das heißt die Anwälte und die Berliner Hungernden, gehen davon aus, daß am Freitag allg. beendet wird, wenn in Paris die Pressekonferenz stattgefunden hat," see *info* entry dated June 28, 1973, in GFA, H 362, F 3169: XVII/13.

9. Wesemann writes of eighty prisoners, see Kristin Wesemann, *Ulrike Meinhof. Kommunistin, Journalistin, Terroristin—eine politische Biographie* (Baden-Baden: Nomos, 2007), 392. Aust had earlier written of forty participants, see Aust, *Der Baader Meinhof Komplex*, 293.

10. Butz Peters, *Tödlicher Irrtum: die Geschichte der RAF* (Berlin: Argon, 2004), 317.

11. Other methods for feeding prisoners were also subsequently used: prisoners in some prisons were force-fed via gastric tubes inserted through the nose instead of the mouth, and some prisoners who were not able to offer physical resistance were fed intravenously. The Federal Ministry of Justice summarized the methods used in the different states on October 7, 1977, see GFA, H 141, F 404858.

12. Kurt Oesterle, *Stammheim. Der Vollzugsbeamte Horst Bubeck und die RAF-Häftlinge* (Munich: Heyne, 2003), 125.

13. For the manual, see GFA, H 362, F 3370: XIV/33.

14. In terms of the physical condition of the prisoners, Psychiatrist Wilfried Rasch attested in September 1975 that all four prisoners (Baader, Meinhof, Ensslin, and Raspe) were underweight, see Martin Jander, "Isolation. Zu den Haftbedingungen der RAF-Gefangenen," in *Die RAF und der linke Terrorismus*, ed. Wolfgang Kraushaar (Hamburg: Hamburger Edition, 2006), 982. Baader, for example, also developed kidney stones, which doctors assumed were the result of water being withheld during a strike, see GFA, H 362, F 3370: XVI/21 RS.

15. "taktisch günstigen Zeitpunkt," see protocol of interrogation of Gerhard Müller from June 10, 1975, in GFA, H 362, F 3363: 6. Müller, who was a RAF member (arrested in 1972) who later turned witness for the prosecution, also testified that part of the reason for the timing of the strike was to protect their lawyers from attacks from the authorities.

16. For a copy of the statement handed out in the courtroom, see "Staatsanwaltschaft bei dem Landgericht Berlin" in GFA, H 362, F 3397.

17. A 2007 article in *Der Spiegel* suggested forty prisoners participated in the strike, see Michael Sontheimer, "Terrorzelle Stammheim," *Der Spiegel* 41 (2007): 100. However, a statement of solidarity signed by "80 prisoners in Stammheim" who joined the strike on November 18, 1974, is held in GFA, H 362, F 3363. This greater number is also in line with RAF policy to strike only in numbers between fifty and one hundred, see "2. Strafsenat Verfügung vom 19. Dezember 1974" in GFA, H 362, F 3172.

18. Kurt Oesterle describes the necessary realism of the strike as descending into farce when the prisoners ate during strikes, see Oesterle, *Stammheim*, 128.

19. Documents relating to the negotiations behind the new section 101 of the Prison Act are held in GFA, H 141, F 404857.

20. Marcel Streng, "'Hungerstreik'. Eine politische Subjektivierungspraxis zwischen 'Freitod' und 'Überlebenskunst' (Westdeutschland, 1970-1990)," in *Das schöne*

Selbst. Zur Genealogie des modernen Subjekts zwischen Ethik und Ästhetik, eds. Jens Elberfeld and Marcus Otto (Bielefeld: transcript Verlag), 353–55.

21. The evolution of the state response to self-starvation outlined here expands on the position taken in Leith Passmore, "The Art of Hunger: Self-Starvation in the Red Army Faction," *German History* 27(1) (2009): 36–37.

22. "Verfügung vom 19. November 1974" in GFA, H 362, F 3172. *Wir wollen alles* was produced monthly from 1973 until 1975 and enjoyed circulation throughout the entire Federal Republic.

23. GFA, H 362, F 3168: 89–92.

24. For documents relating to the shifting conditions associated with, for example, the 1975 kidnapping of Peter Lorenz, see "Verfügung des Vorsitzenden des 2. Strafsenat des Oberlandsgerichts Stuttgart" from April 23, 1975, and "Verfügung des Vorsitzenden des 2. Strafsenat des Oberlandsgerichts Stuttgart" from March 9, 1975, in GFA, H 362, F 3172.

25. Examples of the extremes are an unpublished letter of complaint (held in GFA, H 362, F 3481) by a female inmate in Stammheim—a barely literate American petty criminal with seemingly little vested interest in either domestic German politics or worldwide revolution—and the published recollections of Horst Bubeck, who, from 1972 to 1986, was the acting prison warden of Stammheim Prison (see Oesterle, *Stammheim*).

26. "Bei Frau M., die ich zweimal kurz untersucht habe, ist die Grenze der Belastbarkeit nach psychiatrischer Ansicht *jetzt* erreicht," see GFA, H 362, F 3168: 280. Other doctors—listed as "Regierungsmedizinaldirektor Dr. Allies" and "Diplom-Psychologe Jarmer"—reached similar conclusions.

27. GFA, H 362, F 3168: 290.

28. Ibid.: 93. The other reason given for the conditions imposed on RAF prisoners was that they would attempt to escape (*Fluchtgefahr*).

29. Lists of censored letters and the reasons for censorship are held in GFA, H 362, F 3172. The approval process for newspapers and magazines is described in GFA, H 362, F 3166: 7–8. The concerns regarding radios were twofold: first, prison authorities were worried tools to aid escape could be hidden inside radios, see GFA, H 362, F 3168: 152. Second, authorities refused to allow radios that had a large high-frequency range, including the infamous 27MHz, at which members of illegal groups had been known to transmit messages, see GFA, H 362, F 3167: 218–20. For the regulation of cassette recorders, see "Oberlandsgericht Stuttgart 2. Strafsenat, Verfügung vom 25. Februar 1975" in GFA, H 362, F 3172.

30. "ein infosystem aufzubauen," as cited in Olaf Gäthje, "Das 'info'-System der RAF von 1973 bis 1977 in sprachwissenschaftlicher Perspektive," in *Die RAF und der linke Terrorismus*, ed. Wolfgang Kraushaar (Hamburg: Hamburger Edition, 2006), 719.

31. Wesemann, *Ulrike Meinhof*, 389.

32. The 1974 report *Dokumentation "Baader-Meinhof-Bande"* noted the dual focus—inside and outside—of the communication network and that the goal of the "outside" work was to enable activities and motivate sympathizers, see Ministerium des Innern Rheinland-Pfalz, ed., *Dokumentation "Baader-Meinhof-Bande"* (1974), 21, 32.

33. "das zentrale problem ist verbreitung, veröffentlichung unserer ideen," see "schweigen und handeln" in GFA, H 362, F 3133.
34. For a letter by Meinhof demanding her text be sent to Red Aid only after being read by her fellow prisoners, see GFA, H 362, F 3369: IX/15–IX/17. For a handwritten note by Meinhof her lawyer asking for a particular text not to be delivered to Red Aid, see GFA, H 362, F 3370: XV/46. Prison officials also found in Meinhof's cell a Red Aid booklet entitled *Rote Hilfe Dokumentation. Protest vor dem BGH gegen Psychoterror in deutschen Gefängnissen.* This booklet was put together by Meinhof's sister, Wienke Zitlaff, and included handwritten corrections by Meinhof, see GFA, H 362, F 3370: XVI/113.
35. "bis viell. mal ne rh als org. der poli.gef der knastpol. der guerilla rausspringt," see an *info* entry found in Meinhof's cell on July 16, 1973, in GFA, H 362, F 3369: XI/5.
36. "Auswertungsbericht vom 18.4.74" in HIS, F SO 09/004,002: 95–96.
37. "legaler arm der raf," see "Zunächst ist es irre" in HIS, F Me,U/012,006. For the purposes of the committees, see "NUR ZUM INTERNEN GEBRAUCH" in GFA, H 362, F 3370: 2.
38. A 1972 *info* entry describes local committees with stands on busy street corners handing out 20,000 leaflets every weekend, see GFA, H 362, F 3370: XV/42. Booklets included "Der tote Trakt ist ein Folterinstrument" (43 pages), "Die Systematik der Folter" (35 pages), "Der Kampf gegen die Vernichtungshaft" (285 pages), see Peters, *Tödlicher Irrtum*, 314. For details of demonstrations and teach-ins, see GFA, H 362, F 3363. For details of press conferences and television appearances, see "NUR ZUM INTERNEN GEBRAUCH" in GFA, H 362, F 3370.
39. Alfred Klaus draws the conclusion in his report on material found in RAF cells that Meinhof wrote the texts and Baader and Ensslin exercised some editorial control. Klaus cites an *info* in which Meinhof describes Ensslin as having the "final edit" (*Schlussredaktion*), see HIS, F SO 09/004,003: 151.
40. Jander writes of the strikes being constructed as hooks, a strategy borrowed from the advertising industry, see Jander, "Isolation," 979.
41. "Wir werden in den Durststreik treten," *Der Spiegel* 4 (1975): 54.
42. "politische Inhalte zu vermitteln," see HIS, F Me, U/015,001.
43. See "Sartre ruft Böll zu Solidarität auf," *Frankfurter Allgemeine Zeitung*, December 5, 1974. For other examples, see "Sartre nennt Haftbedingungen Baaders 'Folter,'" *Frankfurter Allgemeine Zeitung*, December 5, 1974; "Sartre spricht von psychischer Folter," *Süddeutsche Zeitung*, December 5, 1974; and "An der Brüstung," *Der Spiegel* 50 (1974): 27.
44. "Holger Meins—ermordet von der bürgerlichen Klassenjustiz," "Kampf der bürgerlichen Klassenjustiz," "Kampf den Mördern von Holger Meins," "Freiheit für alle politischen Gefangenen," see "Demonstration nach Beerdigung von Holger Meins," *Süddeutsche Zeitung*, November 19, 1974.
45. "Holger Meins im Knast ermordet," "Holger Meins verhungert—amen," see "Ermittlungen um Tod von Holger Meins," *Süddeutsche Zeitung*, November 11, 1974. *Der Spiegel* also reported this and other graffiti verbatim as text, see "Es werden Typen dabei kaputtgehen," *Der Spiegel* 47 (1974): 29.

46. See "Kassiber mit Skizze," *Der Spiegel* 9 (1973): 64; and "'Mord beginnt beim bösen Wort.' II," *Der Spiegel* 42 (1977): 54. The text of the posters was also reported, see, for example, "Es werden Typen dabei kaputtgehen," 32.
47. Koenen writes of the public debates surrounding the hunger strikes as ensuring the history of the RAF was not a short one, see Gerd Koenen, "Camera Silens. Das Phantasma der 'Vernichtungshaft,'" in *Die RAF und der linke Terrorismus*, ed. Wolfgang Kraushaar (Hamburg: Hamburger Edition, 2006), 994-5.
48. Alexander Straßner, "Die dritte Generation der RAF," in *Die RAF und der linke Terrorismus*, ed. Wolfgang Kraushaar (Hamburg: Hamburger Edition, 2006), 495–96.
49. During this tenth strike, the RAF prisoners were for the first time also ready to negotiate, see Alexander Straßner, *Die dritte Generation der "Roten Armee Fraktion." Entstehung, Struktur, Funktionslogik und Zerfall einer terroristischen Organisation* (VS Verlag für Sozialwissenschaften: Wiesbaden, 2003), 172.
50. "Wenn in den nächsten 14 Tagen nicht mit Vernunft und Augenmaß gehandelt wird, . . . dann kriegen wir Verhältnisse wie 1977," see "Auf der Kippe," *Der Spiegel* 9 (1989): 109.
51. In theory, the approach to artificially feed prisoners once unconscious largely did away with the practice of force-feeding, where "force-feeding" is defined exclusively as the administration of food against the active resistance of the prisoner. The differentiation between forced and artificial feeding was not clear, however, in the public debate. The term force-feeding was still used by prisoners and their supporters, and it was also used more broadly, almost out of habit, as shorthand for the treatment of prisoners generally. As a result, there was a vagueness to the terminology, and it was consistently used by prisoners and politicians to refer to situations that could have been more accurately described as artificial feeding.
52. George Sweeney, "Irish Hunger Strikes and the Cult of Self-Sacrifice," *Journal of Contemporary History* 28(3) (1993): 422, 435.
53. Feldman, *Formations of Violence*, 219.
54. "essen—an alle / aus 'die IRA, Sinn Fein, sondernummer: folter und kz's in irland, dokumentation,'" HIS, F RA 02/006,002.
55. "'heiligste waffe' wie die ira sagt," see "u,g, (car) ni/hi/ne" in HIS, F RA 02/014,010. See also Pieter Bakker Schut, ed., *das info: briefe von gefangenen aus der RAF aud der diskussion 1973–1977* (Plambeck: Neuer Malik Verlag, 1987), 205.
56. Bakker Schut, ed., *das info*, 212.
57. "die price sisters, sie leben 10 mal 10 mal 10-tausend jahre!" See "zum ein- + vier-zeiler" in HIS, F RA 02/005,004.
58. "Ich denke, wir werden den Hungerstreik diesmal nicht abbrechen. Das heißt, es werden Typen dabei kaputt gehen," Baader as cited in Aust, *Der Baader Meinhof Komplex*, 296. This *info* was from February 4, 1974, see "Vorsitzenden des 2. Strafsenats des OLGs Stgt vom 25. September 1975" in GFA, H 362, F 3480.
59. "Vorsitzenden des 2. Strafsenats des OLGs Stgt vom 25. September 1975" in GFA, H 362, F 3480.
60. GFA, H 362, F 3283: 100.
61. "2. Strafsenat Verfügung vom 19. Dezember 1974," in GFA, H 362, F 3172.

62. For Baader's threat, see Aust, *Der Baader Meinhof Komplex*, 291. For Meinhof's threat, see GFA, H 362, F 3369: XI/11.
63. "Für mich war jedoch klar, daß eine Nichtteilnahme automatisch zum Ausschluß aus der RAF und damit aus dem Info mit all seinen Folgen geführt hätte." The consequences Müller refers to are the withholding of access to avenues of communication, but also legal representation and collective funds. See protocol of interrogation of Gerhard Müller from June 10, 1975, in GFA, H 362, F 3363: 6.
64. "schickt mir sofort wieder 1. ich brauch das, um den hs u. besonders den ds bis zum ende weitermachen zu können," as cited in Gäthje, "Das 'info'-System," 723.
65. "du blöder idiot. / fängst sofort wieder an und machst weiter—wenn du das nicht sowieso schon gemacht hast. das und nichts anderes . . . das einzige was zählt ist der kampf," see "du blöder idiot" in HIS, F RA 02/005,004. See also Bakker Schut, ed., *das info*, 183. Sections of this entry that include insults such as "asshole" (*arschloch*) were omitted from Bakker Schut's edited collection. Gätje has argued that the editing of Bakker Schut's collection renders the source unsuitable or of limited and conditional use for a linguistic study of the *info* system, see Gäthje, "Das 'info'-System," 716; and Olaf Gätje, *Der Gruppenstil der RAF im 'Info'-System. Eine soziostilistische Untersuchung aus systematischer Perspektive* (Berlin: Walter de Gruyter, 2008), 22–26. Colvin cites from the anthology while also conceding the anthology is a problematic source, see Sarah Colvin, *Ulrike Meinhof and West German Terrorism: Language, Violence, and Identity* (New York: Camden House, 2009), 161. Where possible, original passages have been cited.
66. Meinhof's case appears under the name "R. U." (Röhl, Ulrike) in H. Finkemeyer and R. Kautzky, "Das Kavernom des Sinus cavernosus," *Zentralblatt für Neurochirurgie* 29(1) (1968): 23–30.
67. "[N]ach dem Ergebnis der bisher durchgeführten Ermittlungen [kann] eine Beeinträchtigung der strafrechtlichen Verantwortlichkeit der Beschuldigten Ulrike Meinhof für die Zeit von Juni 1970 bis zu ihrer Festnahme am 15. Juni 1972 nicht ohne weiteres ausgeschlossen werden," as cited in Wesemann, *Ulrike Meinhof*, 394.
68. For the ruling recognizing but not implementing the medical recommendations, see GFA, H 362, F 3168: 290.
69. "Die Ergebnisse der Untersuchungen legen vielmehr den Schluß nahe, daß Ulrike Meinhof tot war, als man sie aufhängte, und daß es beunruhigende Indizien gibt, die auf das Eingreifen eines Dritten im Zusammenhang mit diesem Tode hinweisen," see Internationale Untersuchungskommission, ed., *Der Tod Ulrike Meinhofs. Bericht der Internationalen Untersuchungskommission* (Münster: Unrast Verlag, 2007), 6.
70. GFA, H 362, F 3370: XIV/13–XIV/19.
71. "Klar oder krank?" *Der Spiegel* 35 (1973): 55.
72. "Streit um den Kopf der Ulrike Meinhof," *Frankfurter Rundschau*, August 16, 1973.
73. "Ulrike Meinhof, eine 'schwere Psychopathin,' die den Sinn für die Realitäten verloren hat," and "Der Schreck der Nation—ein Fall für den Psychiater? So ist es!" See "Zur Berichterstattung der Presse über die RAF," in *Vorbereitung der*

RAF-Prozesse durch Presse, Polizei und Justiz, ed. Rosa Lévine, *rote hilfe. dokumentation* (Berlin: Eigendruck im Selbstverlag, 1975), 157.

74. HIS, F Me, U/012,007. A subsequent committee publication argued that the main purpose of performing scintigraphy on Meinhof was so that the "rulers" could declare Ulrike Meinhof—and therefore the RAF—to be crazy, and that the doctors and treatments were instrumentalized to lend such "counterpropaganda" (*Gegen-propaganda*) the "appearance of medical and psychiatric 'objectivity'" (*Schein der 'Objektivität' medizinisch-psychiatrischer Wissenschaft*), see "FOLTER MIT MEDIZINSICHEN MITTELN: VERSUCH EINER SZINTIGRAPHIE GEGEN ULRIKE MEINHOF," in *Der Kampf gegen die Vernichtungshaft*, ed. Komitee gegen Folter an politischen Gefangenen in der BRD (Eigenverlag), 130.

75. "und eben auch die idiotie des spk" in HIS, F Me,U/012,001. Such coaching on the use of specific terms was not limited to the "scientific," with Meinhof, for example, suggesting the use of the term "silent wing" (*stille Abteilung*), see a Meinhof letter to RAF lawyer Hans-Christian Ströbele from July 13, 1973, in GFA, H 362, F 3369: I/1.2.

76. "bringt endlich die komitee-argumentation auf das wissenschaftliche niveau, das die bullen haben und auf das politische niveau, das die raf hat," see HIS, F Me,U/008,002. The RAF leaders made no distinction between the police—the "pigs"—and the spread of publications in the commercial media.

77. "Die Wissenschaft ist politisch und die Politik ist wissenschaftlich," see "Teach-in des NRF als Tribunal?" *Rote Volksuniversität* (1972) in HIS, F Publ./007,001.

78. See "croi-stroe-be-kg" in HIS, F Me,U/008,002: 10; and "kg-croi-becker-preuss" in HIS, F Me,U/009,005.

79. "Wir werden in den Durststreik treten," 52–57.

80. "preuss" in HIS, F Me,U/009,005.

81. See Jander, "Isolation," 981; and Gerd Koenen, "Camera Silens," 1005. The poem was published, for example, in a committee publication as the transcript of a press conference given by family members of political prisoners, as read out by Anja Röhl and with the title "A prisoner letter from the death wing" (*Brief einer Gefangenen aus dem Toten Trakt*). The transcript reveals the authorship was withheld at the press conference. When asked who the poem was by, "several people" (*Mehrere*) answered: "That is not so important. No, it's not important—by one of the prisoners" (*Das ist nicht so wichtig. Nein, ist nicht wichtig—Von einer der Gefangenen*), see "DER GEHIRNWÄSCHE—TRAKT IN KÖLN-OSSENDORF," in *Der Kampf gegen die Vernichtungshaft*, ed. Komitee gegen Folter an politischen Gefangenen in der BRD (Eigenverlag), 201–2.

82. "das gefühl, es explodiert einem der kopf (das gefühl, die schädeldecke müßte eigentlich zerreißen, abplatzen)—/ das gefühl, es würde einem das rückenmark ins gehirn gepreßt—/ das gefühl, das gehirn schrumpelte einem allmählich zusammen, wie backobst zB—/ das gefühl, man stünde ununterbrochen, unmerklich, unter Strom, man würde ferngesteuert," see *info* from January 14, 1974, in HIS, F Me,U/009,002.

83. "ich schreib mal hier ein paar sachen auf und ihr sollt mal sagen, ob das überhaupt was für den kampf gegen die schweinerei bringt," see ibid.

84. "weil ich das eben auch genau nicht zur veröffentlichung aufgeschrieben habe, sondern um damit ein material zu liefern, das viell. dazu verhilft, die gegeninformation auf das wissenschaftliche niveau der schweinerei zu bringen," see "lieber klaus" in HIS, F Me,U/013,001. The *info* suggests that Ensslin was pushing for the poem's release. These discussions answer one aspect of the question left open by Koenen as to whether this text was really a poetic transcript of a prison experience or a literary complaint composed for the purposes of the campaign, see Koenen, "Camera Silens," 1005. The may well have been composed as a private description of the prison experience, either at the time or retrospectively, but its release and the timing of its release were certainly strategic moves designed to serve the campaign.

85. "VERTEIDIGERPOST Nr. 15" in HIS, F Me,U/013,001.

86. "Erklärung der Ärzte und Psychologen gegen den TOTEN TRAKT im 'neuen Klingelpütz'" in HIS, F RA 02/006,002. Compare this to the committee leaflet "M O R D AUF RATEN AN POLITISCHEN GEFANGENEN DURCH Ä R Z T E" in HIS, F RA 02/006,002, which looks very much the same.

87. "Ärzte gegen ZWANGSUNTERSUCHUNG" in HIS, F Me,U/012,003.

88. See the leaflet "HUNGERSTREIK. Kampf der politischen Gefangenen," in GFA, H 362, F 3363.

89. "preuss" in HIS, F Me,U/009,005.

90. "in *einem* ausgebreiteten gutachten, das am besten von *mehreren* 'experten' erstellt und unterzeichnet wird (theuns!)," as cited in the internal report *DIE 'KOMITEES GEGEN FOLTER AN POLITISCHEN GEFANGENEN IN DER BRD'. Analyse, Entwicklung und Prognose (Stand: Juli 1974)* in GFA, H 106, F 106992, Folder 626 612/4, Vol. 1.

91. "Anlage zum Protokoll vom 30. September 1975" in GFA, H 362, F 3480.

92. "preuss" in HIS, F Me,U/009,005.

93. Cornelia Brink, "Psychiatrie und Politik: Zum Sozialistischen Patientenkollektiv in Heidelberg," in *Terrorismus in der Bundesrepublik. Medien, Staat und Subkulturen in den 1970er Jahren*, ed. Klaus Weinhauer, Jörg Requate, and Heinz-Gerhard Haupt (Frankfurt: Campus, 2006), 138.

94. "Vermerk" from October 16, 1972, in HIS, F Hu,W/005,007. A newspaper clipping from June 19, 1972, from an unnamed newspaper in HIS, F Publ./010,003 reports Müller meeting Meinhof after attempting suicide and finding his way into the patient collective.

95. Brink, "Psychiatrie und Politik," 138. Overath writes of a total of more than thirty SPK members sentenced to prison for between one and four-and-a-half years in relation to RAF activities. This number includes Müller, Jünschke, Schiller, and Roll, as well as second-generation members Siegfried Hausner, Lutz Taufer, Hanna Krabbe, Sieglinde Hofmann, and Elisabeth von Dyck, see Margot Overath, *Drachenzähne. Gespräche, Dokumente und Recherchen aus der Wirklichkeit der Hochsicherheitsjustiz* (Hamburg: VSA-Verlag, 1991), 74.

96. For the leaflet, see "SPK RAF" in HIS, F Hu,W/003,004. For Meinhof's comments, see "und eben auch die idiotie des spk" in HIS, F Me,U/012,001. For the original statement from July 12, see "Die Revolution ist kein Deckchen" in HIS, F Hu,W/003,004.

97. "Dieses Flugblatt ist das letzte, das von Mitgliedern des ehemaligen SPK verteilt wird," see "ERKLÄRUNG AUS DEM EXIL" in HIS, F Hu,W/003,004.
98. The report attributes the text to Ensslin, see HIS, F SO 09/003,003: IX/4–5.
99. "Der Hauptwiderspruch in den Metropolen des Imperialismus" in HIS, F Me,U/013,002: 18.
100. "einen Mut und eine Kraft dokumentiert," see RAF, "Die Aktion des Schwarzen September in München," in *Rote Armee Fraktion. Texte und Materialien zur Geschichte der RAF*, ed. ID-Verlag (Berlin: ID-Verlag, 1997), 151. Bernd Weisbrod writes of this sort of emotional claim making as one element of the performativity of violence, see Bernd Weisbrod, "Terrorism as Performance: The Assassinations of Walther Rathenau and Hanns-Martin Schleyer," in *Control of Violence: Historical and International Perspectives on Violence in Modern Societies*, ed. Wilhelm Heitmeyer, Heinz-Gerhard Haupt, Andrea Kirschner, and Stefan Malthaner (New York: Springer, 2011), 366–67.
101. "der politische begriff für den toten trakt, köln, sage ich ganz klar ist: das gas. meine auschwitzphantasien dadrin waren realistisch," Bakker Schut, ed., *das info*, 21.
102. "das gefühl, es sei einem die Haut abgezogen worden," see *info* from January 14, 1974, in HIS, F Me,U/009,002.
103. "Unterschied toter Trakt und Isolation: Auschwitz zu Buchenwald. Der Unterschied ist einfach: Buchenwald haben mehr überlebt als Auschwitz . . . Wie wir drin ja, um das mal klar zu sagen, uns nur darüber wundern können, dass wir nicht abgespritzt werden. Sonst über nichts," as cited in Aust, *Der Baader Meinhof Komplex*, 293.
104. Habbo Knoch, *Die Tat als Bild. Fotografien des Holocaust in der deutschen Erinnerungskultur* (Hamburg: Hamburger Edition, 2001), 894. Zelizer also writes of a "visual amnesia," see Barbie Zelizer, *Remembering to Forget: Holocaust Memory through the Camera's Eye* (Chicago: University of Chicago Press, 1998), 141.
105. Petra Terhoeven, "Opferbilder—Täterbilder. Die Fotographie als Medium linksterroristischer Selbstermächtigung in Deutschland und Italien während der 70er Jahre," *Geschichte in Wissenschaft und Unterricht* 58(7/8) (2007): 392.
106. Terhoeven writes of Meins's autopsy image finding great resonance among RAF sympathizers but not being reported in the "mainstream" media. Here, a more prominent photograph of Meins, she writes, was one of the bearded Meins laid out in his coffin, hands folded peacefully, that evoked bizarre Jesus associations, see Terhoeven, "Opferbilder—Täterbilder," 393.
107. "[D]ieser Eindruck sei für sie 'eine der zentralen Weichenstellungen' gewesen, 'weil dieser ausgemergelte Mensch so viel Ähnlichkeit mit KZ-Häftlingen, mit den Toten von Auschwitz' gehabt habe," as cited in Wolfgang Kraushaar, "Mythos RAF. Im Spannungsfeld von terroristischer Herausforderung und populistischer Bedrohungsphantasie," in *Die RAF und der linke Terrorismus*, ed. Wolfgang Kraushaar (Hamburg: Hamburger Edition, 2006), 1193.
108. Terhoeven, "Opferbilder—Täterbilder," 392–93. Collenberg also cites Joachim Klein: "I kept the horrendous photograph of Holger's autopsy with me, so as not to dull the edge of my hatred," see Carrie Collenberg, "Dead Holger," in *Baader-Meinhof Returns: History and Cultural Memory of German Left-Wing Terrorism*,

ed. Gerrit-Jan Berendse and Ingo Cornils, *German Monitor* (New York: Rodopi, 2008), 77.

109. "wenn einer dadurch draufgeht, dann steht der name für das nächste kommando fest," as cited in an internal Ministry of the Interior report in GFA, H 141, F 404871.

110. "Tradition der NS-Medizin im deutschen Faschismus," see "Ärzte gegen ZWANGS-UNTERSUCHUNG" in HIS, F Me,U/012,003. This analogy eventually made it into commercial publications, for example, when *Der Spiegel* quoted directly from submissions, complaints, and other legal documents, as well as press conference statements, in which the RAF lawyer Klaus Croissant compared medical practice in prisons with Nazi methods, see "'Mord beginnt beim bösen Wort'. II," 52.

111. GFA, H 362, F 3165: 8–17, 21–24, and 312. The procedure was eventually deemed unnecessary once the earlier publication of Meinhof's medical history became apparent, see GFA, H 362, F 3164: 407/3–407/4. Electroencephalography uses electrodes placed on the scalp to measure brain activity.

112. See "Erklärung der Ärzte und Psychologen gegen den TOTEN TRAKT im 'neuen Klingelpütz'" in HIS, F RA 02/006,002.

113. "klingelpütz, den 13.11.1973" in HIS, F Me,U/012,001.

114. GFA, H 362, F 3370: XVI/15.

115. Force-feeding was broached as early as January 1973 in the IZRU leaflet "Rote Volksuniversität aktuell," see HIS, F Publ./007,002.

116. "Der Geist der Hitler-KZ'S" and "Isolation ist mit neuer Technologie, die alte Sache des Imperialismus, Endlösung durch Sonderbehandlung von damals zu lebensunwertem, heute (in der Terminologie der Bullen) grundrechtsunwertem Leben erklärten Minderheiten," see HIS, F RA 02/002,012.

117. HIS, F Me,U/008,002: 55.

118. In prison, Meinhof understood "imperialism" increasingly via the works of social scientist Dieter Senghaas, ordering the following titles: Dieter Senghaas, ed., *Imperialismus und strukturelle Gewalt—Analysen über abhängige Reproduktion* (Frankfurt: Suhrkamp, 1972); Dieter Senghaas and Claus Koch, eds., *Texte zur Technokratie-Diskussion* (Frankfurt: Europäische Verlagsanstalt, 1970); and Dieter Senghaas, *Aufrüstung durch Rüstungskontrolle. Über den symbolischen Gebrauch von Politik* (Stuttgart: Verlag Kohlhammer, 1972). For the orders, see GFA, H 362, F 3169: 246 and GFA, H 362, F 3170: 83, 119. In her personal notes, she wrote of the various functions of Senghaas's imperialism, which extended from the political and economic to the military, the medical, and the cultural. She saw his theory as the most important extension of Lenin's "imperialism," see GFA, H 362, F 3370: XV/30.

119. See Helmut Brunn and Thomas Kirn, *Rechtsanwälte, Linksanwälte* (Frankfurt am Main: Eichborn, 2004), 217. The connection to an imperialist torture research network made in alternative texts and activities was eventually also reported in commercial publications, for example, when *Der Spiegel* cited verbatim material produced by the International Committee for the Defense of Political Prisoners in Western Europe: "die Gefangenen aus der RAF [werden] seit sechs Jahren einem bis ins Detail vom CIA entwickelten Haftregiment der Einzel- und

Kleingruppen-Isolation, unterworfen" and "Die 'Mobilisierung' gegen die RAF sei 'ein Produkt der Supervision der amerikanischen Geheimdienste über die deutsche Innenpolitik, in der Bender und das baden-württembergische Landeskabinett nur die Rolle des Henkers übernommen haben,'" see "'Mord beginnt beim bösen Wort'. II."

120. Koenen, "Camera Silens," 997–99.

121. Ibid., 1000–1002. RAF sympathizers knew of such research and freely associated it with the prison conditions experienced by RAF prisoners. A committee text, for example, on the *camera silens* places the work done in the West German "special research field 115" (*Sonderforschungsbereich 115*) in the context of research conducted in the United States—particularly military research—into brainwashing and isolation. It also relies on a study published in Prague to draw parallels between "special research field 115" and torture and brainwashing under National Socialism and in the Stalin era before establishing links between the research conducted and the military. The text cited here is most likely from the early 1980s, but it relies on sources from the early 1970s, see "CAMERA-SILENS-EXPERIMENTE UND FOLTER," in *Der Kampf gegen die Vernichtungshaft*, ed. Komitee gegen Folter an politischen Gefangenen in der BRD (Eigenverlag), 139–42.

122. "das hamburger komitee hat sich die kamera silens vom ksv stehlen lassen," as cited in H. W. Frigge, *DIE "KOMITEES GEGEN FOLTER AN POLITISCHEN GEFANGENEN IN DER BRD." Analyse, Entwicklung und Prognose (1974)*, in GFA, H106, F 106992, Folder 626 612/4, Vol. 1: 11.

123. Such connections did indeed exist: in the early postwar context of behavior modification programs in U.S. prisons, researchers studied the "brainwashing" techniques used in North Korea and China to develop techniques for the U.S. prison system, see Alan Eladio Gómez, "Resisting Living Death at Marion Federal Penitentiary, 1972," *Radical History Review* 96 (2006): 62. Such links were also made at the time, for example, in a committee publication that places the scintigraphy and forced anesthesia in West Germany, and specifically in relation to Meinhof, in context with practices in U.S. prisons, such as the severing of neural pathways, electroshock therapy, and paralyzing drugs that mimic death, see "FOLTER MIT MEDIZINISCHEN MITTELN," 131. In terms of international cooperation, West German Professor Johann M. Burchard brought a Prague researcher to Hamburg in 1968, in what was an act of scientific cooperation across a border that seemed otherwise impenetrable by diplomacy and politics, see Koenen, "Camera Silens," 1001.

124. "der kolonisierte *heilt* sich von den tausend wunden (der krankheit), indem er den kolonialherrn mit waffengewalt davonjagt, er erkämpft sein LEBEN (spk: der gegensatz von krankheit ist leben)," see "und eben auch die idiotie des spk" in HIS, F Me,U/012,001.

125. "wenn kolonisierung eine eroberung war, bei der die vorhandenen gesellschaftlichen (ökonomischen, politischen, kulturellen und kommunikations-) strukturen vernichtet, das heißt: den eingeborenen entzogen wurden, sie stattdessen einem herrschaftsystem unterworfen worden sind—kolonialregime/imperialismus—, an dem sie nicht teilnehmen, / in dem sie nur als ding, als sache vorkommen—/ dann ist das kolonisierte individuum ein depriviertes individuum und der

deprivationsprozeß in der isolation dasselbe, was milliarden bei ihrer kolonisierung erlitten, durchgemacht haben—woran unendlich viele ja auch zugrundegegangen sind," see document 182549 in HIS, F Me, U/009,003. The text was written in 1973 or 1974. A copy in the HIS is stamped as being received (most likely by a RAF lawyer) on April 22, 1974. It was intended for internal discussion and was only published in 2001 as Ulrike Meinhof, "Deprivation und Kolonisierung. Über den Zusammenhang von Rehabilitierung und revolutionärer Aktion," *So oder So: Die Libertad!-Zeitung* 8 (2001).

126. For "kolonisierte gehirne," see GFA, H 362, F 3369: IX/6. For "das kolonialisierte Bewusstsein befreien," see HIS, F SO 09/003,003: XIV/28–31.

127. "psychiatrischen Exploration" and "körperlichen Eingriffe zur Blut- und Urinent-nahme," see Rote Volksuniversität aktuell in HIS, F Publ./007,002. Birgitta Wolf spoke of the integrity of the body in her press release from October 23, 1974, see "in körperliche Unversehrtheit und in die Persönlichkeitsstruktur eingreifen" and "PRESSE-ERKLÄRUNG" in HIS, F Me,U/015,004.

Chapter 4

1. "das ist eben die frage: w e r die öffentlichkeit, die stammheim hat, für sich benutzt: sie oder wir, die bundesanwaltschaft für die durchsetzung ihrer vernich-tungsstrategie gegen die staatguerilla auf dem terrain der justiz oder wir," see Hamburg Institute of Social Research (HIS), File (F) Me,U/025,007.

2. HIS, F Me,U/004,004.

3. "Denkmal aus Stahl und Beton," Stefan Aust, *Der Baader Meinhof Komplex* (Munich: Wilhelm Goldmann Verlag, 1998), 337.

4. "schon Beton gewordenes Urteil," Helmut Brunn and Thomas Kirn, *Rechtsan-wälte, Linksanwälte* (Frankfurt am Main: Eichborn, 2004), 309; and Hanno Balz, "Gesellschaftsformierungen. Die öffentliche Debatte über die RAF in den 70er Jahren," in *Der 'Deutsche Herbst' und die RAF in Politik, Medien und Kunst. Natio-nale und internationale Perspektiven* ed. Nicole Colin, Beatrice De Graaf, Jacco Pekelder, and Joachim Umlauf (Bielefeld: Transcript Verlag, 2008), 175. Ditfurth also cites *The Times* in London as doubting a fair trial was possible given the siege mentality represented by the architecture, and *Der Spiegel* as questioning whether these physical conditions would not inevitably lead to a guilty verdict; see Jutta Ditfurth, *Ulrike Meinhof. Die Biographie* (Berlin: Ullstein, 2007), 400. Similarly, Bakker Schut cites numerous contemporary impressions of the Stammheim facility and associated doubts it could be conducive to a fair trial from both the domestic and international press (the international examples are all from Western Europe); see Pieter Bakker Schut, *Stammheim: Der Prozeß gegen die Rote Armee Fraktion. Die notwendige Korrektur der herrschenden Meinung* (Bonn: Pahl-Rugenstein, 2007), 170–73.

5. "von Unschuldvermutung zu sprechen, ist lächerlich . . . Die Formulierung vom Schuldspruch, der in Gestalt dieses Gebäudes längst und im vorhinein in Beton gegossen wurde, ist in diesem Zusammenhang durchaus zutreffend," see German Federal Archive (GFA), Holding (H) 362, File (F) 3445: 2016–17.

6. "die architektur dieses prozeßbunkers sieht aus wie die amerikanische botschaft in saigon. das entspricht—wenn die vermittlungen auch kompliziert sind, der situation . . . die architektur dieser betonfestung bildet die besonderen beziehungen zwischen dem deutschen und us-imperialismus, die spezifische situation der revolution in deutschland aus ihrer geschichte von niederlagen und der rolle, die der westdeutsche imperialismus in der kette des us-imperialismus hat, ab . . . die architektur dieser betonfestung, der aufmarsch der polizei und des bgs, die ausweiskontrollen und leibesvisitationen, die fahrzeugkontrollen, der charakter dieses verfahren als ausnahmeverfahren—reine propagandistische vorbereitung seit 3 jahren um als gebrochene menschen, zerstörte kämpfer hier vorgeführt zu werden, sitzen wir seit 3 jahren in toten trakts und totaler sozialer isolation," HIS, F Me,U/008,004.

7. See Jörg Requate, " 'Terroristenanwälte' und Rechtsstaat: Zur Auseinandersetzung um die Rolle der Verteidiger in den Terroristenverfahren der 1970er Jahre," in *Terrorismus in der Bundesrepublik. Medien, Staat und Subkulturen in den 1970er Jahren*, ed. Klaus Weinhauer, Jörg Requate, and Heinz Gerhard Haupt (Frankfurt: Campus Verlag, 2006), 271; Klaus Eschen, "Das Sozialistische Anwaltskollektiv," in *Die RAF und der linke Terrorismus*, ed. Wolfgang Kraushaar (Hamburg: Hamburger Edition, 2006), 969; and Stefan Reinecke, "Die linken Anwälte. Eine Typologie," in *Die RAF und der linke Terrorismus*, ed. Wolfgang Kraushaar (Hamburg: Hamburger Edition, 2006), 953–54. A number of high-profile incidents led to this perception of collusion beyond defense: not least of all the *Kassiber-Affäre*, which saw Otto Schily accused of smuggling a written note from the freshly arrested Ensslin to the still at large Meinhof. Ensslin's note describing the prison conditions inside was found on Meinhof when she was arrested.

8. See Bakker Schut, *Stammheim*, 142; and Heinrich Hannover, *Terroristenprozesse. Erfahrungen und Erkenntnisse eines Strafverteidigers* (Hamburg: VSA-Verlag, 1991), 160.

9. "1. an der Tat, die den Gegenstand der Untersuchung bildet, beteiligt ist, / 2. den Verkehr mit dem nicht auf freiem Fuß befindlichen Beschuldigten dazu mißbraucht, Straftaten zu begehen oder die Sicherheit einer Vollzugsanstalt erheblich zu gefährden, oder / 3. eine Handlung begangen hat, die für den Fall der Verurteilung des Beschuldigten Begünstigung, Strafvereitelung oder Hehlerei wäre," see Bundesministerium der Justiz, ed., *Strafprozessordnung* (2008).

10. Requate, " 'Terroristenanwälte' und Rechtsstaat," 273 and 83–84.

11. "zum taktisch günstigen Zeitpunkt," as cited in Ditfurth, *Ulrike Meinhof*, 397.

12. See Bakker Schut, *Stammheim*, 45–46 and 143–45; and Hannover, *Terroristenprozesse*, 146, 200.

13. Ditfurth, *Ulrike Meinhof*, 401. Similar legislation was controversially tested in 2007 in Germany in the context of the post-9/11 "war on terror." In 2003 the German parliament amended section 129a that defines a "terrorist organization" (*terroristische Vereinigung*), and in 2007 the police used the powers of this section to keep the homes of academics Andrej H. and Matthias B. under surveillance, track their mobile phones, read their emails, and bug their phones for almost a year. The federal prosecutor suspected sociologist Andrej and political scientist Matthias of being the intellectual masterminds behind the group *militante gruppe*

("mg") after Google searches identified a doctoral thesis and a 1998 article on Kosovo "key words and phrases" that also appeared in "mg" declarations: "draconian," "implodes," "propaganda of the deed," "gentrification," "inequality." Evidence collected during the surveillance and additional raids on private residences included two occasions that Andrej met with another suspect for coffee and the fact that Matthias—in his capacity as an academic—had access to libraries, which he could potentially use to compose texts for a terrorist group, although he was not accused of doing so. Andrej was kept in remand for four weeks, which meant 23 hours a day isolation, before the Federal Court of Justice ruled in late November 2007 that "mg" did not constitute a "terrorist organization." It found that, despite the group's textual aggression, the string of arson attacks carried out since 2001 on police cars, employment offices, and empty supermarkets were not capable, as required under section 129a, of "substantially damaging the fundamental structures of the state" or "substantially intimidating the population." The "mg" case revived memories of the RAF not only because of the targets and the mode of attack, the expressed goal of bringing down the capitalist world order, or the fact that "mg" produced declarations justifying its struggle against the "symbols of capitalism" and imperialism that explicitly referenced a text by former RAF terrorist Christian Klar, but also because of the controversial scope of the legislation used to counter the threat. Interestingly, unlike splinter groups of the 1980s and 1990s inspired by the RAF, and indeed the second generation of the RAF, which looked to the RAF martyrs of Stammheim and RAF texts by Meinhof in particular, "mg" cited texts from the second generation of the RAF. See Dietmar Hipp, Caroline Schmidt, and Michael Sontheimer, "Gebildet, unauffällig, verdächtig," *Der Spiegel* 47 (2007) 52–55; Dietmar Hipp and Caroline Schmidt, "Mit aller Härte," *Der Spiegel* 35 (2007) 48–49: "Bundesrichter sehen 'militante gruppe' nicht als Terrorvereinigung," *Spiegel-Online*, November 28, 2007, http://www.spiegel.de/politik/deutschland/0,1518,520245,00.html (accessed March 28, 2011); and Philipp Wittrock, "Wissenschaftler im Visier der Linksterror-Fahnder," *Spiegel-Online*,August2,2007,http://www.spiegel.de/politik/deutschland/0,1518,497923,00.html (accessed March 28, 2011).

14. "alle verfahren gegen die gefangenen aus der raf sind e i n prozeß," HIS, F Me,U/025,007.

15. Andreas Baader et al., "Vor einer solchen Justiz verteidigen wir uns nicht. Schlußwort im Kaufhausbrandprozeß," *VoltaireFlugschrift* 27 (1969): 6. Thorwald Proll has since claimed sole authorship of the closing statement; see Thorwald Proll and Daniel Dubbe, *Wir kamen vom anderen Stern. Über 1968, Andreas Baader und ein Kaufhaus* (Hamburg: Edition Nautilus, 2003), 43.

16. "die autoritären Strukturen zum Übereinanderfallen . . . bringen," Proll and Dubbe, *Wir kamen vom anderen Stern*, 34.

17. "Wie verschafft man den Ermittlungsrichtern Magengeschwüre?" GFA, H 362, F 3167: 37c.

18. "Einige Gefangene sollen auf Veranlassung des Gerichts im Asdonk-Prozeß gehört werden. Gesagt wird nichts," GFA, H 362, F 3370: XIII/21.

19. "1. Nur Angaben zur Person machen . . . 2. Sonst keinerlei Aussagen machen! Jedes Wort kann gegen euch verwendet werden" and "NICHTS SAGEN,"

see Georg-von-Rauch-Haus, Tommy-Weißbecker-Haus, and Schöneberger Jungarbeiter- und Schülerzentrum, eds., *Dokumentation über die Polizeiüberfälle am 5.3.75*, 110–11. The booklet is undated, but given the content, was most likely produced in mid-1975.

20. Meinhof had the option of instead serving three days in prison; see GFA, H 362, F 3168: 515–16.

21. Four trial days later Meinhof complains of being prevented from taking part in the *Vernehmung zur Person*; see GFA, H 362, F 3445.

22. "teil der maschine," see "der bewaffnete kampf ist der operator" in HIS, F Me,U/025,005.

23. "wir bestimmen unser verhältnis zu den anwälten nach den kriterien proletarischer bündnispolitik . . . wir bestimmen es aus unserm interesse," see HIS, F Me,U/025,007.

24. HIS, F Me,U/008,010.

25. GFA, H 362, F 3171: 411–21.

26. Meinhof's letters adding and removing counsel from 1974 to 1976 are held in GFA, H 362, F 3172.

27. "es ist einfach. Es handelt sich bei diesen Zwangsverteidigern um Instrumente der B.Anwaltschaft," GFA, H 362, F 3441.

28. "bei ASDONK wurden genaue Untersuchungen gemacht: Blut/Urin. Sie wurde als *krank* erklärt, d.h. Prozeß fiel aus, keine Freistunde, Besuch etc," HIS, F Me,U/008,010: 152 7 RS.

29. "ist jemand krank, kann also nicht kommen, kann nicht verhandelt werden, ist jemand länger als 10 Tage krank, ist der Prozeß geplatzt," ibid.

30. "Dieser Umstand kann vom Angeklagten dazu mißbraucht werden, durch absichtliche Herbeiführung der Verhandlungsunfähigkeit die Weiterführung des gegen ihn gerichteten Strafverfahrens zu verhindern," see report from September 25, 1975, justifying continuation in absence of defendants in GFA, H 362, F 3480.

31. In the context of the debate over the fitness of the accused to stand trial, RAF lawyer Otto Schily requested the prisoners be examined by a doctor other than Dr. Henck, as Henck had not been able to perform an examination because the prisoners had refused to cooperate; see GFA, H 362, F 3443: 981.

32. Ibid.: 1128–29.

33. The expert medical witnesses are listed as professors Rasch, Müller, Schröder and Mende, see GFA, H 362, F 3446: 3112.

34. "Die Hauptverhandlung wird in Abwesenheit der Angeklagten fortgesetzt. / Gründe: / Die Angeklagten sind verhandlungsunfähig im Sinne von § 231 a StPO.* Die Vorschrift des § 231 a StPO will sicherstellen, daß ein Angeklagter die Durchführung des Verfahrens nicht durch wissentlich herbeigeführte Verhandlungsunfähigkeit verhindert . . . Der Senat hat keine Zweifel, daß die Hungerstreiks wenigstens mit-ursächlich für den heutigen Gesundheitszustand der Angeklagten sind," ibid.: 3124–28.

35. "Vor Gericht endet in Deutschland die Würde des Individuums, jenseits des Kreidekreises, von der Publikumsschranke an bis in den letzten dörflichen, städtischen, sozialen und asozialen Winkel setzt mit dem ersten Verhandlungstag der Rechtsstaat aus, das Volksempfinden ein," see Ulrike Marie Meinhof, "Von

Mördern und Menschen," *konkret* 5 (1962): 3. The "chalk circle" is a reference to Bertolt Brecht's play *The Caucasian Chalk Circle* (*Der kaukasische Kreidekreis*).

36. Ditfurth, *Ulrike Meinhof*, 397–98.
37. Bakker Schut, *Stammheim*, 124–25.
38. Brunn and Kirn, *Rechtsanwälte, Linksanwälte*, 314–15; and Balz, "Gesellschafts-formierungen," 175.
39. Bakker Schut, *Stammheim*, 238.
40. Ulf G. Stuberger, *Die Tage von Stammheim. Als Augenzeuge beim RAF-Prozeß* (Munich: Herbig, 2007), 43–44.
41. As cited in Sarah Colvin, *Ulrike Meinhof and West German Terrorism: Language, Violence, and Identity* (New York: Camden House, 2009), 131.
42. GFA, H 362, F 3397.
43. "habt ihr den arsch auf oder was ist los!???! / ihr hattet in frankfurt die möglichkeit, den schinken platzen zu lassen—die chance, eine irre attacke gegen die isolations-folter zu reiten—und gegen den toten trakt köln—wo astrid drin gefoltert worden ist, bis auf die knochen, durch und durch,—warte—und ihr ergreift sie nicht. ihr prozessiert weiter." This *info* entry from January 9, 1974, is cited in a report from September 25, 1975, that was used to help justify the decision to continue the trial in the absence of the defendants and is held in GFA, H 362, F 3480.
44. The full title is "Der Hauptwiderspruch in den Metropolen des Imperialismus ist der Widerspruch zwischen Produktivitäten und Produktionsverhältnissen." Also referred to by the RAF as the "Proll-Rede" or "Frankfurter-Erklärung," see GFA, H 362, F 3185. A copy of the speech is held in HIS, F Me,U/013,002.
45. GFA, H 362, F 3185.
46. "es ist noch lange nicht klar, daß in stgt. verteidigt wird. wir haben an dieser veranstaltung nur interesse wenn wir sie umdrehen können . . . aber nochmal, prozeße, die nichts transportieren können, keine öffentlichkeit haben—werden nicht g e f ü h r t . sie kriegen nur die erklärung, danach keine verteidiger + keine angeklagten," see a prison text by Baader from June 1974 found in the cell of RAF member Monika Berberich in GFA, H 362, F 3480.
47. "das aus der erfahrung von den 4 monaten hier. er hilft einem nicht durchblicken, er stört einem nur. anträge sind n u r vehikel und hebel, sonst nichts. weil's so ist, dass es die funktion und so auch struktur der juristischen rituale. des para-graphendschungels ist unterdrückung zu produzieren. das heisst: man kann sie nicht umdrehen. auf dem terrain hat der staat die macht und nur eine ratte wie b kann darauf kommen, zu behaupten, es liesse sich mit juristischen tricks und finten das kraftverhältnis verändern," see "der bewaffnete kampf ist der operator" in HIS, F Me,U/025,005.
48. "ob ne verteidigung mit juristischen argumenten durchkommt hängt auch—aber immer mehr erst in zweiter und dritter linie vom juristischen niveau der argu-mente ab. wenn damit überhaupt noch was zu machen ist—ist primär eine macht-frage. das heißt, macht vermittelt durch das, was sich in bezug auf öffentlichkeit abspielt," HIS, F Me,U/008,002.
49. "unsere linie ganz klar [ist]: alles, was wir tun, tun wir mit bezug zur proletarischen und internationalen antiimperialistischen öffentlichkeit. alles . . . du sagst: ein

schriftsatz, der veröffentlicht wird, wirkt immer besser, wenn er sich auf juristische argumente beschränkt—bei wem?" Ibid.

50. Bakker Schut, *Stammheim*, 311–12. For recordings on YouTube of Baader and Ensslin during the trial and arguing that proceedings should be understood in the context of the "dramaturgy" (*Dramaturgie*) of the contemporaneous election campaign, see *andreas baader im originalton. 4. mai 1976*, http://www.youtube .com/watch?v=LxRI8--EgEU&feature=related (accessed March 13, 2011), and *gudrun ensslin im originalton. 4. mai 1976*, http://www.youtube.com/watch?v=gTO 62ML75fY&NR=1 (accessed March 13, 2011).

51. Baaker Schut writes of two strategies of the defense: to frame the 1972 bomb attacks as "self-defense," that is, as resistance in terms of an "international proletarianism," and to demand treatment as POWs in line with the Geneva Conventions; see Bakker Schut, *Stammheim*, 317–18. These are treated here as aspects of the one strategy of presenting the "urban guerilla" of the RAF as part of an international resistance movement. Importantly, it was via these strategies that the group maintained the sympathy that had mounted around the prison campaigns.

52. Prinzing as cited in Aust, *Der Baader Meinhof Komplex*, 361. Balz argues that politicians' open speculation on the verdict before the trial concluded, and the attention paid to prisoners, which manifested in tailored prison conditions and the building of the Stammheim courthouse, undermine the notion that the authorities considered this a "normal criminal trial," Balz, "Gesellschaftsformierungen," 174.

53. "der erste politische Prozeß in der Bundesrepublik seit 1945," as cited in Aust, *Der Baader Meinhof Komplex*, 361.

54. HIS, F Me,U/025,007.

55. Ibid.

56. Rolf Gössner, *Das Anti-Terror-System. Politische Justiz im präventiven Sicherheitsstaat* (Hamburg: VSA-Verlag, 1991), 95–98.

57. "Verfolgung richtet sich ausschließlich gegen das kriminelle Tun und nicht gegen deren etwaige politische Motivation," as cited in Balz, "Gesellschaftsformierungen," 173.

58. Colvin, *Ulrike Meinhof and West German Terrorism*, 137. Colvin also notes the contradictory situation the state found itself in: accepting the RAF's inflammatory declaration of war, while dismissing the group as mere criminals.

59. "verteidigung wird politische opposition gegen die politik der bundesanwaltschaft, die innerstaatliche strategie des neuen faschismus: counterinsurgency, / oder / sie ist teil des projekts der bundesanwaltschaft—indem sie an deren verschleierung mitwirkt—/ ihrer verschleierung in der form des vorgetäuschten 'normalen strafverfahrens,' " HIS, F Me,U/025,007. Bakker Schut includes an almost identical quote with the additional word "*resistance*" (italics his), which is extremely loaded in the postwar German context, particularly when used in combination with "fascism," see Bakker Schut, *Stammheim*, 314–15.

60. "es geht in diesem prozeß darum, das 'normale strafverfahren' zu zerstören . . . zerstörung des normalen strafverfahrens ist eben genau n i c h t prozeßsabotage sondern aufdeckung der wahrheit dieses verfahrens gegen uns und damit der wahrheit der sozialdemokratie und damit der wahrheit des westdeutschen staats

als einer funktion des us-imperialismus, des hauptfeindes der völker der welt," HIS, F Me,U/025,007.

61. "die rolle 'normales strafverfahren' . . . spielen," HIS, F Me,U/025,005.

62. "Im normalen Sprachgebrauch umfaßt der Begriff des 'pG' [politischen Gefangenen] zwei Gruppen: 1.) von den pigs aus jeden Straftäter gegen die §§ 80-109 k StGB (Landesverrat, Vereins-/Parteiverbot etc.) und §§ 125-131 (Landfriedensbruch . . .) 2.) im liberalen/herkömmlich linken Sprachgebrauch, jeden Gefangenen, der aus politischen Gründen eingelocht worden ist, d.h. aus politischer Motivation heraus ein Delikt begangen hat (haben soll) . . . Unter Führung der RH ist versucht worden, diesen Begriff zu erweitern auf 3.) jeden Knastologen, der den Knast als *politisches* Unterdrückungsmittel der herrschenden Klasse begreift und schließlich 4.) auf jeden Knastologen überhaupt, der dagegen Widerstand leistet, auch wenn er noch politisch 'unbewußt' ist . . . Im Ergebnis hat das alles jedoch dazu geführt, daß jeder unter dem Begriff 'pG' etwas anderes versteht, und auch die RH in der Regel den Begriff im Sinne 2.) benutzt (trotz gegenteiliger Beteuerungen) / Ein derart schillernder Begriff ist daher unbrauchbar," see "Einige individuelle GEDANKENSPLITTER" held in GFA, H 362, F 3370: XIII/16. The term "prisonologist" (*knastologe*) is used to lend an air of professionalism to someone who has been in and out of prison.

63. "und wieder andere votierten für die Unterstützung der revolutionären Arbeiterklasse, was immer das auch hieß," Volker Speitel, " 'Wir wollten alles und gleichzeitig nichts,' " *Der Spiegel* 31 (1980): 37.

64. GFA, H 362, F 3370: XIII/11–XIII/15.

65. "Alle Anwälte, mit Ausnahme von zweien, sind für die Parole '*politische* Gefangene.' Ebenfalls für den Begriff Pg sind das IZRU und der KSV, allerdings verstehen beide etwas Anderes darunter. / Die Roten Hilfen und ehemalige Gefangene (Schiller, Herzog, Mauer) meinen, dieser Begriff sei spalterisch, nicht zu vermitteln im Knast. / Dagegen argumentieren die Anwälte voll mit der Meinung der RAF-Prominenten. Allerdings tauchten Zweifel darüber auf, ob die Anwälte die Meinung der RAF richtig vermittelten," GFA, H 362, F 3370: XIII/2.

66. The IZRU position recalls the argument by the SPK that it does not matter if in prison or not—prison is merely an extension of the same capitalist oppression experienced on the outside. The extrapolated argument is that everyone is a prisoner and all prisoners are political; see HIS, F Hu,W/003,004.

67. GFA, H 362, F 3370: XIII/1–3.

68. Ibid.: XIII/2.

69. "politischer gefangener ist jeder gefangene, der seine lage begreift, sich als den gefangenen der herrschenden klasse—des geldes—begriffen hat, gegen den vernichtungsvollzug an den isolierten gefangenen und kretinisierenden behandlungsvollzug an allen gefangenen widerstand leistet, deswegen in isolation oder von isolation jeden augenblick bedroht ist," HIS, F RA 02/005,004.

70. The term *Staatsschutz* is an umbrella term for measures taken to protect a state from politically motivated acts.

71. "Politischer Gefangener zu sein heißt, der p o l i t i s c h e n Klassenjustiz gegenüberzustehen: dem Staatsschutz. Politischer Gefangener in der BRD zu sein heißt, Gefangener des Staats zu sein, der im Interesse der Feinde des Volkes,

der Feinde der RAF (Rote Armee Fraktion) die Revolutionäre anklagt . . . / Zum politischen Gefangenen wird auch der, der als Gefangener begreift, daß das Gefängnissystem Disziplinierungsinstrument, Institution des permanenten Faschismus gegen Teile des Volkes ist zur Aufrechterhaltung der kapitalistischen Herrschaft, und danach handelt; der den unsolidarischen Privatstandpunkt 'Fresse halten—dann passiert dir nix—dann kommste hoch' als Ausdruck des Elends, der Unterwerfung, der Ohnmacht überwunden hat und sich mit anderen Gefangenen auflehnt. / Politischer Gefangener in der BRD zu sein heißt schließlich, einer schleichenden Exekution, der unblutigen und äußerlich spurlosen Folter durch soziale Isolation/sensorische Deprivation unterworfen zu werden," Komitees gegen Folter an politischen Gefangenen in der BRD und Westberlin, "COUNTERINSURGENCY GEGEN DIE RAF," in *Der Kampf gegen die Vernichtungshaft*, ed. Komitee gegen Folter an politischen Gefangenen in der BRD (Eigenverlag), 33.

72. "Application 6166/73. Andreas BAADER, Holger MEINS, Ulrike MEINHOF, Wolfgang GRUNDMANN v/the FEDERAL REPUBLIC OF GERMANY," *Decisions and Reports of the European Commission of Human Rights* 2 (1975): 59.

73. "Application 6166/73," 62.

74. HIS, F Me,U/008,010.

75. "Application 6166/73," 59–60.

76. "was wir . . . von den schriftstellern jetzt erwarten, ist, daß ihr nicht nur in resolutionen auf eurem treffen, sondern danach in den medien und verlagshäusern, zu denen ihr zugang habt—im funk, im fernsehen, in zeitungen, in zeitschriften über die ziele unseres hungerstreiks informiert; . . . daß ihr / 1. unsere hungerstreikerklärung aktiv verbreitet—/ . . . 3. daß ihr den begriff des POLITISCHEN GEFANGENEN als das was er ist: ein kampfbegriff durchsetzt, vertretet," see "AN DAS SCHRIFTSTELLERTREFFEN IN FRANKFURT" in HIS, F Me,U/015,001.

77. GFA, H 362, F 3454.

78. Other names included former West German Chancellors Ludwig Erhard, Kurt Georg Kiesinger, and Willi Brandt, and former President of the Federal Republic Gustav Heinemann.

79. Volker Speitel, " 'Wir wollten alles und gleichzeitig nichts' (II)," *Der Spiegel* 32 (1980): 32.

80. The International Committee of the Red Cross (ICRC) prompted negotiations in 1965 when it raised concerns about the protection of civilian populations and the risk of indiscriminate warfare. At its 1968 Tehran meeting, the International Conference on Human Rights adopted a resolution requesting the General Assembly of the United Nations invite the Secretary-General to investigate the measures necessary to ensure better application of existing humanitarian law. The General Assembly in turn invited the Secretary-General to undertake a study in consultation with the ICRC, which resulted in reports handed down in 1969, 1970, and 1971. Particularly important for the discussion here are amendments made to articles 1, 43, and 44. Article 1 was broadened to include "armed struggles waged by peoples for the exercise of their right to self-determination," that is, national liberation movements. At the 1974 Diplomatic Conference, the ICRC draft was amended to make the law governing international conflicts apply also to conflicts of "self-determination," a wording that was adopted as article 1,

section 4 in 1977. Article 43 sets out the legal definition of the parties to a conflict. The ICRC draft of 1972 reads that "armed forces shall be organized and subject to an internal discipline system, which should enforce respect for the applicable rules of international law." In 1973 "armed forces" was expanded to include "the armed forces of resistance movements." This definition was further widened at the 1976 conference (and later adopted in 1977) to read: "The armed forces of a Party to the conflict consist of all organized armed forces, groups and units which are under a command responsible to that Party for the conduct of its subordinates, even if that Party is represented by a government or an authority not recognized by an adverse Party." Article 44 addresses the definition of POWs, and as early as the 1971 conference experts argued that traditional criteria—the fixed distinctive sign and the open carrying of arms—were inconsistent with the requirements of guerilla warfare. A subsequent 1972 ICRC draft article stipulated that "organized resistance or independence movements" were entitled to POW status when captured, even if represented by an unrecognized government or authority. This protection was, however, on the conditions that they comply with the law, distinguish themselves from the civilian population by carrying arms openly or by wearing a fixed distinctive sign, and be organized under a responsible commander. These conditions were retained in the 1973 draft "New category of prisoners of war" with one amendment, which clarified "compliance with the law" as the conducting of "military operations in accordance with the Conventions [of 1949] and the present Protocol." The adopted article proceeds on the assumption that the nature of contemporary warfare dictated that an armed combatant cannot always distinguish himself, but he is still entitled to POW status if he carries his arms during a military engagement. See W. Thomas Mallison and Sally V. Mallison, "The Juridical Status of Privileged Combatants under the Geneva Protocol of 1977 Concerning International Conflicts," *Law and Contemporary Problems* 42(2) (1978): 6–22; and International Committee of the Red Cross, *Commentary on the Additional Protocols of 8 June 1977 to the Geneva Conventions of 12 August 1949* (Geneva: Martinus Nijhoff, 1987), 384–86, 505.

81. "internationaler zusammenhang der unterdrückung" and "internationaler zusammenhang der guerillabewegung," as cited in Bakker Schut, *Stammheim*, 311.

82. "wir verlangen n u r , dass ihr die gefangenen aus der stadtguerilla im rahmen der p o l i t i s c h e n verteidigungsLINE, also mit der perspektive ner rechtspolitik im internationalen zusammenhang verteidigt," HIS, F Me,U/025,007.

83. "weiter—kriegsgefangene: / ihr braucht da nur, was die uno längst macht, diese definitionen (partisanen usw.) in die spezifik dieses verfahrens umzusetzen / und wir *erinnern* da mal so arschlöcher wie pfaff daran, dass diese initiative in der uno auch wesentlich durch *uns* entwickelt wurde—zumindest was westeuropa angeht. / die defintion der uno meint in diesem begriff 'international [illegible],' das nicht als eigennutz oder psychologisch definiert ist, sondern 'einer sache verpflichtet' explizit auch uns. wissen wir definitiv. / das kam in den zusatzanträgen zu moynihan [sic] jetzt zum ausdruck," ibid.

84. By consensus at the 1974 session, recognized national liberation movements were invited to participate: African National Congress, Angola National Liberation Front, Mozambique Liberation Front, Palestine Liberation Organization, Panafricanist

Congress, People's Movement for the Liberation of Angola, Seychelles People's United Party, South West African People's Organization, Zimbabwe African National Union, and Zimbabwe African People's Union: see Mallison and Mallison, "The Juridical Status of Privileged Combatants," 8, 16–17.

85. "Der Imperialismus des internationalen Kapitals und seine Agenten," HIS, F RA 02/011,009: 62.

86. "Diesem neuen Inhalt kriegerischer Konflikte muß auch eine brauchbare Definition dessen, was völkerrechtlich als Krieg zu betrachten ist, Rechnung tragen. Auf das hergebrachte formale Kriterium, daß Nationalstaaten die Konfliktpartner sein müssen, kann es nicht mehr ankommen," ibid.: 68.

87. "internationale öffentlichkeit sei nur über den prozess und durch die verteidigung zu erreichen—eben. es geht auch nicht darum, gremien anzurufen, von denen nur ne abfuhr zu erwarten ist—es geht darum, im prozess und aus der konfrontation im prozess eine politische initiative zu entwickeln . . . es gibt ein projekt: status kriegsgefangene . . . die taktik in dem verfahren kann nur: widerstand sein. widerstand der anwälte gegen . . . und sinn hat das in stammheim und nur in stammheim, weil hier die öffentlichkeit ist," HIS, F Me,U/008,002.

88. "und kampf um den status kriegsgefangene. wir scheißen natürlich auf den status. es ist der operator, internationale öffentlichkeit für unseren kampf gegen die vernichtungshaft zu mobilisieren. / und allerdings um die völkerrechtliche anerkennung der s o z i a l revolutionären bewegungen als kriegsführender partei—/ es ist die einzige möglichkeit der vermittlung von verteidigung auf der ebene der justiz: völkerrecht," HIS, F Me,U/025,007.

89. "die brd darf keine weiteren gefangenen in den gefängnissen mehr ermorden," HIS, F Me,U/015,006.

90. "das ganze sollte von einem verlag oder einer ko-operation verschiedener verlage herausgebracht werden. / zwischen die einzelnen dokumente sollten texte geschaltet werden, die klarmachen, daß die anwendung der genfer konvention über die behandlung von krieggefangenen notwendig ist, um die vernichtung der gefangenen unter dem mantel des 'normalen strafverfahrens' zu verhindern," HIS, F RA 02/011,008.

91. Alexander Straßner, *Die dritte Generation der "Roten Armee Fraktion." Entstehung, Struktur, Funktionslogik und Zerfall einer terroristischen Organisation* (Wiesbaden: VS Verlag für Sozialwissenschaften, 2003), 172.

92. The RAF called for the formation of a Western European Front in its 1982 *May Paper* (*Mai-Papier*). In 1985 Action Directe and the RAF coauthored the text *For the Unity of Western European Revolutionaries* (*Für die Einheit der Revolutionäre in Westeuropa*), and carried out simultaneous attacks shortly thereafter. A significant factor in the failure of the Front was the lack of support from the powerful groups in Western Europe: Spain's Basque Homeland and Freedom (Euskadi Ta Askatasuna, ETA) and the IRA. For example, when the RAF commando that assassinated Ernst Zimmermann in February 1985 took the name of an IRA prisoner who died during the 1981 hunger strike—Patsy O'Hara—the Irish organization rebuked the move as a defilement of O'Hara's name, see Alexander Straßner, "Die dritte Generation der RAF," in *Die RAF und der linke Terrorismus*, ed. Wolfgang Kraushaar (Hamburg: Hamburger Edition, 2006), 504–6.

Chapter 5

1. "Das Fehlen des Abschiedsbriefes ist ein entscheidender Faktor. Dieser spricht m.E. entschieden gegen Selbstmord und steht auch im Gegensatz zu allem, was wir sonst über sie wissen . . . Es ist ausgeschlossen, daß Ulrike Meinhof einen Selbstmord begangen hätte, ohne einen Abschiedsbrief zu hinterlassen," see Internationale Untersuchungskommission, ed., *Der Tod Ulrike Meinhofs. Bericht der Internationalen Untersuchungskommission* (Münster: Unrast Verlag, 2007), 34–35.
2. For more on the "Stammheim myth" and its role in sustaining the RAF, see Andreas Elter, *Propaganda der Tat. Die RAF und die Medien* (Frankfurt am Main: Suhrkamp Verlag, 2008), 181–95.
3. The pattern of interpretation of the RAF prison deaths taps into ideas on suicide with long traditions: from the noble self-killing of the ancients to the modern idea of illness. Classical Greek suicide was emptied of primitive horror and developed as a rational, "noble" option when external societal circumstances became intolerable. Heroic sacrifice, political protest, and dignity in death are themes that have resonated throughout antiquity and the centuries following. Roman culture adopted the classical lack of fear or revulsion toward suicide, and among the elites of Rome, the way one died became an important validation of the way one lived. This inherited tolerance of suicide was also reflected in Roman law, under which suicide was not punishable as a crime except under certain (mainly economic) conditions. The Christian conception of suicide as a crime evolved relatively late, in part because early Christians adopted the contemporaneous Roman attitude toward suicide. Jesus's self-sacrifice and an initially ambiguous Christian stance on self-murder meant early generations of Christians embraced the martyrdom of self-destruction. Consequently the suicide rate was high among this group until the fourth century, when self-murderers were denied Christian burials. Saint Augustine formally prohibited the act a century later in his *City of God* because it violated the sixth commandment "thou shalt not kill," was an affront to God's dominion, and therefore was the work of the devil. Suicide as a consciously subversive act reemerged in the late eighteenth century as romantic and philosophical suicide. With his *The Sorrows of Young Werther*, Goethe rode the wave of the existing fashion of self-murder and went on to inspire copycat suicides among disaffected young lovers throughout Europe. An older Goethe offered Europe *Faust*, which turned on another eighteenth-century trend: philosophical suicide. More than a mere rejection of society, suicide on philosophical grounds was a highly refined expression of dissatisfaction with life itself. Suicide was not significantly recast into its modern understanding until the late seventeenth century, when Europe began an intense and lasting preoccupation with the conflict between individual freedom and individual responsibility. Whereas the main concern had previously been questions of (primarily religious) morality, the Enlightenment and the aftermath of the French Revolution saw the slow emergence of empiricist and medical approaches: the gradual "secularization" of suicide. Throughout the nineteenth century the disciplines of psychiatry and sociology, in particular, cultivated the idea that "self-murderers" were either sick or victims of social dysfunction. Accordingly, legal prohibitions against suicide in Europe were softened or removed altogether. For more on the cultural history of suicide, see A. Alvarez, *The Savage*

God: A Study of Suicide (London: Penguin Books, 1971); Norman L. Farberow, "Cultural History of Suicide," in *Suicide in Different Cultures*, ed. Norman L. Farberow (London: University Park Press, 1975); Georges Minois, *History of Suicide: Voluntary Death in Western Culture*, trans. Lydia G. Cochrane (London: John Hopkins University Press, 1995); Émile Durkheim, *Suicide: A Study in Sociology*, trans. John A. Spaulding and George Simpson (London: Routledge, 2002); Lisa Lieberman, *Leaving You: The Cultural Meaning of Suicide* (Chicago: Ivan R. Dee, 2003); and Susan K. Morrissey, *Suicide and the Body Politic in Imperial Russia* (Cambridge: Cambridge University Press, 2006).

4. "Zwischen Ulrike Meinhof und den übrigen Angeklagten im Stuttgarter Anarchistenprozeß bestanden nach den Erkenntnissen der Bundesanwaltschaft bereits Wochen vor dem Selbstmord der 41-jährigen 'gewisse Spannungen,'" as cited in Internationale Untersuchungskommission, ed., *Der Tod Ulrike Meinhofs*, 59.

5. Ibid.

6. Felix Kaul as cited in Jutta Ditfurth, *Ulrike Meinhof. Die Biographie* (Berlin: Ullstein, 2007), 435. The official reporting of Meinhof's death was recognized by the remaining RAF prisoners as a deliberate construction of a suicide motive, see "die linie hat ow am telefon bekommen" in Hamburg Institute for Social Research (HIS), File (F) Me,U/015,006.

7. Internationale Untersuchungskommission, ed., *Der Tod Ulrike Meinhofs*, 60–61.

8. Ben Lewis, dir., *Baader-Meinhof: In Love with Terror* (BBC4, 2002).

9. "das Beste, was sie mit ihrem verkorksten Leben noch machen könnte," as cited in Stefan Aust, *Der Baader Meinhof Komplex* (Munich: Wilhelm Goldmann Verlag, 1998), 390.

10. "Nach den verwertbaren Befunden der Nachsektion handelt es sich bei Frau Meinhof um einen Tod durch Erhängen. Nach den bisher vorliegenden Untersuchungsbefunden besteht kein Anhalt für Fremdeinwirkung," as cited in ibid., 388.

11. "Wir glauben, daß Ulrike hingerichtet worden ist; wir wissen nicht, wie, aber wir wissen, von wem, und wir können das Kalkül der Methode bestimmen . . . Als Hinrichtung bedeutet der Tod von Ulrike, daß die internationale Auseinandersetzung—Guerillastaat—in dieser Exekution nach Bedingungen, die wir kennen, über die wir jetzt nicht reden werden, kulminieren mußte. Strategisch begriffen: Gegen die Politik der illegalen Gruppen in der B.Republik, für die Ulrike eine wesentliche ideologische Funktion hat, war das Ziel, wie in jeder staatlichen Maßnahme und Reaktion gegen die RAF seit es sie gibt, die physische und moralische Vernichtung und so die Zerstörung ihrer Politik," see German Federal Archive (GFA), Holding (H) 362, File (F) 3454: 9609–10.

12. Ibid.: 9613.

13. Aust, *Der Baader Meinhof Komplex*, 390.

14. Ditfurth, *Ulrike Meinhof*, 437–44.

15. The IUK was founded at a press conference on August 26, 1976, and the members were Denis Payot (Swiss lawyer and general secretary from the International Federation for Human Rights), Henrik Kaufholz (Danish journalist), Professor Lolle Nauta (Dutch professor of philosophy), Johann von Minnen (Dutch television Ombudsman), Professor Paul Jensen (Danish professor of psychology), Professor Joachim Israel (Swedish professor of sociology), Lelio Basso (one of the authors of

the Italian constitution, leading Italian constitutional lawyer, and elected member of the Italian senate), and Michele Beauvilar (French lawyer), see "An die Unterzeichner der Forderung" in HIS, F Me,U/015,006.

16. Internationale Untersuchungskommission, ed., *Der Tod Ulrike Meinhofs*, 39–62.
17. Ibid., 34–35.
18. Ibid., 20–22.
19. Aust, *Der Baader Meinhof Komplex*, 389.
20. "Sollte es jemals heißen, ich hätte Selbstmord gemacht, so war es Mord—äußere Gewalteinwirkung—oder totaler Widerstand," as cited in Helmut Brunn and Thomas Kirn, *Rechtsanwälte, Linksanwälte* (Frankfurt am Main: Eichborn, 2004), 329.
21. This description appeared as a handwritten note in the margins of an *info* entry, see Stefan Aust and Helmar Büchel, "Der letzte Akt der Rebellion," *Der Spiegel* 37 (2007): 53.
22. Wolfgang Kraushaar, "Mythos RAF. Im Spannungsfeld von terroristischer Herausforderung und populistischer Bedrohungsphantasie," in *Die RAF und der linke Terrorismus*, ed. Wolfgang Kraushaar (Hamburg: Hamburger Edition, 2006), 1191.
23. Ortrud Gutjahr, "Königinnenstreit. Eine Annäherung an Elfriede Jelineks *Ulrike Maria Stuart* und ein Blick auf Friedrich Schillers *Maria Stuart*," in *Ulrike Maria Stuart*, ed. Ortrud Gutjahr (Würzburg: Königshausen und Neumann, 2007), 29. The idea that Meinhof prepared the ground for the reception of her own death as it is presented in this chapter does not require such a preparation to have been Meinhof's intent. In fact, she very rarely applied the logic of her social critique to her own experience. Despite delving into the personal histories of her research subjects, Meinhof wrote in a private 1972 letter cited by Bettina Röhl that tracing her situation backward through a biographical context could establish a misleading chain of causation. Also, Röhl noted her mother's 1961 *konkret* article "Hitler in you" (*Hitler in euch*) as an example of this tendency to set herself apart from society and outside the rules she applied to others. In the article Meinhof places herself outside of the generation of Germans she addressed as "you," despite her background and age demanding, as Röhl argues, the article be entitled "Hitler in us," see Bettina Röhl, *So macht Kommunismus Spaß. Ulrike Meinhof, Klaus Rainer Röhl und die Akte KONKRET* (Hamburg: Europäische Verlagsanstalt, 2006), 179, 348.
24. Ditfurth, *Ulrike Meinhof*, 436.
25. "es gibt keinen Selbstmord, es gibt nur Treiber und Getriebene!" as cited in ibid., 443.
26. "Für den Fall, daß ich in der Haft vom Leben in den Tod komme, war's Mord. Gleich was die Schweine behaupten werden" and "Rache für Holger," see Aust, *Der Baader Meinhof Komplex*, 305.
27. GFA, H 362, F 3169: 214.
28. GFA, H 362, F 3166: 64–76.
29. GFA, H 362, F 3170: 141–42.
30. GFA, H 362, F 3183.

31. "An die Genossen im Knast: Wir würden gern mehr Genossen herausholen, sind aber dazu bei unserer jetzigen Stärke nicht in der Lage," as cited in Aust, *Der Baader Meinhof Komplex*, 326–27.
32. See interview in Lewis, dir., *Baader-Meinhof: In Love with Terror.*
33. Kraushaar, "Mythos RAF," 1195.
34. "Ich habe weder einen Selbstmordversuch begangen noch intendiert, noch war eine Absprache dagewesen," Möller as cited in Aust, *Der Baader Meinhof Komplex*, 636.
35. "Etwa um 5.00 Uhr hörte ich es knallen und quietschen. / Diese Geräusche waren sehr leise und dumpf geblieben, wie wenn etwas herunterfällt oder ein Schrank verschoben wird. Ich habe die Knallgeräusche nicht sofort als Schüsse identifiziert . . . / Ich bin danach auch wieder eingeschlafen. Plötzlich sackte ich weg und verlor das Bewußtsein, es ist alles sehr schnell gegangen. / Mein letzter sinnlicher Eindruck, an den ich mich erinnere, war ein sehr starkes Rauschen im Kopf. Ich hatte keine Person gesehen und keine Zellenöffnung bemerkt. / Ich bin dann erst auf dem Flur auf einer Bahre aufgewacht, als zusammengekrümmtes, wimmerndes Häufchen, furchtbar frierend, voll von Blut, und habe Stimmen—befriedigt, gehässig—gehört: Baader und Ensslin sind kalt," Möller as cited in ibid., 636.
36. Sven Felix Kellerhoff, "Die Mord-Legende von Stammheim," *Die Welt* 35 (2007): 20.
37. Aust, *Der Baader Meinhof Komplex*, 18.
38. Ibid.
39. "Könnt ihr die Stammheimer wirklich nur als Opfer sehen? Das war eine Aktion, habt ihr verstanden, eine Aktion! Ihr könnt aufhören zu flennen, ihr Arschlöcher!" as cited in Kraushaar, "Mythos RAF," 1196.
40. "Die Bundesregierung hat nur die Wahl, die Gefangenen umzubringen oder sie irgendwann zu entlassen," see Kellerhoff, "Die Mord-Legende von Stammheim," 20.
41. "Keiner von uns hat die Absicht, sich umzubringen. Sollten wir hier tot aufgefunden werden, sind wir in der guten Tradition justizieller und politischer Maßnahmen dieses Verfahrens ermordet worden," see ibid.
42. "Wenn Du hörst, ich hätte mich umgebracht, dann kannst Du sicher sein, es war Mord!" See Internationale Untersuchungskommission, ed., *Der Tod Ulrike Meinhofs*, 34.
43. "Guck, da haben wir die Bescherung, da liegt die andere Pistole," see Aust and Büchel, "Der letzte Akt der Rebellion," 54.
44. "die Linke [hat] mit dem angeblichen Mord an den Gefangenen endlich ein Thema in die Hände bekommen, an das sie schon selbst nicht mehr glaubte: der offen faschistisch auftretende Staat," see Volker Speitel, "'Wir wollten alles und gleichzeitig nichts' (II)," *Der Spiegel* 32 (1980): 38.
45. "die Linke [hat] mit dem angeblichen Mord an den Gefangenen endlich ein Thema in die Hände bekommen, an das sie schon selbst nicht mehr glaubte: der offen faschistisch auftretende Staat," and "es wird besonders schlau festgestellt, daß eine Minox-Kamera ja nur die halbe Größe einer Knarre hat," see ibid.
46. "es gibt keinen Freitod hinter Gittern," see Mario Krebs, *Ulrike Meinhof. Ein Leben im Widerspruch* (Reinbeck bei Hamburg: Rowohlt Taschenbuch Verlag,

1988), 267. For Krebs's use of Meinhof's suicide as part of his narrative of resistance see ibid, 21.

47. Internationale Untersuchungskommission, ed., *Der Tod Ulrike Meinhofs*, 70.

48. "Die Herrschenden wissen, daß diese gewaltsame Reduzierung des Menschen zum Lohnsklaven und Konsumtier als Voraussetzung für ihre weitere Anhäufung von Kapital in der Metropole BRD eine ungeheuerliche Verelendung produziert, die sich ausdrückt in: / hunderttausenden von 'Selbst'mordversuchen—15 000 'Selbst'morden darin, daß 120 000 Menschen dauernd in Irrenanstalten zusammengepfercht sind. / in 600 000 'Schizophrenen,'" see "Die Kritik, die sich mit diesem Inhalt befaßt" in HIS, F Me,U/026,004.

49. "das problem in den metropolen ist, daß, obwohl das system politisch und ökonomisch reif ist, abgeschafft zu werden, die revolutionären kräfte im volk noch zu schwach sind—es mehr resignation, lethargie, depression, agonie, mehr kranke und selbstmörder, mehr leute gibt, die sich hinlegen und sterben, weil man in diesem system nicht mehr leben kann, als aufstehen und kämpfen," see die gefangenen aus der raf, "PROVISORISCHES KAMPFPROGRAMM FÜR DEN KAMPF UM DIE POLITISCHEN RECHTE DER GEFANGENEN ARBEITER," in *Der Kampf gegen die Vernichtungshaft*, ed. Komitee gegen Folter an politischen Gefangenen in der BRD (Eigenverlag), 17.

50. "20 000 Menschen sterben jedes Jahr—weil die Aktionäre der Automobilindustrie nur für ihre Profite produzieren lassen und dabei keine Rücksicht auf die technische Sicherheit der Autos und den Straßenbau nehmen. / 5 000 Menschen sterben jedes Jahr—am Arbeitsplatz oder auf dem Weg dahin oder auf dem Heimweg, weil es den Produktionsmittelbesitzern nur auf ihre Profite ankommt und nicht auf einen Unfalltoten mehr oder weniger. / 12 000 Menschen begehen jedes Jahr Selbstmord, weil sie nicht im Dienst des Kapitals hinsterben wollen, machen sie lieber selber mit allem Schluß. / 1 000 Kinder werden jedes Jahr ermordet, weil die zu kleinen Wohnungen nur da sind, daß die Haus- und Grundbesitzer eine hohe Rendite einstreichen können. / Den Tod im Dienst der Ausbeuter nennen die Leute einen natürlichen Tod. Die Weigerung, im Dienst der Ausbeuter zu sterben, nennen die Leute einen 'unnatürlichen Tod,'" see RAF, "Dem Volk dienen. Stadtguerilla und Klassenkampf," in *Rote Armee Fraktion. Texte und Materialien zur Geschichte der RAF*, ed. ID-Verlag (Berlin: ID-Verlag, 1997), 112.

51. GFA, H 362, F 3164: 305.

52. RAF, "Dem Volk dienen," 129–30.

53. "Im Märkischen Viertel fehlt alles: Spielplätze, Verkehrsmittel, Schulen, billige Einkaufsmöglichkeiten, Ärzte, Anwälte. Brutstätten von Armut, Kindesmißhandlungen, Selbstmord, Bandenkriminalität, Verbitterung, Not. Das Märkische Viertel ist soziale Zukunft . . . Das Fernsehen gibt dem Satz 'Die Bundesrepublik ist nicht Lateinamerika,' die Armen in der Bundesrepublik haben selbst schuld, sie sind kriminell, es gibt nur wenige Arme—die anschauliche Evidenz. Die Springerpresse druckt sowas nach. Faschismusmaterial," see ibid., 131.

54. The quotation "lethal world" (*tötende Welt*) is from Brecht's *The Measures Taken* (*Die Maßnahme*). Brecht was a favorite author of the RAF and *The Measures Taken* was a favorite work, often cited by Ensslin and Meinhof. See Aust and Büchel, "Der letzte Akt der Rebellion," 53; and "lieber Klaus" in HIS, F Me,U/012,002.

55. "materielles Elend und gesellschaftliche Ächtung sind tödlich, Mordwerkzeuge der kapitalistischen Gesellschaft," see the newsletters "Patienten-info Nr. 37 *Neuer Unispiegel* Nr. 8" and "Patienten-info Nr. 35 *Neuer Unispiegel* Nr. 6" in HIS, RAF, A Hu,W/003,004.

56. "Vom Glauben an die Sinnlosigkeit und Unerklärbarkeit Benno Ohnesorgs Tod, vom Glauben an die Unschuld des Systems ist es nur noch ein Schritt zu der Formel, nicht der Mörder, sondern der Ermordete sei schuldig," see Ulrike Marie Meinhof, "Wasserwerfer—auch gegen Frauen," *konkret* 4 (1968): 38.

57. The German word *Weib* is difficult to translate. It is an older word for a woman that now has largely derogatory connotations.

58. "Heute sind es nicht mehr biologische, sondern gesellschaftliche Schranken, die die Frauen daran hindern, sich ihrer Chance bewusst zu werden, sie zu nutzen . . . Die Idylle von Heimchen am Herd konnte fast nahtlos in die Idylle von Heimchen am Fließband umgewandelt werden," see Ulrike Marie Meinhof, *Frauen sind billiger: Ein Bericht über Frauenarbeit in der Bundesrepublik* (Abendstudio, 1967).

59. Ulrike Marie Meinhof, "Frauenkram," *konkret* 7 (1968): 24–27, 52.

60. "Eine sich ihnen gegenüber kriminell verhaltende Umwelt macht sie zu Kriminelle," see Ulrike Marie Meinhof, "Doof—weil arm. Hilfsschulkinder," *konkret* 5 (1969): 41. "Ihre Lernbehinderung ist das Produkt ihrer Armut," see Ulrike Marie Meinhof, "Doof—weil arm. Hilfsschulkinder, 2. Teil," *konkret* 6 (1969): 37.

61. Ulrike Marie Meinhof, *Ausgestossen oder aufgehoben: Heimkinder in der Bundesrepublik* (Abendstudio, 1965).

62. Ulrike Marie *Meinhof*, "Flucht aus dem Mädchenheim," *konkret* 9 (1966): 18–23.

63. Ibid., 23.

64. Ulrike Marie Meinhof, *Bambule: Fürsorgeerziehung aus der Sicht von drei ehemaligen Berliner Heimmädchen* (Abendstudio, 1969); and Ulrike Marie Meinhof, *Guxhagen—Mädchen in Fürsorgeerziehung. Ein Heim in Essen* (Abendstudio, 1969).

65. Elter writes of the deaths of Meins and Meinhof as preparing the "fruchtbare[n] Boden" for the theories of state murder, the "Stammheim myth" surrounding the 1977 deaths, see Elter, *Propaganda der Tat*, 183–84. Kraushaar has suggested that the longevity of the "Stammheim myth" is bound up with the question of whether or not, given the constant and intense observation, the authorities could have prevented the deaths, see Kraushaar, "Mythos RAF," 1196. Ditfurth argues the lasting suspicions surrounding Meinhof's death are due to the arrogance, lack of professionalism, and haste with which her body was treated, see Ditfurth, *Ulrike Meinhof*, 444. The argument presented in this chapter is that the deaths of the RAF prisoners remain a topic due to the active conditioning of the sympathetic audience in the years, even decade, prior to the deaths.

66. Tobias Wunschik, "Aufstieg und Zerfall. Die zweite Generation der RAF," in *Die RAF und der linke Terrorismus*, ed. Wolfgang Kraushaar (Hamburg: Hamburger Edition, 2006), 485; and Bernd Weisbrod, "Terrorism as Performance: The Assassinations of Walther Rathenau and Hanns-Martin Schleyer," in *Control of Violence: Historical and International Perspectives on Violence in Modern Societies*, ed. Wilhelm Heitmeyer et al. (New York: Springer, 2011), 383.

67. Alexander Straßner, "Die dritte Generation der RAF," in *Die RAF und der linke Terrorismus*, ed. Wolfgang Kraushaar (Hamburg: Hamburger Edition, 2006), 500.
68. "Ich will das ganz klar machen, ich persönlich war damals überzeugt und bin bis heute absolut davon überzeugt, daß sie ermordet worden ist," see "Veranstaltung zum 20. Todestag von Ulrike Meinhof am 3. Mai 1996 im Auditorium Maximum der TU Berlin," http://www.nadir.org/nadir/archiv/PolitischeStroemungen/Stadtguerilla+RAF/RAF/ulrike_meinhof/va20/va20podium.html (accessed March 13, 2011).

Conclusion

1. "jeder (außer nat. dir) weiß, daß DU DIE STIMME WARST BIST SEIN WIRST," as cited by Alfred Klaus in a report on material found in RAF cells during searches carried out between July 16 and 19, 1973, in Hamburg Institute for Social Research (HIS), RAF, A SO 09/004,003: 151.
2. Colvin writes of the two private voices in Meinhof's later works: her voice of determination and resolve, and her voice of anger and regret that her identity did not overlap completely with that of the RAF, see Sarah Colvin, *Ulrike Meinhof and West German Terrorism: Language, Violence, and Identity* (New York: Camden House, 2009), 225. The voices referred to in this conclusion are the voice Meinhof was constantly looking for in private and the voice she had in public.
3. The kidnap and murder of Schleyer, the hijacking of the *Landshut*, and the Stammheim suicides were preceded by the murders of Attorney General Siegfried Buback (April 1977) and Jürgen Ponto (July 1977), chairman of Dresdner Bank.
4. Weisbrod writes of the brutal murder as having a performative effect that the terrorists did not expect: it transformed Schleyer from an object of hate to an object of sympathy; see Bernd Weisbrod, "Terrorism as Performance: The Assassinations of Walther Rathenau and Hanns-Martin Schleyer," in *Control of Violence: Historical and International Perspectives on Violence in Modern Societies*, ed. Wilhelm Heitmeyer et al. (New York: Springer, 2011), 386.
5. These attacks included attempts on the lives of NATO Supreme Commander Alexander Haig (June 1979), U.S. Army General Frederik Kroesen (September 1981), and high-ranking public servants Hans Tietmeyer (September 1988) and Hans Neusel (June 1990). Other attacks claimed the lives of industrial figure Dr. Ernst Zimmermann (February 1985), U.S. soldier Edward Pimental (August 1985), U.S. soldier Frank Scarton, and U.S. civilian Becky Bristol in the bombing of the U.S. Air Force base near Frankfurt (August 1985); Siemens board member Karl Heinz Beckurts and his driver Eckhard Groppler (July 1986); diplomat Gerold von Braunmühl (October 1986); chairman of Deutsche Bank Alfred Herrhausen (November 1989); and politician Detlev Karsten Rohwedder (April 1991).
6. There was a brief period where the agendas of the RAF prison leaders and the external commando leaders diverged in the mid-1980s, but the definitive split—the prelude to the group's dissolution—came in the early 1990s. This gulf opened up between the commandos and the prisoners, but also opposing camps of prisoners: the "hardliners" (*Hardliner*) and those prepared to compromise (*Freunde der Vernunft*). For more on this split and the dissolution of the RAF, see Alexander Straßner, *Die dritte Generation der "Roten Armee Fraktion." Entstehung, Struktur,*

Funktionslogik und Zerfall einer terroristischen Organisation (VS Verlag für Sozial-wissenschaften: Wiesbaden, 2003), 235–53.

7. The "legal arm" supported what developed into a tiered structure led by the "commandos," who lived in the underground and carried out deadly attacks against people. Below the commandos were the "illegal militants," who carried out attacks on objects and were prepared to enter the underground if required to do so by the commandos. Below the illegal militants were the "militants," who carried out the most risk-free, illegal operations, such as renting safe houses, hiding weapons, and establishing contacts with foreign terrorist groups. See Alexander Straßner, "Die dritte Generation der RAF," in *Die RAF und der linke Terrorismus*, ed. Wolfgang Kraushaar (Hamburg: Hamburger Edition, 2006), 494–95.

8. Ibid., 495.

9. After the loss of the first-generation leaders, the RAF restructured, producing the tiered structure and competing leaderships of the third generation. The defeat of the urban guerilla also produced a shift in strategy, with the group launching targeted assassinations once it regrouped. In terms of a theoretical framework, the RAF worldview as articulated by Meinhof was upheld by the second generation, but a shift toward a more pragmatic conception of the armed struggle was evident in the 1982 *May Paper*. Finally, in the wake of losing important figures in 1977, the RAF was rocked by waves of high-profile arrests in 1982 and 1984.

10. Bernd Weisbrod, "Terrorism as Performance: The Assassinations of Walther Rathenau and Hanns-Martin Schleyer," in *Control of Violence: Historical and International Perspectives on Violence in Modern Societies*, ed. Wilhelm Heitmeyer et al (New York: Springer, 2011), 383.

11. For the 1992 communiqué announcing the de-escalation, see RAF, *Die Eskalation zurücknehmen*, http://www.rafinfo.de/archiv/raf/raf-10-4-92.php (accessed March 17, 2011).

12. "Vor fast 28 Jahren, am 14. Mai 1970, entstand in einer Befreiungsaktion die RAF: Heute beenden wir dieses Projekt," see RAF, "RAF-Auflösungserklärung," http://www.rafinfo.de/archiv/raf/raf-20-4-98.php (accessed March 17, 2011).

13. Sarah Colvin writes of the lingering idolization of Meinhof; see Colvin, *Ulrike Meinhof and West German Terrorism*, 4–5.

Bibliography

Meinhof Texts

"Die Rote Armee aufbauen." In *Rote Armee Fraktion. Texte und Materialien zur Geschichte der RAF*. Edited by ID-Verlag, 24–26. Berlin: ID-Verlag, 1997.

Holtkamp, Jürgen, and Ulrike Marie Meinhof. "Ulbricht löst die DDR auf. Eine Presseparodie." *konkret* 12 (1964): 11–17.

Holtkamp, Jürgen, Ulrike Marie Meinhof, and Klaus Rainer Röhl. "Eine Presseparodie. Political fiction." *konkret* 12 (1966): 18–24.

———. "Political fiction: 'Spiegel' an Springer verkauft." *konkret* 6 (1967): 48–53.

Meinhof, Ulrike. "Deprivation und Kolonisierung. Über den Zusammenhang von Rehabilitierung und revolutionärer Aktion." *So oder So: Die Libertad!-Zeitung* 8 (2001): 16–17.

Meinhof, Ulrike Marie. "Der unaufhaltsame Aufstieg des 'Spiegel'—oder Der Fall Nirumand." *konkret* 12 (1967): 26.

———. "Die Herausforderung und die Antwort." *konkret* 5 (1964): 5.

———. "Doof—weil arm. Hilfsschulkinder." *konkret* 5 (1969): 38–42.

———. "Doof—weil arm. Hilfsschulkinder, 2. Teil." *konkret* 6 (1969): 34–37.

———. "Ein Mann mit guten Manieren. Ein Tag Karl-Wolff-Prozess." *konkret* 9 (1964): 15–17.

———. "Enteignet Springer!" *konkret* 9 (1967): 2–3.

———. "Flucht aus dem Mädchenheim." *konkret* 9 (1966): 18–23.

———. "Frauenkram." *konkret* 7 (1968): 24–27, 52.

———. "Früchte der Knappheit." *konkret* 8 (1963): 13–15.

———. "Gegen-Gewalt." *konkret* 2 (1968): 2–3.

———. "Gipfelschatten westwärts." *konkret* 3 (1960): 1.

———. "Hitler in Euch." *konkret* 10 (1961): 8.

———. "Jürgen Bartsch und die Gesellschaft." *konkret* 1 (1968): 2–3.

———. "Kolumnismus." *konkret* 2 (1969): 2.

———. "Kranker Mann, was nun?" *konkret* 7 (1963): 7–9.

———. "Kuli oder Kollege. Gastarbeiter in Deutschland." *konkret* 11 (1966): 22–27.

———. "Lohnkampf." *konkret* 2 (1966): 2–3.

———. "Napalm und Pudding." *konkret* 5 (1967): 2–3.

———. "Notstand? Notstand!" *konkret* 18 (1960): 1.

———. "Offener Brief an Farah Diba." *konkret* 6 (1967), 21–22.
———. "Spiegels Spiegelbilder. Ein sehr offener Brief an Rudolf Augstein." *konkret* 1 (1968): 49–51.
———. "Springer-Fernsehen." *konkret* 4 (1965): 3.
———. "Vietnam und die Deutschen." In *Die Würde des Menschen ist antastbar*. Edited by Klaus Wagenbach, 108–11. Berlin: Klaus Wagenbach, 2004.
———. "Vom Protest zum Widerstand." *konkret* 5 (1968): 5.
———. "Von Mördern und Menschen." *konkret* 5 (1962): 3.
———. "Warenhausbrandstiftung." *konkret* 14 (1968): 5.
———. "Wasserwerfer—auch gegen Frauen." *konkret* 4 (1968): 36–40.
———. "Zum Kanzlerwechsel. Adenauer und die Volksmeinung." *konkret* 11 (1963): 8.
———. "Zum neuen Jahr." *konkret* 1 (1963): 4.
"'Natürlich kann geschossen werden.' Ulrike Meinhof über der Baader-Aktion." *Der Spiegel* 25 (1970): 74–75.

Meinhof Radio Features

Meinhof, Ulrike Marie. *Ausgestossen oder aufgehoben: Heimkinder in der Bundesrepublik*. Abendstudio, 1965.
———. *Bambule: Fürsorgeerziehung aus der Sicht von drei ehemaligen Berliner Heimmädchen*. Abendstudio, 1969.
———. *Frauen sind billiger: Ein Bericht über Frauenarbeit in der Bundesrepublik*. Abendstudio, 1967.
———. *Gefahr vom Fließband: Arbeitsunfälle, beobachtet und kritisch beschrieben*. Abendstudio, 1965.
———. *Guxhagen—Mädchen in Fürsorgeerziehung. Ein Heim in Essen*. Abendstudio, 1969.
———. *Halb Weib—halb Mensch: Ein Diskussionsbeitrag zur Situation der Frau zwischen Familie und Erwerbstätigkeit*. Abendstudio, 1967.

RAF Texts

RAF. "Anschlag auf das Hauptquartier der US-Army in Frankfurt/Main." In *Rote Armee Fraktion. Texte und Materialien zur Geschichte der RAF*. Edited by ID-Verlag, 145. Berlin: ID-Verlag, 1997.
———. "Anschlag auf den BGH-Richter Buddenberg in Karlsruhe." In *Rote Armee Fraktion. Texte und Materialien zur Geschichte der RAF*. Edited by ID-Verlag, 146. Berlin: ID-Verlag, 1997.
———. "Anschläge in Augsburg und München." In *Rote Armee Fraktion. Texte und Materialien zur Geschichte der RAF*. Edited by ID-Verlag, 145–46. Berlin: ID-Verlag, 1997.
———. "Bombenanschlag auf das Hauptquartier der US-Army in Europa in Heidelberg. Erklärung vom 25. Mai 1972." In *Rote Armee Fraktion. Texte und Materialien zur Geschichte der RAF*. Edited by ID-Verlag, 147–48. Berlin: ID-Verlag, 1997.

———. "Das Konzept Stadtguerilla." In *Rote Armee Fraktion. Texte und Materialien zur Geschichte der RAF*. Edited by ID-Verlag, 27–48. Berlin: ID-Verlag, 1997.
———. "Dem Volk dienen. Stadtguerilla und Klassenkampf." In *Rote Armee Fraktion. Texte und Materialien zur Geschichte der RAF*. Edited by ID-Verlag, 112–44. Berlin: ID-Verlag, 1997.
———. "Die Aktion des Schwarzen September in München." In *Rote Armee Fraktion. Texte und Materialien zur Geschichte der RAF*. Edited by ID-Verlag, 151–77. Berlin: ID-Verlag, 1997.
———. *Die Eskalation zurücknehmen*. http://www.rafinfo.de/archiv/raf/raf-10-4-92.php (accessed March 17, 2011).
———. "Erklärung der RAF zum Bombenanschlag im Hamburger Hauptbahnhof." In *Rote Armee Fraktion. Texte und Materialien zur Geschichte der RAF*. Edited by ID-Verlag, 196–98. Berlin: ID-Verlag, 1997.
———. "Hungerstreikerklärung vom 1. Februar 1989." In *Rote Armee Fraktion. Texte und Materialien zur Geschichte der RAF*. Edited by ID-Verlag, 389–91. Berlin: ID-Verlag, 1997.
———. "Hungerstreikerklärung vom 27. Juli 1994." In *Rote Armee Fraktion. Texte und Materialien zur Geschichte der RAF*. Edited by ID-Verlag, 498–99. Berlin: ID-Verlag, 1997.
———. "RAF-Auflösungserklärung." http://www.rafinfo.de/archiv/raf/raf-20-4-98.php (accessed March 17, 2011).
———. "Sprengstoffanschlag auf das Springer-Hochhaus in Hamburg." In *Rote Armee Fraktion. Texte und Materialien zur Geschichte der RAF*. Edited by ID-Verlag, 147. Berlin: ID-Verlag, 1997.

Files in the RAF Collection at the Hamburg Institute of Social Research (*Hamburger Institut für Sozialforschung*)

Hu,W/003,004: *Flugblätter, Informationen und Patienten-Infos des Sozialistisches Patientenkollektivs. 1970–1971.*
Hu,W/005,007: *Handakte Klaus Croissant: Presse und Presseerklärung zum SPK-Verfahren; Ablehnungsanträge gegen Gohl; Anträge zur Terminierung der Hauptverhandlung; Ermittlungen zum "inneren Kreis" des Sozialistisches Patientenkollektiv; Ermittlungsergebnisse gegen Ursula Hubler. 1972.* KOK 03/003.
Me,U/004,004: *Ulrike Meinhof—Personenakten Band IV—Postkontrolle, Verteidigerpost und Informationssystem. 1973.*
Me,U/008,001: *Selbstkritik von Ulrike Meinhof. 1974.*
Me,U/008,002: *Briefe von Ulrike Meinhof. 1973–1976.*
Me,U/008,004: *Text von Ulrike Meinhof zum Prozessgebäude, Kissingers Politik, Imperialismus und Schriftwechsel zum Revisionsverfahren. 1975.*
Me,U/008,010: *Informationssystem: Hungerstreik, die Politik der "Vietnamisierung" und Presse zu den RAF-Anwälten. 1973.*

Me,U/009,002: *Schriftwechsel zu Postkontrolle, Haftprüfung, Hungerstreikserklärung, Vertrauensärzte, Gedicht aus dem Toten Trakt und Haftbedingungen. 1973–1974.*

Me,U/009,003: *Materialien und Schriftwechsel zur Isolationsfolter. 1974.*

Me,U/009,005: *Informationssystem der RAF-Gefangenen: Briefe von Ulrike Meinhof zum Totem Trakt und Isolationsfolter. 1973–1974.*

Me,U/012,001: *Handakte Croissant: Briefwechsel Ulrike Meinhof mit Croissant. 1973–1974.*

Me,U/012,002: *Handakte Croissant: Briefwechsel Ulrike Meinhof mit Croissant. 1973–1974.*

Me,U/012,003: *Handakte Croissant: Briefwechsel Ulrike Meinhof mit Croissant. 1973.*

Me,U/012,006: *Handakte Croissant: Briefwechsel Ulrike Meinhof mit Croissant, Briefe von Meinhof an ihre Schwester. 1974.*

Me,U/012,007: *Handakte Croissant: Briefe von Ulrike Meinhof, Schriftwechsel im Informationssystem der RAF und der Anwälte. 1973–1974.*

Me,U/013,001: *Handakte Croissant: Briefe von Ulrike Meinhof, Schriftwechsel im Informationssystem der RAF und der Anwälte. 1974.*

Me,U/013,002: *Handakte Croissant: Der Hauptwiderspruch in den Metropolen des Imperialismus ist der Widerspruch zwischen Produktivitäten und Produktionsverhältnissen—Rede von Astrid Proll; verschiedene Korrespondenzen. 1973–1974.*

Me,U/015,001: *Handakte Klaus Croissant zu Ulrike Meinhof mit Strategiepapier zum antiimperialistischen Kampf in der BRD und Westberlin. 1974–1975.*

Me,U/015,004: *Handakte Klaus Croissant: Schriftwechsel, Berichte und Erklärungen zu Bambule, zum Buch von Brückner "Ulrike Meinhof und die deutschen Verhältnisse" und zu den "Konkret"-Kolumnen. 1975–1977.*

Me,U/015,006: *Handakte Hans Heinz Heldmann: Briefe der Gefangenen zum Tod von Ulrike Meinhof, zur Prozeßstrategie, zur Rolle der Bundesanwaltschaft; Texte von Ulrike Meinhof; Interview mit Debray zu Tamara Bunke; Zertifikat von Basaglio zu Roll mit Brief von Roll dazu aus Triest; Zusammenstellung von Schreiben zur Haft von Meinhof in der JVA Köln-Ossendorf, Bericht zur Zellendurchsuchung von Meinhof und Berichte and Analysen aus dem Informationssystem der RAF-Gefangenen; Ulrike Meinhof und die Stammheimer Mord-Legende von Klaus Rainer Röhl. 1972–1977.*

Me,U/016,001: *Todesermittlungssache: Tatort und Spurensicherung; beschlagnahmte Texte von Ulrike Meinhof, Gudrun Ensslin und Jan Carl Raspe aus der Gemeinschaftszelle in der JVA Stuttgart-Stammheim. 1976.*

Me,U/025,005: *Informationssystem der RAF-Gefangenen: Briefe von Ulrike Meinhof vom Sommer 1974 bis März 1976. 1974–1976.*

Me,U/025,007: *Informationssystem der RAF-Gefangenen: zu den Anwälten und zur Prozessstrategie. 1975–1976.*

Me,U/026,004: *Leserbrief von Hannover; Entwurf der Hungerstreikerklärung; Vorläufige endgültige Fassung des allgemeinen Teiles der Dokumentation über die Haftbedingungen; Briefe von Ulrike Meinhof zur Haft in der JVA Köln Ossendorf; Der Leiter der Justizvollzugsanstalt Köln wegen zerbrochenen Zellenspiegel und Fliegedraht; Ulrike Meinhof zu den Linken, zur geplanten Ermordung von Andreas Baader und der revolutionären Praxis. 1974.*

Publ./007,001: *Rote Volksuniversität 1972–1973.*

Publ./007,002: *Flugblätter und Erklärungen zum Hungerstreik der Rechtsanwälte und Angehörigen vor dem Bundesgerichtshof. 1973.*

Publ./010,003: *Pressearchiv Frauböse II: Röhls Buch "Die Genossin"; Kaul in da das; Posser zu den Angehörigen; Szintigrafie; Festnahme von Ulrike Meinhof; Bombenleger entdeckt; Herold zur Fahndung u.a. 1972–1975.*

RA 02/002,012: *Handakte Klaus Croissant zum Stammheim-Verfahren: Hungerstreiker-klärung der Gefangenen; Flugblätter und Erklärungen zum Hungerstreik; Fragebogen von Amnesty International. 1974.*

RA 02/005,004: *Informationssystem der RAF-Gefangenen 1974.*

RA 02/005,005: *Informationssystem der RAF-Gefangenen 1975.*

RA 02/006,002: *Deutsche und Internationale Presse zur Folter In- und Ausland, zu den politischen Gefangenen in Westdeutschland; Erklärungen von Ärztenzur Isolationshaft; Informationssystem der RAF-Gefangenen zur IRA und Folter in Irland; Folter in Ost und West: Länder und Methoden der unmenschlichen Torut von Ralf Giordano. 1973–1974.*

RA 02/011,008: *Konzept einer Veröffentlichung zu "Guerilla und Kriegsgefangenenstatus" von Croissant; Antrag von Croissant auf Anwendung der Genfer Konvention über die Behandlung von Kriegsgefangenen; RAF-Erklärungenzu den Anschlägen in Frankfurt und Heidelberg. 1972–1976.*

RA 02/011,009: *Anträge, Erklärungen und Schreiben zum Kriegsgefangenstatus, zum Hungerstreik und Zwangsernährung; Prozeßerklärung in Stammheim am 29.03.1977 mit den Forderungen nach Genfer Konvention; Artikel 3 der Genfer Konvention und Texte dazu; Papier der Gefangenen vno Anfang März 1976 zur Verteidigungslinie; Presse zur Rot-Kreuz-Konferenz u.a. 1975–1977.*

RA 02/014,010: *Informationssystem der RAF-Gefangenen zum Hungerstreik vom 21.11.1974–25.02.1975 mit Presse, Grußadresse der ETA und Erklärung des Verbandes Deutscher Schriftsteller. 1974–1975.*

SO 09/002,005.

SO 09/003,003: *Zellenmaterial von Ulrike Meinhof und Ermittlungen dazu. 1973–1974.*

SO 09/004,002: *Bericht von Alfred Klaus über die Auswertung des am 16.07. bzw. 19.07.1973 in den Zellen von acht RAF-Gefangenen gefundenen Beweismatierials. 1974.*

SO 09/004,003: *Bericht von Alfred Klaus über die Auswertung des am 16.07. bzw. 19.07.1973 in den Zellen von acht RAF-Gefangenen gefundenen Beweismatierials. 1974.*

SO 09/005,004: *Ermittlungen zur 2. RAF-Schrift "Rote Armee Fraktion: Stadtguerilla und Klassenkampf". 1972–1973.*

SO 09/005,005: *Ermittlungen zur 3. RAF-Schrift "Die Aktion des Schwazen September in München: Zur Strategie des antiimperialistischen Kampfes." 1972–1973.*

SO 09/006,003: *Ermittlungen zum Brief der RAF an die Partei der Abeit der Volksrepublik Korea. 1971–1972.*

SO 09/006,007.

SO 09/006,008: *Ermittlungen zur Tonbanderklärung von Ulrike Meinhof am 31.05.1972. 1972–1973.*

Files in the German Federal Archive (*Bundesarchiv*)

Holding 106, File 106992: *Komitee gegen Folter an politischen Gefangenen in der BRD. Analyse, Entwicklung und Prognose. Bd. 1–2: 1974–1977.*

Holding 141, File 404857: *Zwangsweise Durchführung des Gesundheitsschutzes bei Gefangenen, insbesondere Zwangsernährung: Vom 6.5.1975 bis 23.1.1978.*

Holding 141, File 404858: *Zwangsweise Durchführung des Gesundheitsschutzes bei Gefangenen, insbesondere Zwangsernährung.*

Holding 141, File 404871: *Zwangsweise Durchführung des Gesundheitsschutzes bei Gefangenen. Hungerstreik inhaftierter Terroristen.*

Holding 362, File 3130: *Bekennerbriefe Bd. I.*

Holding 362, File 3132: *Zellenmaterial Bd. I/1.*

Holding 362, File 3133: *Zellenmaterial Bd. I/2.*

Holding 362, File 3155: *Ensslin, Gudrun: Personensachakten Bd. I.*

Holding 362, File 3164: *Meinhof: Personensachakten Bd. I.*

Holding 362, File 3165: *Meinhof: Personensachakten Bd. II.*

Holding 362, File 3166: *Meinhof: Personensachakten Bd. III.*

Holding 362, File 3167: *Meinhof: Personensachakten Bd. IV.*

Holding 362, File 3168: *Meinhof: Personensachakten Bd. V.*

Holding 362, File 3169: *Meinhof: Personensachakten Bd. VI.*

Holding 362, File 3170: *Meinhof: Personensachakten Bd. VIII.*

Holding 362, File 3171: *Meinhof: Personensachakten Bd. VII.*

Holding 362, File 3172: *Meinhof: Personensachakten Bd. IX.*

Holding 362, File 3183: *Meinhof: Ersatz-Personensachakten Bd. II.*

Holding 362, File 3185: *Meins: Ersatz-Personensachakten.*

Holding 362, File 3283: *III, 2. Strafsenat BM-Sammelakten: Haftbedinungen, geordnet nach Eingang der Anträge 2 StE 1/74.*

Holding 362, File 3352: *Unterlagen für den GBA für eine evtl. Gegenüberstellung der ULRIKE MEINHOF.*

Holding 362, File 3363: *Müller (II).*

Holding 362, File 3369: *Meinhof, Zellendurchsuchung 16.7.73: Positionen I-XII/1.*

Holding 362, File 3370: *Meinhof, Zellendurchsuchung 16.7.73: Positionen XII/2-XVII.*

Holding 362, File 3377: *Anklage—Hauptakten—1StE 1/74.*

Holding 362, File 3397: *2BJs 6/71, 2StE OLG Stgt 1/74: BM-Verfahren Verschiedenes.*

Holding 362, File 3409: *B.*

Holding 362, File 3416: *C.*

Holding 362, File 3424: *C.*

Holding 362, File 3435: *B 13.1 13.2 SA.*

Holding 362, File 3441: *Original Protokoll: Seite 1–540, Tonband 1–17.*

Holding 362, File 3443: *Original Protokoll: Seite 981–1485, Tonband 39–58.*

Holding 362, File 3445: *Original Protokoll: Seite 1998–2478, Tonband 89–128.*

Holding 362, File 3446: *Original Protokoll: Seite 2479–3260, Tonband 129–183.*

Holding 362, File 3454: *Original Protokoll: Seite 9127–10043, Tonband 511–573.*

Holding 362, File 3477: *Originalanlage zum Urteil.*

Holding 362, File 3480: *Teil I: a) Begutachtung der Angeklagten / b) rechtl. Folgerungen aus Gutachten.*

Holding 362, File 3481: *Teil II: b) rechtl. Folgerungen aus Gutachten.*

Published Sources

Aijmer, Göran. 2000, "The Idiom of Violence in Imagery and Discourse." In *Meanings of Violence: A Cross Cultural Perspective.* Edited by Göran Aijmer and Jon Abbink, 1–21. New York: Berg, 2000.

Alvarez, A. *The Savage God. A Study of Suicide.* London: Penguin, 1971.

"An der Brüstung." *Der Spiegel* 50 (1974): 27–29.

andreas baader im originalton. 4. mai 1976. http://www.youtube.com/watch?v=LxRI8 --EgEU&feature=related (accessed March 13, 2011).

"Application 6166/73. Andreas BAADER, Holger MEINS, Ulrike MEINHOF, Wolfgang GRUNDMANN v/the FEDERAL REPUBLIC OF GERMANY." *Decisions and Reports of the European Commission of Human Rights* 2 (1975): 58–67.

Aretxaga, Begoña. "Dirty Protest: Symbolic Overdetermination and Gender in Northern Ireland Ethnic Violence." *Ethos* 23(2) (1995): 123–48.

———. "Terror as a thrill: First thoughts on the 'war on terrorism.'" *Anthropological Quarterly* 75(1) (2001): 138–50.

"Auf der Kippe." *Der Spiegel* 9 (1989): 109–10.

Aust, Stefan. *Der Baader Meinhof Komplex.* Munich: Wilhelm Goldmann Verlag, 1998.

Aust, Stefan, and Helmar Büchel. "'Der letzte Akt der Rebellion.'" *Der Spiegel* 37 (2007): 52–78.

Austin, J. L. *How to do Things With Words.* Oxford: Clarendon Press, 1975.

Baader, Andreas, Gudrun Ensslin, Thorwald Proll, and Horst Söhnlein. "Vor einer solchen Justiz verteidigen wir uns nicht. Schlußwort im Kaufhausbrandprozeß." *VoltaireFlugschrift* 27 (1969).

"Baader/Meinhof. Bis irgendwohin." *Der Spiegel* 25 (1970): 71–75.

Bakker Schut, Pieter, ed. *das info: briefe von gefangenen aus der raf aus der diskussion 1973–1977.* Plambeck: Neuer Malik Verlag, 1987.

———. *Stammheim: Der Prozeß gegen die Rote Armee Fraktion. Die notwendige Korrektur der herrschenden Meinung.* Bonn: Pahl-Rugenstein, 2007.

Balz, Hanno. "Gesellschaftsformierungen. Die öffentliche Debatte über die RAF in den 70er Jahren." In *Der 'Deutsche Herbst' und die RAF in Politik, Medien und Kunst. Nationale und internationale Perspektiven.* Edited by Nicole Colin, Beatrice De Graaf, Jacco Pekelder, and Joachim Umlauf, 170–84. Bielefeld: Transcript Verlag, 2008.

Barthes, Roland. *Camera Lucida.* New York: Hill and Wang, 1981.

———. *Image, Music, Text.* Translated by Stephen Heath. London: Flamingo, 1984.

———. *Mythologies.* Translated by Annette Lavers. London: Vintage, 2000.

Bauer, Karin, ed. *Everybody Talks About the Weather . . . We Don't: The Writings of Ulrike Meinhof.* New York: Seven Stories Press, 2008.

Becker, Jillian. *Hitler's Children: the Story of the Baader-Meinhof Terrorist Gang.* London: Joseph, 1977.

Berkowitz, Dan. "Suicide Bombers as Women Warriors: Making News Through Mythical Archetypes." *Journalism and Mass Communication Quarterly* 82(3) (2005): 607–22.

Bielby, Clare, "Remembering the Red Army Faction." *Memory Studies* 3(2) (2010): 137–50.

Blok, Anton. "The Enigma of Senseless Violence." In *Meanings of Violence. A Cross Cultural Perspective*. Edited by Göran Aijmer and Jon Abbink, 23–38. Oxford: Berg, 2000.

Bohrer, Karl Heinz. "Surrealismus und Terror, oder die Aporien des Juste-milieu." In *Die gefährdete Phantasie, oder Surrealismus und Terror*, 32–61. Munich: Carl Hanser Verlag, 1970.

Böll, Heinrich. "Will Ulrike Meinhof Gnade oder freies Geleit?" *Der Spiegel* 3 (1972): 54–56.

Brink, Cornelia. "Psychiatrie und Politik: Zum Sozialistischen Patientenkollektiv in Heidelberg." In *Terrorismus in der Bundesrepublik. Medien, Staat und Subkulturen in den 1970er Jahren*. Edited by Klaus Weinhauer, Jörg Requate, and Heinz-Gerhard Haupt, 134–53. Frankfurt: Campus Verlag, 2006.

Brumberg, Joan Jacobs. *Fasting Girls: The History of Anorexia Nervosa*. New York: Vintage Books, 2000.

Brunn, Helmut, and Thomas Kirn. *Rechtsanwälte, Linksanwälte*. Frankfurt: Eichborn, 2004.

Bundesministerium der Justiz, ed. *Strafprozessordnung*. http://www.gesetze-im-internet.de/stpo/__138a.html (accessed March 28, 2011).

"Bundesrichter sehen 'militante gruppe' nicht als Terrorvereinigung." *Spiegel-Online* http://www.spiegel.de/politik/deutschland/0,1518,520245,00.html (accessed March 28, 2011).

Butler, Judith. *Bodies That Matter: On the Discursive Limits of "Sex."* New York: Routledge, 1993.

———. *Excitable speech. A Politics of the Performative*. New York: Routledge, 1997.

———. *Gender Trouble. Feminism and the Subversion of Identity*. New York: Routledge, 2008.

Bynum, Caroline Walker. *Holy Feast and Holy Fast: The Religious Significance of Food to Medieval Women*. Berkeley: University of California Press, 1987.

"CAMERA-SILENS-EXPERIMENTE UND FOLTER." In *Der Kampf gegen die Vernichtungshaft*. Edited by Komitee gegen Folter anpolitischen Gefangenen in der BRD, 139–43. Berlin: Eigenverlag, 1983.

Carlson, Andrew R. *Anarchism in Germany*. Metuchen: Scarecrow Press, 1972.

Carruthers, Susan L. *The Media at War. Communication and Conflict in the Twentieth Century*. London: Macmillan, 2000.

Colin, Nicole, Beatrice De Graaf, Jacco Pekelder, and Joachim Umlauf. "Einleitung: 'Terrorismus' als soziale Konstruktion." In *Der 'Deutsche Herbst' und die RAF in Politik, Medien und Kunst. Nationale und internationale Perspektiven*. Edited by Nicole Colin, Beatrice De Graaf, Jacco Pekelder, and Joachim Umlauf, 7–13. Bielefeld: Transcript Verlag, 2008.

Collenberg, Carrie. "Dead Holger." In *Baader-Meinhof Returns: History and Cultural Memory of German Left-Wing Terrorism*. Edited by Gerrit-Jan Berendse and Ingo Cornils, 65–81. New York: Rodopi, 2008.

Colvin, Sarah. *Ulrike Meinhof and West German Terrorism. Language, Violence, and Identity*. New York: Camden House, 2009.

———. "Witch, Amazon, or Joan of Arc? Ulrike Meinhof's Defenders, or How to Legitimize a Violent Woman." In *Women and Death 2: Warlike Women in the German Literary and Cultural Imagination since 1500*. Edited by Sarah Colvin and Helen Watanabe-O'Kelly, 250–72. New York: Camden House, 2009.

———. "Ulrike Meinhof as Woman and Terrorist: Cultural Discourses of Violence and Virtue." In *Baader-Meinhof Returns. History and Cultural Memory of German Left-Wing Terrorism*. Edited by Gerrit-Jan Berendse and Ingo Cornils, 83–101. New York: Rodopi, 2008.

———. " 'Wenn deine Identität Kampf ist': violence, gendered language and identity in the writing of Ulrike Marie Meinhof." In *Violence, Culture and Identity. Essays on German and Austrian Literature, Politics and Society*. Edited by Helen Chambers, 287–305. Bern: Peter Lang, 2006.

Conradt, Gerd. "Nicht oder Sein—Ikonen der Zeitgeschichte." In *Zur Vorstellung des Terrors: Die RAF*. Edited by Klaus Biesenbach, 131–34. Göttingen: Steidl Verlag, 2005.

de Graaf, Beatrice, and Bob de Graaff. "Bringing politics back in: the introduction of the 'performative power' of counterterrorism." *Critical Studies on Terrorism* 3(2) (2010): 261–75.

"Demonstration nach Beerdigung von Holger Meins." *Süddeutsche Zeitung*, November 19, 1974.

Der Baader Meinhof Report. Dokumente—Analysen—Zusammenhänge. Aus den Akten des Bundeskriminalamtes, der "Sonderkommission, Bonn" und dem Bundesamt für Verfassungsschutz. Mainz: v. Hase & Koehler Verlag, 1972.

"DER GEHIRNWÄSCHE—TRAKT IN KÖLN-OSSENDORF." In *Der Kampf gegen die Vernichtungshaft*. Edited by Komitee gegen Folter an politischen Gefangenen in der BRD, 168–230. Berlin: Eigenverlag.

die gefangenen aus der raf. "PROVISORISCHES KAMPFPROGRAMM FÜR DEN KAMPF UM DIE POLITISCHEN RECHTE DER GEFANGENEN ARBEITER." In *Der Kampf gegen die Vernichtungshaft*. Edited by Komitee gegen Folter an politischen Gefangenen, 17–23. Berlin: Eigenverlag, [1983?].

Diederichs, Helmut H. *Konzentration in den Massenmedien: systematischer Überblick zur Situation in der BRD*. Munich: C. Hanser, 1973.

Ditfurth, Jutta. *Ulrike Meinhof. Die Biographie*. Berlin: Ullstein, 2007.

Durkheim, Émile. *Suicide: a Study in Sociology*. Translated by John A. Spaulding and George Simpson. London: Routledge, 2002.

Edel, Uli, dir. *Der Baader-Meinhof Komplex*. 2008.

Ellmann, Maud. *The Hunger Artists: Starving, Writing, and Imprisonment*. London: Virago Press, 1993.

Elter, Andreas. "Die RAF und die Medien. Ein Fallbeispiel für terroristische Kommunikation." In *Die RAF und der linke Terrorismus*. Vol. 2. Edited by Wolfgang Kraushaar,
1060–74. Hamburg: Hamburger Edition, 2006.

———. *Propaganda der Tat. Die RAF und die Medien*. Frankfurt: Suhrkamp Verlag,
2008.

Enzensberger, Hans Magnus. *Bewußtseins-Industrie*. Frankfurt: Suhrkamp Verlag, 1962.

"Ermittlungen um Tod von Holger Meins." *Süddeutsche Zeitung*, November 11, 1974.

"'Es werden Typen dabei kaputtgehen.'" *Der Spiegel* 47 (1974): 28–34.

Eschen, Klaus. "Das Sozialistische Anwaltskollektiv." In *Die RAF und der linke Terrorismus*. Vol. 2. Edited by Wolfgang Kraushaar, 957–72. Hamburg: Hamburger Edition,
2006.

Farberow, Norman L. "Cultural History of Suicide." In *Suicide in Different Cultures*.
Edited by Norman L. Farberow, 1–15. London: University Park Press, 1975.

Feldman, Allen. *Formations of Violence. The Narrative of the Body and Political Terror in
Northern Ireland*. Chicago: University of Chicago Press, 1991.

Fest, Joachim. *Begegnungen. Über nahe und ferne Freunde*. Reinbeck bei Hamburg:
Rowohlt, 2004.

Fetscher, Iring, Herfried Münkler, and Hannelore Ludwig. "Ideologien der Terroristen in der Bundesrepublik Deutschland." In *Analysen zum Terrorismus. Ideologien
and Strategien*. Edited by Federal Ministry of the Interior, 16–271. Opladen: Westdeutscher Verlag, 1981.

Finkemeyer, H., and R. Kautzky. "Das Kavernom des Sinus cavernosus." *Zentralblatt für
Neurochirurgie* 29(1) (1968): 23–30.

"FOLTER MIT MEDIZINSICHEN MITTELN: VERSUCH EINER SZINTIGRA-
PHIE GEGEN ULRIKE MEINHOF." In *Der Kampf gegen die Vernichtungshaft*.
Edited by Komitee gegen Folter an politischen Gefangenen in der BRD, 129–36.
Berlin: Eigenverlag, [1983?].

"FREIE UNIVERSITÄT BERLIN 1948–1973—Hochschule im Umbruch Teil VI."
http://fuberlin.tripod.com (accessed March 11, 2011).

Galli, Matteo. "'Mit dem Einkaufswagen durch den Geschichts-Supermarkt'? Zu einigen Bestandteilen des so genannten Mythos RAF in den Künsten: Entstehung, Entwicklung und Neukontextualisierung." In *Mythos Terrorismus. Vom Deutschen Herbst
zum 11. September*. Edited by Matteo Galli and Heinz-Peter Preusser, 101–66. Heidelberg: Universitätsverlag Winter, 2006.

Gasser, Hans-Peter, Sylvie-S. Junod, Claude Pilloud, Jean de Preux, Yves Sandoz, Chris-
tophe Swinarski, Claude F. Wenger, and Bruno Zimmerman. *Commentary on the
Additional Protocols of 8 June 1977 to the Geneva Conventions of 12 August 1949*.
Geneva: Martinus Nijhoff, 1987.

Gäthje, Olaf. "Das 'info'-System der RAF von 1973 bis 1977 in sprachwissenschaftlicher
Perspektive." In *Die RAF und der linke Terrorismus*. Vol. 1. Edited by Wolfgang Kraushaar, 714–33. Hamburg: Hamburger Edition, 2006.

Gätje, Olaf. *Der Gruppenstil der RAF im 'Info'-System. Eine soziostilistische Untersuchung
aus systematischer Perspektive*. Berlin: Walter de Gruyter, 2008.

Georg-von-Rauch-Haus, Tommy-Weißbecker-Haus, and Schöneberger Jungarbeiter- und Schülerzentrum, ed. *Dokumentation über die Polizeiüberfälle am 5.3.75.*

Goethe, Johann Wolfgang von. *The Sufferings of Young Werther.* Translated by Harry Steinhauer. New York: W. W. Norton & Company, 1970.

Gómez, Alan Eladio. "Resisting Living Death at Marion Federal Penitentiary, 1972." *Radical History Review* 96 (2006): 58–86.

Gössner, Rolf. *Das Anti-Terror-System. Politische Justiz im präventiven Sicherheitsstaat.* Hamburg: VSA-Verlag, 1991.

gudrun ensslin im originalton. 4. mai 1976. http://www.youtube.com/watch?v=gTO 62ML75fY&NR=1 (accessed March 13, 2011).

Gutjahr, Ortrud. "Königinnenstreit. Eine Annäherung an Elfriede Jelineks *Ulrike Maria Stuart* und ein Blick auf Friedrich Schillers *Maria Stuart.*" In *Ulrike Maria Stuart.* Edited by Ortrud Gutjahr, 19–35. Würzburg: Königshausen und Neumann, 2007.

Hahn, Michael. "Land der Superpigs. Wie Agit 883 mit Black Panthers und Weather- men die 'zweite Front in den Metropolen' eröffnete." In *agit 883. Bewegung, Revolte, Underground in Westberlin 1969–1972.* Edited by rotaprint 25, 141–54. Hamburg: Assoziation A, 2006.

Hakemi, Sara. "'Burn, baby, burn!' Die andere Vorgeschichte der RAF." In *Zur Vorstel- lung des Terrors: Die RAF.* Edited by Klaus Biesenbach, 69–71. Göttingen: Steidl Verlag, 2005.

———. "Terrorismus und Avantgarde." In *Die RAF und der linke Terrorismus.* Vol. 1. Edited by Wolfgang Kraushaar, 604–19. Hamburg: Hamburger Edition, 2006.

Hannover, Heinrich. *Die Republik vor Gericht 1954–1995. Erinnerungen eines unbeque- men Rechtsanwalts.* Berlin: Aufbau Taschenbuch Verlag, 2005.

———. *Terroristenprozesse. Erfahrungen und Erkenntnisse eines Strafverteidigers.* Vol. 1, *Terroristen und Richter.* Hamburg: VSA-Verlag, 1991.

Hebdige, Dick. *Subculture: the Meaning of Style.* London: Methuen & Co, 1979.

Hecken, Thomas. *Avantgarde und Terrorismus. Rhetorik der Intensität und Programme der Revolte von den Futuristen bis zur RAF.* Bielefeld: Transcript Verlag, 2006.

Herrmann, Jörg. "Ulrike Meinhof und Gudrun Ensslin—Vom Protestantismus zum Terrorismus." In *Zur Vorstellung des Terrors: Die RAF.* Edited by Klaus Biesenbach, 112–14. Göttingen: Steidl Verlag, 2005.

———. "'Unsere Söhne und Töchter'. Protestantismus und RAF-Terrorismus in den 1970er Jahren." In *Die RAF und der linke Terrorismus.* Vol. 1. Edited by Wolfgang Kraushaar, 644–56. Hamburg: Hamburger Edition, 2006.

Heskin, Ken. "The Psychology of Terrorism in Ireland." In *Terrorism in Ireland.* Edited by Yonah Alexander and Alan O'Day, 88–105. New York: St. Martin's Press, 1984.

Hipp, Dietmar, and Caroline Schmidt. "Mit aller Härte." *Der Spiegel* 35 (2007): 48–49.

Hipp, Dietmar, Caroline Schmidt, and Michael Sontheimer. "Gebildet, unauffällig, verdächtig." *Der Spiegel* 47 (2007): 52–55.

Holzer, Horst. *Kommunikationssoziologie.* Reinbeck bei Hamburg: Rowohlt, 1973.

Horgan, John. *The Psychology of Terrorism.* New York: Routledge, 2005.

Horkheimer, Max, and Theodor W. Adorno. "The Culture Industry: Enlightenment as Mass Deception." In *The Dialectic of Enlightenment. Philosophical Fragments.* Edited by Gunzelin Schmid Noerr, 94–136. Stanford: Stanford University Press, 2002.

Hund, Wulf D., ed. *Kommunikationstopologie: exemplarische Figuren gesellschaftlicher Nachrichtenvermittlung.* Frankfurt am Main: Europäische Verlagsanstalt, 1973.

Internationale Untersuchungskommission, ed. *Der Tod Ulrike Meinhofs. Bericht der Internationalen Untersuchungskommission.* Münster: Unrast Verlag, 2007.

Itzenplitz, Eberhard. "Über die Filmarbeit mit Ulrike Meinhof." In *Bambule. Fürsorge— Sorge für wen?* Berlin: Verlag Klaus Wagenbach, 2002.

Jäger, Herbert, Gerhard Schmidtchen, and Lieselotte Süllwold, ed. *Lebenslaufanalysen.* Opladen: Westdeutscher Verlag, 1981.

Jander, Martin. "Isolation. Zu den Haftbedingungen der RAF-Gefangenen." In *Die RAF und der linke Terrorismus.* Vol. 2. Edited by Wolfgang Kraushaar, 973–94. Hamburg: Hamburger Edition, 2006.

Jenkins, Brian. *International Terrorism. A New Mode of Conflict.* Los Angeles: Crescent Publications, 1975.

Juergensmeyer, Mark. *Terror in the Mind of God. The Global Rise of Religious Violence.* Berkeley: University of California Press, 2000.

Kafka, Franz. "A Hunger Artist." In *The Complete Stories.* Edited by Nahum N. Glatzer. New York: Schocken Books, 1971.

"Kassiber mit Skizze." *Der Spiegel* 9 (1973): 64.

Kellerhoff, Sven Felix. "Die Mord-Legende von Stammheim." *Die Welt* 35 (2007): 20.

"Klar oder krank?" *Der Spiegel* 35 (1973): 54–56.

Knoch, Habbo. *Die Tat als Bild. Fotografien des Holocaust in der deutschen Erinnerungskultur.* Hamburg: Hamburger Edition, 2001.

Koenen, Gerd. "Armed Innocence, or 'Hitler's Children' Revisited." In *Baader-Meinhof Returns. History and Cultural Memory of German Left-Wing Terrorism.* Edited by Gerrit-Jan Berendse and Ingo Cornils, 23–38. Amsterdam: Rodopi, 2008.

———. "Camera Silens. Das Phantasma der 'Vernichtungshaft.'" In *Die RAF und der linke Terrorismus.* Vol. 2. Edited by Wolfgang Kraushaar, 994–1010. Hamburg: Hamburger Edition, 2006.

Komitees gegen Folter an politischen Gefangenen in der BRD und Westberlin. "COUNTERINSURGENCY GEGEN DIE RAF." In *Der Kampf gegen die Vernichtungshaft.* Edited by Komitee gegen Folter anpolitischen Gefangenen, 33–54: Eigenverlag, [1983?].

Kraushaar, Wolfgang. "Der Vietcong als Mythos des bewaffneten Volksaufstandes." In *Die RAF und der linke Terrorismus.* Vol. 2. Edited by Wolfgang Kraushaar, 751–67. Hamburg: Hamburger Edition, 2006.

———. "Kleinkrieg gegen einen Großverleger. Von der Anti-Springer-Kampagne der APO zu den Brand- und Bombenanschlägen der RAF." In *Die RAF und der linke Terrorismus.* Vol. 2. Edited by Wolfgang Kraushaar, 1075–116. Hamburg: Hamburger Edition, 2006.

————. "Mythos RAF. Im Spannungsfeld von terroristischer Herausforderung und populistischer Bedrohungsphantasie." In *Die RAF und der linke Terrorismus*. Vol. 2. Edited by Wolfgang Kraushaar, 1186–210. Hamburg: Hamburger Edition, 2006.

Krebs, Mario. *Ulrike Meinhof. Ein Leben im Widerspruch.* Reinbeck bei Hamburg: Rowohlt Taschenbuch Verlag, 1988.

Kropotkin, Petr. "The Spirit of Revolt." In *The Essential Kropotkin.* Edited by Emile Capouya and Keitha Tompkins, 3–9. London: Macmillan, 1976.

Kruglanski, Arie W., and Shira Fishman. "The Psychology of Terrorism: 'Syndrome' Versus 'Tool' Perspectives." *Terrorism and Political Violence* 18 (2006): 193–215.

Laqueur, Walter. *No End to War: Terrorism in the Twenty-First Century.* New York: Continuum, 2003.

————. *Terrorism.* London: Wiendenfeld and Nicolson, 1977.

————. *The New Terrorism and the Arms of Mass Destruction.* Oxford: Oxford University Press, 1999.

Lewis, Ben, dir. *Baader-Meinhof: In Love with Terror.* BBC4, 2002.

Lieberman, Lisa. *Leaving You: The Cultural Meaning of Suicide.* Chicago: Ivan R. Dee, 2003.

Ligthart, Theo. "avantgarde, 2000/2004." In *Zur Vorstellung des Terrors: Die RAF.* Edited by Klaus Biesenbach, 68. Göttingen: Steidl Verlag, 2005.

Mahler, Horst. "Über den bewaffneten Kampf in Westeuropa." In *Rote Armee Fraktion. Texte und Materialien zur Geschichte der RAF.* Edited by ID-Verlag, 49–111. Berlin: ID-Verlag, 1997.

Mallison, W. Thomas, and Sally V. Mallison. "The Juridical Status of Privileged Combatants under the Geneva Protocol of 1977 Concerning International Conflicts." *Law and Contemporary Problems* 42(2) (1978): 4–35.

Marighella, Carlos. *Mini-Manual of the Urban Guerilla.* Montreal: Abraham Guillen Press & Arm The Spirit, 2002.

Ministerium des Innern Rheinland-Pfalz, ed. *Dokumentation "Baader-Meinhof-Bande."* 1974.

Minois, Georges. *History of Suicide. Voluntary Death in Western Culture.* Translated by Lydia G. Cochrane. Baltimore: Johns Hopkins University Press, 1995.

Mitchell, W. J. T. *Picture Theory. Essays on Verbal and Visual Representation.* Chicago: University of Chicago Press, 1994.

"'Mord beginnt beim bösen Wort'. II." *Der Spiegel* 42 (1977): 28–57.

Morrissey, Susan K. *Suicide and the Body Politic in Imperial Russia.* Cambridge: Cambridge University Press, 2006.

Müller, Hans Dieter. *Der Springer-Konzern: eine kritische Studie.* Munich: R. Piper & Co., 1968.

Musolff, Andreas. "Bürgerkriegs-Szenarios und ihre Folgen. Die Terrorismusdebatte in der Bundesrepublik 1970–1993." In *Die RAF und der linke Terrorismus*. Vol. 2. Edited by Wolfgang Kraushaar, 1171–84. Hamburg: Hamburger Edition, 2006.

————. *Krieg gegen die Öffentlichkeit. Terrorismus und politischer Sprachgebrauch.* Opladen: Westdeutscher Verlag, 1996.

————. "Terrorismus im öffentlichen Diskurs der BRD: Seine Deutung als Kriegsgeschehen und die Folgen." In *Terrorismus in der Bundesrepublik. Medien, Staat und Subkulturen in den 1970er Jahren.* Edited by Klaus Weinhauer, Jörg Requate, and Heinz-Gerhard Haupt, 302–19. Frankfurt: Campus Verlag, 2006.

Nacos, Brigitte L. "The Portrayal of Female Terrorists in the Media: Similar Framing Patterns in the News Coverage of Women in Politics and in Terrorism." *Studies in Conflict & Terrorism* 28 (2005): 435–51.

Negt, Oskar. "Rede zum Angela-Davis-Kongress 1972. Im Zeichen der Gewalt." http://www.linksnet.de/artikel.php?id=374 (accessed March 24, 2011).

Ness, Cindy D. "In the Name of the Cause: Women's Work in Secular and Religious Terrorism." *Studies in Conflict & Terrorism* 28 (2005): 353–73.

Neumann, Robert. "Baute Lübke KZs?" *konkret* 12 (1966): 14–15.

————. "Ein Lübke zuviel?" *konkret* 7 (1966): 15–21.

Nirumand, Bahman. *Persien. Modell eines Entwicklungslandes oder Die Diktatur der freien Welt.* Reinbeck bei Hamburg: Rowohlt, 1967.

Oesterle, Kurt. *Stammheim. Der Vollzugsbeamte Horst Bubeck und die RAF-Häftlinge.* Munich: Heyne, 2003.

Overath, Margot. *Drachenzähne. Gespräche, Dokumente und Recherchen aus der Wirklichkeit der Hochsicherheitsjustiz.* Hamburg: VSA-Verlag, 1991.

Passmore, Leith. "Another New Illustrated History: The visual turns in the memory of West German terrorism." *EDGE* 1(1) (2009): art. 2.

————. "The Art of Hunger: Self-Starvation in the Red Army Faction." *German History* 27(1) (2009): 32–59.

Patkin, Terri Toles. "Explosive Baggage: Female Palestinian Suicide Bombers and the Rhetoric of Emotion." *Women and Language* 27(2) (2004): 79–88.

Peters, Butz. *RAF. Terrorismus in Deutschland.* Stuttgart: Deutsche Verlags-Anstalt, 1991.

————. *Tödlicher Irrtum. Die Geschichte der RAF.* Berlin: Argon, 2004.

Piekalkiewicz, Janusz. *Secret Agents, Spies and Saboteurs: Secret Missions of the Second World War.* Translated by Francisca Garvie and Nadia Fowler. London: Garden City Press, 1974.

Possony, Stefan T., and L. Francis Bouchey. *International Terrorism: The Communist Connection. With a case study of West German terrorist Ulrike Meinhof.* Washington, DC: American Council for World Freedom, 1978.

Preece, Julian. "The lives of the RAF revisited: The biographical turn." *Memory Studies* 3(2) (2010): 151–63.

Preußer, Heinz-Peter. "Warum *Mythos* Terrorismus? Versuch einer Begriffsklärung." In *Mythos Terrorismus. Vom Deutschen Herbst zum 11. September.* Edited by Matteo Galli and Heinz-Peter Preußer, 69–83. Heidelberg: Universitätsverlag Winter, 2006.

Prinz, Alois. *Lieber wütend als traurig. Die Lebensgeschichte der Ulrike Meinhof.* Berlin: Suhrkamp, 2005.

Proll, Astrid, ed. *Hans und Grete. Bilder der RAF 1967–1977.* Berlin: Aufbau-Verlag, 2004.

Proll, Thorwald, and Daniel Dubbe. *Wir kamen vom anderen Stern. Über 1968, Andreas Baader und ein Kaufhaus.* Hamburg: Edition Nautilus, 2003.

Rasch, Wilfried. "Psychological Dimensions of Political Terrorism in the Federal Republic of Germany." *International Journal of Law and Psychiatry* 2 (1979): 79–85.

Reinecke, Stefan. "Die linken Anwälte. Eine Typologie." In *Die RAF und der linke Terrorismus.* Vol. 2. Edited by Wolfgang Kraushaar, 948–56. Hamburg: Hamburger Edition, 2006.

———. "Die RAF und die Politik der Zeichen." In *Zur Vorstellung des Terrors: Die RAF.* Edited by Klaus Biesenbach, 219–21. Göttingen: Steidl Verlag, 2005.

Requate, Jörg. "'Terroristenanwälte' und Rechtsstaat: Zur Auseinandersetzung um die Rolle der Verteidiger in den Terroristenverfahren der 1970er Jahre." In *Terrorismus in der Bundesrepublik. Medien, Staat und Subkulturen in den 1970er Jahren.* Edited by Klaus Weinhauer, Jörg Requate, and Heinz-Gerhard Haupt, 271–99. Frankfurt: Campus Verlag, 2006.

Rhodes, Joel. *The Voice of Violence: Performative Violence as Protest in the Vietnam Era.* Westport, CT: Praeger, 2001.

Roberts, Michael. "Postmodernism and the linguistic turn." In *Making History. An introduction to the history and practices of a discipline.* Edited by Peter Lambert and Phillipp Schofield, 227–40. New York: Routledge, 2004.

Röhl, Bettina. *So macht Kommunismus Spaß. Ulrike Meinhof, Klaus Rainer Röhl und die Akte KONKRET.* Hamburg: Europäische Verlagsanstalt, 2006.

———. "Warum ging Ulrike Meinhof in den Untergrund? Das Hirn der RAF." *Rheinische Post*, November 9, 2002.

Rohrmoser, Günter, and Jörg Fröhlich. "Ideologische Ursachen des Terrorismus." In *Analysen zum Terrorismus. Ideologien and Strategien.* Edited by Federal Ministry of the Interior, 274–339. Opladen: Westdeutscher Verlag, 1981.

Ruby, Charles L. "Are Terrorists Mentally Deranged?" *Analyses of Social Issues and Public Policy* 2(1) (2002): 15–26.

Sabatini, Arthur J. "Terrorismus und Performance." *Kunstforum International* 117 (1992): 147–51.

Sachsse, Rolf. "Pentagramm hinter deutscher Maschinenpistole unter Russisch Brot. Zur Semiosphäre der Erinnerung an die Rote Armee Fraktion." In *Der 'Deutsche Herbst' und die RAF in Politik, Medien und Kunst. Nationale und internationale Perspektiven.* Edited by Nicole Colin, Beatrice De Graaf, Jacco Pekelder, and Joachim Umlauf, 131–40. Bielefeld: Transcript Verlag, 2008.

"Sartre nennt Haftbedingungen Baaders 'Folter.'" *Frankfurter Allgemeine Zeitung*, December 5, 1974.

"Sartre ruft Böll zu Solidarität auf." *Frankfurter Allgemeine Zeitung*, December 5, 1974.

"Sartre spricht von psychischer Folter." *Süddeutsche Zeitung*, December 5, 1974.

Schechner, Richard, ed. *Performance Studies. An Introduction.* New York: Routledge, 2002.

Schmid, Alex P., and Janny de Graaf. *Violence as Communication. Insurgent Terrorism and the Western News Media.* London: Sage Publications, 1982.

Schmidt, Regina, and Egon Becker. *Reaktionen auf politische Vorgänge. Drei Meinungsstudien aus der Bundesrepublik.* Frankfurt am Main: Europäische Verlagsanstalt, 1967.

Schmidtchen, Gerhard. "Terroristische Karrieren." In *Lebenslaufanalysen*. Edited by Herbert Jäger, Gerhard Schmidtchen, and Lieselotte Süllwold, 14–77. Opladen: Westdeuscher Verlag, 1981.

Schneider, Peter. "BILD macht dumm." *konkret* 3 (1968): 14–17.

Schütte, Uwe. "Was ist und zu welchem Ende studieren wir den 'Kunst-Terrorismus'? Einige vorläufige Überlegungen zum Verhältnis von Kultur, Gewalt und Politik im 20. Jahrhundert und darüber hinaus." In *Mythos Terrorismus. Vom Deutschen Herbst zum 11. September*. Edited by Matteo Galli and Heinz-Peter Preusser, 191–206. Heidelberg: Universitätsverlag Winter, 2006.

Scribner, Charity. "Buildings on Fire: The Situationist International and the Red Army Faction." *Grey Room* 26 (2007): 30–55.

Senghaas, Dieter. *Aufrüstung durch Rüstungskontrolle. Über den symbolischen Gebrauch von Politik*. Stuttgart: Verlag Kohlhammer, 1972.

———, ed. *Imperialismus und strukturelle Gewalt—Analysen über abhängige Reproduktion*. Frankfurt: Suhrkamp, 1972.

Senghaas, Dieter, and Claus Koch, ed. *Texte zur Technokratie-Diskussion*. Frankfurt: Europäische Verlagsanstalt, 1970.

Serke, Jürgen. "Terror in Deutschland. Die Bombenleger." *Stern* 24 (1972): 18–24.

"Solange sie nicht die Fresse voll kriegen." *Der Spiegel* 8 (1972): 83.

Sontag, Susan. *On Photography*. New York: Anchor Books, 1990.

———. *Regarding the Pain of Others*. New York: Picador, 2004.

Sontheimer, Michael. "Terrorzelle Stammheim." *Der Spiegel* 41 (2007): 98–108.

Speitel, Volker. "'Wir wollten alles und gleichzeitig nichts.'" *Der Spiegel* 31 (1980): 36–49.

———. "'Wir wollten alles und gleichzeitig nichts' (II)." *Der Spiegel* 32 (1980): 30–39.

———. "'Wir wollten alles und gleichzeitig nichts' (III)." *Der Spiegel* 33 (1980): 30–36.

Steinseifer, Martin. "'Fotos wie Brandwunden'?—Überlegungen zur deontischen Bedeutung von Pressefotografien am Beispiel von Hanns Martin Schleyer als Opfer der Roten Armee Fraktion." In *Brisante Semantik. Neuere Konzepte und Froschungsergebnisse einer kulturwissenschaftlichen Linguistik*. Edited by Dietrich Busse, Thomas Niehr, and Thomas Wengeler, 269–90. Tübingen: Max Niemeyer Verlag, 2005.

———. "Terrorismus als Medienereignis im Herbst 1977: Strategien, Dynamiken, Darstellungen, Deutungen." In *Terrorismus in der Bundesrepublik. Medien, Staat und Subkulturen in den 1970er Jahren*. Edited by Klaus Weinhauer, Jörg Requate, and Heinz-Gerhard Haupt, 351–81. Frankfurt: Campus Verlag, 2006.

Straßner, Alexander. "Die dritte Generation der RAF." In *Die RAF und der linke Terrorismus*. Vol. 1. Edited by Wolfgang Kraushaar, 489–519. Hamburg: Hamburger Edition, 2006.

———. *Die dritte Generation der "Roten Armee Fraktion." Entstehung, Struktur, Funktionslogik und Zerfall einer terroristischen Organisation*. Wiesbaden: VS Verlag für Sozialwissenschaften, 2003.

"Streit um den Kopf der Ulrike Meinhof." *Frankfurter Rundschau*, August 16, 1973.

Streng, Marcel. "'Hungerstreik'. Eine politische Subjektivierungspraxis zwischen 'Freitod' und 'Überlebenskunst' (Westdeutschland, 1970—1990)." In *Das schöne Selbst*.

Zur Genealogie des modernen Subjekts zwischen Ethik und Ästhetik. Edited by Jens Elberfeld and Marcus Otto. Bielefeld: transcript Verlag, 333–65.

Stuberger, Ulf G. *Die Tage von Stammheim. Als Augenzeuge beim RAF-Prozeß.* Munich: Herbig, 2007.

Sturm, Beate. "Man kann nur zurückbrüllen." *Der Spiegel* 7 (1972): 57–63.

Sweeney, George. "Irish Hunger Strikes and the Cult of Self-Sacrifice." *Journal of Contemporary History* 28(3) (1993): 421–37.

Terhoeven, Petra. "Opferbilder—Täterbilder. Die Fotographie als Medium linksterroristischer Selbstermächtigung in Deutschland und Italien während der 70er Jahre." *Geschichte in Wissenschaft und Unterricht* 58(7/8) (2007): 380–99.

Teuns, Sjef. "Isolation/Sensorische Deprivation: die programmierte Folter." *Kursbuch* 32 (1973): 118–26.

"Unklarheit über neue Terror-Drohungen." *Frankfurter Rundschau*, May 29, 1972.

Vandereycken, Walter, and Ron van Deth. *From Fasting Saints to Anorexic Girls: The History of Self-Starvation.* London: Athlone Press, 1996.

"Veranstaltung zum 20. Todestag von Ulrike Meinhof am 3. Mai 1996 im Auditorium Maximum der TU Berlin." http://www.nadir.org/nadir/archiv/PolitischeStroemungen/Stadtguerilla+RAF/RAF/ulrike_meinhof/va20/va20podium.html (accessed March 13, 2011).

Victoroff, Jeff. "The Mind of the Terrorist: A Review and Critique of Psychological Approaches." *Journal of Conflict Resolution* 49(1) (2005): 3–42.

Waldmann, Peter. *Terrorismus. Provokation der Macht.* Hamburg: Murmann Verlag, 2005.

Weimann, Gabriel, and Conrad Winn. *The Theatre of Terror. Mass Media and International Terrorism.* New York: Longman, 1994.

Weinhauer, Klaus, and Jörg Requate. "Einleitung: Die Herausforderung des 'Linksterrorismus.'" In *Terrorismus in der Bundesrepublik. Medien, Staat und Subkulturen in den 1970er Jahren.* Edited by Klaus Weinhauer, Jörg Requate, and Heinz-Gerhard Haupt, 9–32. Frankfurt am Main: Campus Verlag, 2006.

Weisbrod, Bernd. "Terrorism as Performance: The Assassinations of Walther Rathenau and Hanns-Martin Schleyer." In *Control of Violence. Historical and International Perspectives on Violence in Modern Societies.* Edited by Wilhelm Heitmeyer, Heinz-Gerhard Haupt, Andrea Kirschner, and Stefan Malthaner, 365–94. New York: Springer, 2011.

Wesemann, Kristin. *Ulrike Meinhof. Kommunistin, Journalistin, Terroristin—eine politische Biographie.* Baden-Baden: Nomos, 2007.

"'Wir werden in den Durststreik treten.'" *Der Spiegel* 4 (1975): 52–57.

Wittrock, Philipp. "Wissenschaftler im Visier der Linksterror-Fahnder." *Spiegel-Online*, August 2, 2007. http://www.spiegel.de/politik/deutschland/0,1518,497923,00.html (accessed March 28, 2011).

Wunschik, Tobias. "Aufstieg und Zerfall. Die zweite Generation der RAF." In *Die RAF und der linke Terrorismus.* Vol. 1. Edited by Wolfgang Kraushaar, 472–88. Hamburg: Hamburger Edition, 2006.

Zelizer, Barbie. *Remembering to Forget. Holocaust Memory through the Camera's Eye.* Chicago: University of Chicago Press, 1998.

Zulaika, Joseba. "The Self-Fulfilling Prophecies of Counterterrorism." *Radical History Review* 85 (2003): 191–99.

"Zur Berichterstattung der Presse über die RAF." In *Vorbereitung der RAF-Prozesse durch Presse, Polizei und Justiz.* Edited by Rosa Léviné, 156–59. Berlin: Eigendruck im Selbstverlag, 1975.

Index

camera silens, 80–81, 164n121
capitalism
  as the cause of illness, 76–77,
    113–15
  as prerequisite for the "consciousness
    industry," 18
  structural violence of, 24, 120
CDU (*Christlich Demokratische Union
  Deutschlands*), ix, 18, 109, 140n50
Cellules Communistes Combattantes, 101
Central Intelligence Agency (CIA), 111
Christian Democratic Union. *See* CDU
*Christlich Demokratische Union
  Deutschlands* (CDU), ix, 18, 109,
  140n50
CIA, 111
civil rights movement, 39
Code of Criminal Procedure. See
  Strafprozessordnung
Cold War, ix, xii, 14, 36, 47
Cologne-Ossendorf prison, 65, 75, 79,
  108, 154n4
colonialism
  of the individual, 81
  as negation, 81
  viral, 81
  See also anticolonialism
Colvin, Sarah, vii, 3, 7–8, 127n3,
  132n46, 134n2, 141n70, 141n72,
  142n76, 143n92, 144n19, 148n79,
  148n81, 150n101, 159n65,
  170n58, 181n2, 182n13
coma solution, 64
Committees against the torture of
  political prisoners, 67, 69, 75–76,
  80, 94, 98, 157nn37–38
  events, 74
  formation, 67
  publications, 74, 75, 79–80, 95,
    97, 160n74, 160n81, 161n86,
    161n121, 164n123
  support of doctors, 76
communism
  Meinhof's commitment to, 14, 16,
    26, 133

Communist Party of Germany, 14, 26,
  36, 94
Development Organization (KPD/
  AO), 67
Communist Student Union. *See* KSV
concentration camps (Nazi), 77–78, 122
consciousness industry, 18, 137n30
"Of Course we can Shoot" (RAF
  statement), 28, 37, 40
criminology, 8, 133n53
Croissant, Klaus, 20, 47, 62, 68, 78, 85,
  163n110
culture industry, 18, 137n30, 138n33

das argument (student newspaper), 14, 21
*Das Konzept Stadtguerilla. See Urban
  Guerilla Concept, The*
death wing, 62, 77–78, 84, 91
  letter from a prisoner in the (poem),
    75, 160n81, 161n84
Debray, Regis, 58, 137n25
Debus, Sigurd, 79, 117
defense mail, 66
*Dem Volk dienen. Stadtguerilla und
  Klassenkampf* (RAF treatise), 19, 37,
  38, 51–52, 57–59, 113–15
Der Kampf hat erst begonnen (RAF
  statement), 37, 44
Deutscher Herbst. See German Autumn
*Die Aktion des Schwarzen September in
  München* (RAF treatise), 37, 52,
  56–58, 77
*Die beiden aus Buchstaben
  zusammengestückelten
  Bombendrohungen* (RAF
  statement), 37
*Die neue Straßenverkehrsordnung (The
  New Traffic Regulations). See On the
  Armed Struggle in Western Europe*
Die Rote Armee aufbauen (RAF
  statement), 37–40, 56
Die Welt (newspaper), 16, 21, 104
Die Zeit (newspaper), 21, 27
Ditfurth, Jutta, 8, 133nn51–52, 139n41,
  141n70, 165n4, 180n65